THE CASSANDRA ARCHITECTURE:
Distributed Control in a Blackboard System

ELLIS HORWOOD BOOKS IN INFORMATION TECHNOLOGY

General Editor: Dr JOHN M. M. PINKERTON, Principal, J. & H. Pinkerton Associates, Surrey (Consultants in Information Technology), and formerly Manager of Strategic Requirements, ICL

EXPERT SYSTEMS IN BUSINESS: A Practical Approach
M. BARRETT, Expertech Limited, Slough, and A. C. BEEREL, Lysia Limited, London
ELECTRONIC DATA PROCESSING IN PRACTICE, Vols. 1 and 2
M. BECKER, R. HABERFELLNER and G. LIEBETRAU, Zurich, Switzerland
EXPERT SYSTEMS: Strategic Implications and Applications
A. C. BEEREL, Lysia Limited, London
APPLICATIONS OF OPTICAL STORAGE*
A. BRADLEY, Congleton, Cheshire
SOFTWARE ENGINEERING ENVIRONMENTS
P. BRERETON, Department of Computer Science, University of Keele
SMART CARDS: Principles, Practice and Applications
R. BRIGHT, Information Technology Strategies International Limited, Orpington, Kent
PRACTICAL MACHINE TRANSLATION*
D. CLARKE and U. MAGNUSSON-MURRAY, Department of Applied Computing and Mathematics, Cranfield Institute of Technology, Bedford
ENCYCLOPAEDIA OF IT*
V. CLAUS and A. SCHWILL, FRG
KNOWLEDGE-BASED SYSTEMS: Implications for Human–Computer Interfaces
D. CLEAL, PA Computers and Telecommunications, London, and N. HEATON, Central Computer and Telecommunications Agency, London
THE CASSANDRA ARCHITECTURE: Distributed Control in a Blackboard System
I. CRAIG, Dept. of Computer Science, University of Warwick, Coventry
KNOWLEDGE ELICITATION: Principles, Techniques and Applications
D. DIAPER, Section of Psychology, Liverpool Polytechnic
KNOWLEDGE-BASED MANAGEMENT SUPPORT SYSTEMS
G. I. DOUKIDIS, F. LAND and G. MILLER, Department of Information Management, London Business School, London
KNOWLEDGE-BASED SYSTEMS: Applications in Administrative Government
P. DUFFIN, CCTA, Riverwalk, London
MULTI-LINGUAL SPEECH ASSESSMENT*
A. FOURCIN, Dept. of Phonetics and Linguistics, University College London
KNOWLEDGE ENGINEERING FOR EXPERT SYSTEMS
M. GREENWELL, Expert Systems International, Oxford
EXPERT SYSTEMS: Safety and Risks*
E. HOLLNAGEL, Computer Resources International, Denmark
KNOWLEDGE-BASED EXPERT SYSTEMS IN INDUSTRY
J. KRIZ, Head of AI Group, Brown Boveri Research Systems, Switzerland
ARTIFICIAL INTELLIGENCE: Current Applications*
A. MATTHEWS and J. RODDY, Aregon International Ltd, London
INFORMATION TECHNOLOGY: An Overview*
J. M. M. PINKERTON, J & H Pinkerton Associates, Esher, Surrey
PRACTICAL TOOLS IN HUMAN–COMPUTER INTERFACES*
S. RAVDEN and G. JOHNSON, MRC/ESRC Social and Applied Psychology Unit, University of Sheffield
EXPERT SYSTEMS IN THE ORGANIZATION: An Introduction for Decision-makers
S. SAVORY, Nixdorf Computer AG, FRG
ARTIFICAL INTELLIGENCE AND EXPERT SYSTEMS
S. SAVORY, Nixdorf Computer AG, FRG
BUILDING EXPERT SYSTEMS: Cognitive Emulation
P. E. SLATTER, Telecomputing plc, Oxford
SOFTWARE ENGINEERING MANAGEMENT
H. M. SNEED, FRG
SPEECH AND LANGUAGE-BASED COMMUNICATION WITH MACHINES: Towards the Conversational Computer
J. A. WATERWORTH and M. TALBOT, Human Factors Division, British Telecom Research Laboratories, Ipswich
THE IMPLEMENTATION OF COMPUTER SYSTEMS
R. J. WHIDDETT, Dept. of Computing, University of Lancaster

* In preparation

THE CASSANDRA ARCHITECTURE:
Distributed Control in a Blackboard System

IAIN D. CRAIG, M.A., Ph.D.
Department of Computer Science
University of Warwick

ELLIS HORWOOD LIMITED
Publishers · Chichester

Halsted Press: a division of
JOHN WILEY & SONS
New York · Chichester · Brisbane · Toronto

First published in 1989 by
ELLIS HORWOOD LIMITED
Market Cross House, Cooper Street,
Chichester, West Sussex, PO19 1EB, England
The publisher's colophon is reproduced from James Gillison's drawing of the ancient Market Cross, Chichester.

Distributors:
Australia and New Zealand:
JACARANDA WILEY LIMITED
GPO Box 859, Brisbane, Queensland 4001, Australia
Canada:
JOHN WILEY & SONS CANADA LIMITED
22 Worcester Road, Rexdale, Ontario, Canada
Europe and Africa:
JOHN WILEY & SONS LIMITED
Baffins Lane, Chichester, West Sussex, England
North and South America and the rest of the world:
Halsted Press: a division of
JOHN WILEY & SONS
605 Third Avenue, New York, NY 10158, USA
South-East Asia
JOHN WILEY & SONS (SEA) PTE LIMITED
37 Jalan Pemimpin # 05–04
Block B, Union Industrial Building, Singapore 2057
Indian Subcontinent
WILEY EASTERN LIMITED
4835/24 Ansari Road
Daryaganj, New Delhi 110002, India

British Library Cataloguing in Publication Data
Craig, Iain D.
The Cassandra architecture: distributed control in a blackboard system.
1. Expert systems. Design
I. Title
006.5'3

Library of Congress CIP available

ISBN 0–7458–0579–5 (Ellis Horwood Limited)
ISBN 0–470–21353–1 (Halsted Press)

Printed in Great Britain by Hartnolls, Bodmin

To Ted and to Claire
(without permission).

Table of Contents

1. INTRODUCTION

1.1. INTRODUCTION

The problems being tackled by knowledge-based systems are becoming increasingly complex. This complexity is reflected in the diversity of knowledge required to solve problems and in the difficulty of finding adequate solutions. An immediate consequence of this increased complexity is that the structure of a knowledge-based system is, itself, becoming complex. As the complexity of systems increases, they become progressively more difficult to construct, extend and maintain. This book is concerned with a new problem solving architecture designed to overcome some of these problems.

The traditional way to construct knowledge-based systems has been to use production rules. However, because productions represent comparatively small amounts of knowledge, any complex system will contain many thousands of rules and it becomes difficult to record dependencies and similarities between rules.* This property has led to the use of rulesets (collections of related rules). Rulesets, though, on their own, do not genuinely simplify system design and construction because they do not adequately divide the knowledge used to solve problems into sufficiently differentiated units, nor do they, often, reflect the structure of the problem in any obvious way. In addition, complex problems requiring a diversity of knowledge frequently also require complex control strategies: this is not reflected in either the production rule or ruleset architectures. Also, rules do not immediately suggest a decomposition of the problem so that a system can be built: that is, they do not immediately suggest a method for running projects.

The blackboard architecture (e.g., Nii, 1986a, 1986b) is becoming increasingly used in the construction of complex systems. The architecture is based on the metaphor of a team of experts co-operating to solve a difficult problem, and provides a basis for building complex systems: it also suggests a methodology. The architecture provides support for sophisticated control of problem solving. The architecture is based on the concept of a central, publicly accessible database through which all intermediate results pass. The organisation of this central database suggests ways in which one can construct systems from a practi-

* The XCON computer configuration system (McDermott, 1984) now contains approximately 10,000 rules. Peter Sell of Digital Equipment Corporation has informed me (personal communication) that this appears to be the limit of the feasible as far as maintenance and updating is concerned.

cal standpoint. This architecture forms the basis of the new architecture described in this book: I have called the new architecture the CASSANDRA architecture after the first system to be built with it.**

It is always, of course, possible, to devise *ad hoc* organisations for problem solving systems. One, popular, basis is object-oriented programming (for example, systems based on Smalltalk (Goldberg, 1983)). The problem with devising a one-shot solution is that it may not be applicable to other problems, even to problems from the same domain. I belive that it is necessary to devise *architectures* for the construction of systems. An architecture provides a set of principles which are to be followed and also provides a set of guidelines with which one can analyse the task to be carried out by a system. It is for this reason that, in this book, I will be concerned very much with architectural principles and their application.

The CASSANDRA architecture, described in this book, is based on the blackboard architecture. The blackboard architecture is often claimed to be a highly modular framework within which to construct systems. However, closer inspection shows that there is a number of deficiencies with it in this respect. There are also problems with the fact that the blackboard architecture must be taken intact -- one cannot take subsets -- and this has the immediate consequence that it may not be applicable to certain problems. Blackboard systems require considerable computational resources and they are difficult to construct. Although one might want the modularity of an architecture like the blackboard for a particular problem, the overheads incurred may be excessive.

The CASSANDRA architecture attempts to remedy some of the problems inherent in blackboard systems. In particular, it attempts to be a more modular and additive architecture; it also attempts to simplify the control problem. It is more modular because it requires the decomposition of problem solving knowledge into totally independent, though communicating, units. The units, called Level Managers, communicate by passing messages of various sorts. The new architecture is claimed to be additive because it is possible to introduce additional Level Managers into an existing system without the need to make fundamental changes to those Level Managers already present. This last property is supported, in part, by the requirement that each Level Manager provide a local control facility which is responsible for controlling its

** Cassandra was the Trojan prophetess who foresaw the sack of Troy by the Greeks. I would prefer a less pessimistic name, but, to date, I have found no acceptable alternative.

problem solving actions. The architecture requires only local control, so the addition of a new Level Manager requires only changes to be made to those Level Managers with which it communicates.

The new architecture uses concepts from parallel computation. Concurrent processes which communicate only by message-passing may not directly share data structures, but, must, instead, pass messages containing the data required to continue processing. Processes such as those just outlined are *a fortiori* modular because the interfaces between them are defined by the message-passing system and its protocols. By adopting a vocabulary in which concurrency is highly prominent, the goal of modularity can be emphasised and supported by the architecture: it does not matter whether a CASSANDRA system is actually implemented as a concurrent, distributed or serial program as long as the constraints made by the architecture are met.

The CASSANDRA architecture is an attempt at the knowledge-based management of complexity. It manages complexity by requiring and enforcing high levels of modularity.

1.2. AIMS OF THIS RESEARCH

The research work described below had two main and one subsidiary aims. The two main aims were as follows.

1. The definition of a problem solving architecture which was more modular than the blackboard architecture and which would form the basis for the construction of systems with a structure more explicit than blackboard systems. A major problem with the blackboard architecture is that the relationships between abstraction levels is often implicitly represented within the modules representing problem solving knowledge. This makes the job of determining how intermediate results and problem solving knowledge are related more difficult; it also allows designers to short-cut the abstraction hierarchy and place information at any point on the blackboard. Modular systems are easier to understand and the constraints imposed by requiring modularity force a clearer structure on a system by making the designer define the relationships between components in an explicit fashion.

2. The architecture was to be aimed at the structuring of the knowledge required to construct systems solving complex problems so that they would be highly modular. The desire for modularity was

motivated by the need to add or replace knowledge during system construction and maintenance, and by the need to expand the functionality of a system once it had been constructed. In order to fulfill these aims, well-defined interfaces between system components would have to be defined. The organisational problem in systems solving complex problem is how to organise diverse knowledge into an effective framework. In addition, the control problem poses severe difficulties for systems operating in complex domains. It was necessary, therefore, to be able to provide a framework for control which would also be modular and which could also easily be extended. For these reasons, each system component, it was decided, should provide its own control component: this approach factors the control problem and makes it easier to provide controllers tailored to the specific needs of each system component.

The subsidiary aim was to discover a method for deleting solution elements which were no longer required by the solution process. It is not generally possible to find simple, algorithmic methods because any solution element may, potentially, be of utility at some future time. This fact suggested that a heuristic method, based upon knowledge of problem characteristics, would be more appropriate. The deletion problem is in need of solution for systems which must be in continuous operation or which are constrained to run in real time: this problem frequently occurs in blackboard systems for they are often constructed to solve real time problems.

The aims can be summarised as the knowledge-based management of complexity and deletion.

1.3. THE ARCHITECTURE

The architecture which evolved from these ideas is the CASSANDRA architecture. The architecture's principal component is the *Level Manager*. Level Managers are encapsulation mechanisms which form independent, autonomous units in a system. A Level Manager is composed of a local database in which partial solution elements are stored, a set of Knowledge Sources which procedurally encode problem solving knowledge, a local controller and an interface to a communication medium. Each Level Manager in a CASSANDRA system is an autonomous unit: its Knowledge Sources operate on information which is held locally in the Level Manager's working memory (its *entry* or *local* database) and may directly update only the local state. When a Knowledge Source in a Level Manager wishes to make information available to another Level Manager, it must send a message along a communication channel connecting the Level Manager in which it resides to the Level Manager to which the message is to be sent. In the CASSANDRA architecture, communication channels determine the relationships between Level Managers.

All communication channels between Level Managers must be pre-defined: that is, they must be declared to the system before they can be used. The channel definition process is static and may be only be performed *before* the system is called upon to solve a problem: currently, dynamic communication channel definition is not permitted. The fact that channels are explicitly and statically defined means that the relationships between Level Managers in a CASSANDRA system are also static. The requirement that channels be declared also entails that modularity is enforced: it is not permitted for a Knowledge Source to send messages to Level Managers which have not been connected by channels to the Knowledge Source's Level Manager. Because of the introduction of message-passing in the CASSANDRA architecture, additional constraints have been imposed on Knowledge Source behaviour: this is so that possible problems which arise from implementation as a concurrent system are minimised.

Finally, it should be stated that it is possible to consider the CASSANDRA architecture as providing a more constrained representation for blackboard systems. One does not need to take on board the assumptions of the CASSANDRA architecture, but use it in the design of conventional systems: this is possible because it is possible to express any blackboard system in CASSANDRA terms. The concepts in the CASSANDRA architecture, I will argue, are more tightly defined than in blackboard systems and that the new architecture promotes highly modular descriptions of systems. Since the functionalities of the two architectures are similar and because they employ similar constructs, mappings can be introduced between them -- the CASSANDRA concepts can be mapped onto blackboard concepts by a front-end, thus improving the structure of the blackboard system being constructed. However, this is not the main aim of this book: the book definitely concentrates on the CASSANDRA architecture as an independent entity and examines its properties. Even though one may think of mapping systems described in CASSANDRA terms onto the blackboard architecture, the intent of this book is to show that the CASSANDRA architecture is a framework within which to construct problem-solving systems and that this new framework has more desirable properties than the older architecture.

1.4. TRIAL SYSTEMS

Two experimental systems have been constructed to test the CASSANDRA architecture. The larger system is called CASSANDRA-II. CASSANDRA-II's task is to monitor the progress of aircraft through controlled airspace and to report violations of Air Traffic Control rules to the user. CASSANDRA-II contains nine Level Managers arranged in sets of very loose hierarchies. The message-passing features of the CASSANDRA architecture are not exploited in any complex way in this system, but all Level Managers are architecturally complete and interact in ways prescribed by the architecture specification. CASSANDRA-II was designed to test the Level Manager construct and the possibility and effectiveness of local control: it provides a number of generic control regimes which are used by Level Managers as appropriate.

The second experimental system, WordSys, is very much smaller than CASSANDRA-II. WordSys performs a cognitive modelling task (although the modelling is interpreted in a comparatively loose way). It was constructed to test those aspects of the architecture not well-motivated by the airspace monitoring problem. Unlike CASSANDRA-II, the message-passing facilities defined by the architecture are exploited in WordSys, with message interpretation facilities provided by each Level Manager in the system. WordSys contains three Level Managers arranged in a strict abstraction hierarchy. The task performed by WordSys is the identification of English words from noisy input data representing letter images.

In both systems, deletion Knowledge Sources were provided so that the local database of each Level Manager would not contain out-of-date information and so that each local database would remain at a fairly small size. Both systems contributed to the testing of the idea that entry deletion in blackboard and CASSANDRA systems should be performed as a knowledge-based activity.

By implementing two experimental systems, it has been shown that the CASSANDRA architecture is not tied to any one particular type of domain. The tasks assigned to each system are sufficiently different and make different demands on the architecture to permit one to make this assertion. With only two systems implemented using the architecture, it is not possible reasonably to claim that the architecture is completely general. However, the two experiments afford some grounds for optimism.

1.5. GLOBAL CONTROL

This book addresses the purely *local* issues raised by the new architecture. In particular, I do not investigate issues of global control. There are good reasons for this. Firstly, I want to define the architecture in a fairly complete fashion and the architecture is concerned with local control (with the provision that there *may* be global control if the application demands it). Second, I believe that global control is a problem-specific issue and that general statements are not possible at this time because there have been too few systems similar to those which can be built using the CASSANDRA architecture. It may well be the case that there are useful generalisations which can be stated, but, at present, I suggest we are just too ignorant of them for any such statements to be made. In addition, the two systems examined in this book have extremely simple global control (in fact, the second, WordSys, has no global control at all).

A third and equally important reason why global control is not discussed is that it is possible to build a perfectly legal CASSANDRA system which consists of only *one* Level Manager. In such a system, the question of global control simply does not arise. The position I have taken, therefore, is that global control is a matter for the individual system and should not be prescribed in the architecture definition. Despite these caveats, I will make a few suggestions during the course of the book about how to *think* about global control.

1.6. CONTRIBUTIONS TO KNOWLEDGE

This section lists the contributions to knowledge made by the project reported in this book. The major contribution is the CASSANDRA architecture itself. The architecture can be viewed as a considerably more modular interpretation of the blackboard model of problem solving. The architecture carries over some concepts and ideas from the blackboard architecture. Specifically, it retains the concept of the Knowledge Source and assumes that Knowledge Sources have the same general structure (precondition-action) as they do in blackboard systems. Secondly, the local controllers in CASSANDRA systems are constructed on the basis of knowledge of the characteristics of the problem under attack: they can be implemented as knowledge-based controllers, in other words. Third, intermediate results are explicitly stored in publicly accessible databases: here, though, there is a restriction because each Level Manager has its own database which is shared only by its Knowledge Sources -- there is no truly global database in CASSANDRA systems. Finally, there is the idea of dividing problem solving into different areas and different vocabularies: in blackboard systems, the different areas are represented by abstraction levels and Knowledge Sources, in CASSANDRA systems they are Level Managers and Knowledge Sources.

The components and properties of the architecture which I claim to be new are as follows.

- The Level Manager construct. Level Managers are the primary components of systems built using the CASSANDRA architecture. A Level Manager consists of a wholly local database containing partial solution elements relevant to the activities of the Level Manager, a set of Knowledge Sources which act wholly locally and a local control mechanism tailored to the needs of the Level Manager. Knowledge Sources belonging to a particular Level Manager may not directly interact with other Level Managers: instead, they send messages containing information likely to be of use to the receiving Level Manager. Level Managers are intended to be able to solve small portions of problems (how this is achieved will become clearer below). The contents of the local database are wholly private to the Level Manager which owns the database.
- Local control. Each Level Manager has a purely local control component which is responsible for scheduling the Knowledge Sources belonging to it. Each local controller implements control regimes which are specifically tailored to the activities and needs of its Level Manager. Local controllers may not perform any global control activities: these are performed by a completely separate mechanism if they are required by a particular task.
- Increased modularity. Because the CASSANDRA architecture requires that systems be composed of Level Managers and because each Level Manager is an autonomous, encapsulated object, the result is a very much more modular structure. Modularity is also promoted by the requirement that all inter-Level Manager communication be conducted by the explicit passing of messages. Since communication channels must be declared before they can be used, the interfaces between Level Managers are well-defined and enforceable. The CASSANDRA architecture extends the modularity of blackboard systems by modularising the working memory and control aspects of the system.
- Additivity. Systems constructed using the architecture are modular and the interactions between Level Managers are limited by the message-passing mechanism. This entails that the introduction of

new Level Managers into a system is far easier and far more disciplined than it is in blackboard systems. In addition to the ease of addition of Level Managers, this property entails the fact that CASSANDRA systems can be built according to the needs of the problem: when adopting the blackboard architecture, one has to accept the architecture intact -- one can build a legal CASSANDRA system which contains only *one* Level Manager.

In addition to these features and properties of the architecture, the systems constructed to examine the viability of the architecture include Knowledge Sources which delete solution elements from working memory when they are no longer required. The approach to deletion is knowledge-based: in order to be able to delete something, one must *know* that it is no longer required and one must *know* the conditions under which it may be deleted. The only blackboard system in which the problem of removal of information from working memory has been considered is the HASP/SIAP blackboard system (Feigenbaum, 1982). HASP/SIAP did not delete entries from the blackboard, but, instead, summarised information so that it consumed less memory. Although deletion is common (and rather undisciplined) in production systems, it has been left an open problem for systems with highly structured working memories such as blackboard systems. The solution to the deletion problem reported here is, I believe, not limited to CASSANDRA systems: it is the case that the approach adopted here can be applied directly to blackboard systems.

1.7. RELATIONSHIP TO PREVIOUS WORK

Although there has been a certain amount of work on distributed problem-solving, there has, to date, been no proposal similar to that presented in this book.

Lesser and Corkhill have been active for a number of years in the area of distributed problem-solving (e.g., (Lesser, 1983)), but have concentrated their efforts on systems composed of nodes built from architecturally intact blackboard systems (in fact, copies of HEARSAY-II -- (Erman, 1975) -- but without the speech understanding knowledge). The TRICERO system (Williams, 1984) again, relies upon intact copies of blackboard systems (in this case, AGE (Nii, 1979)) running on separate processors. From the blackboard perspective, there is nothing similar to the CASSANDRA architecture in the literature.

Davis and Smith (Davis, 1983) have proposed a protocol, the Contract Net, for synchronisation and task assignment within a distributed network of problem-solving agents. They make no comments on how the agents in such a network should be organised internally, and concentrate on specifying the external behaviours of agents in terms of a bid-based protocol.

Nilsson and Konolige (Konolige, 1980) have examined planning in a distributed processing environment, but they assume that some form of theorem-prover is provided for each planner. Nilsson and Konolige are more concerned with a specification of the logic of belief necessary for distributed planning than with a general architecture to support such processing.

Rice (Rice, 1986) has developed a formalism for describing distributed problem-solving activities. This notation is similar in some ways to the Actor formalism (e.g., (Lieberman, 1981)) and could form the basis for an architecture. However, Rice's proposals are very different from those presented in this document.

Viewed in another way, the CASSANDRA architecture is a development of the blackboard architecture: in fact, one which increases the modularity and flexibility of the older architecture. Under this interpretation, the CASSANDRA architecture is a descendent of the blackboard architecture (e.g., (Nii, 1986a)) and of object-oriented programming languages (e.g., (Goldberg, 1983)). If one views the CASSANDRA architecture in this way (and this suggests that it is also a knowledge-based technique for system complexity management), one need not consider any of the facilities it provides for exploiting concurrent, distributed execution, and one can root it firmly in both of these traditions. There have, though, to my knowledge, been no formal suggestions that one can construct blackboard systems in the way proposed in this document.

Finally, one can view the architecture as being the result of speculations on the structure of Mind. Fodor (Fodor, 1983) has already been cited as presenting arguments close to the ideas which led to the development of the architecture. The CASSANDRA architecture differs from Fodor's analysis in the way in which it treats horizontal and vertical structure: the architecture allows the system builder to decide upon these distinctions and merely provides a set of standard units from which to compose a system.

Despite these links with previous work, the architecture presented in this book is not the result of taking a previous system or architecture or theory and directly extending it or applying it. The connections with the blackboard architecture are the strongest, but, I would suggest, even here, there are significant differences. Certainly, there are no systems in the literature which are similar in detail to the CASSANDRA architecture presented here.

1.8. BOOK STRUCTURE

This book is organised as follows.

Chapters Two and Three are concerned with the blackboard architecture. The architecture was the basis for the development of the CASSANDRA architecture and many features of the latter were suggested by or adapted from the former. Chapter Two contains descriptions of some of the more important implementations of the blackboard architecture: the descriptions are motivated by a discussion of the blackboard metaphor or model which informally supports the architecture. Chapter Three is concerned with a more rigorous definition of the blackboard architecture and with a discussion of the role of opportunism. Opportunism is frequently cited as the main characteristic of the blackboard architecture, but is less in evidence in the CASSANDRA architecture. The discussion of opportunism is aimed at providing a better understanding of the phenomenon of opportunism (it tends to be treated as an informal construct in the literature) and at trying to dispell the myth that opportunism *is* the blackboard architecture. The latter aim is required so that a fair comparison of the blackboard and CASSANDRA architectures can be made. Chapter Three concludes with a discussion of some problems with the blackboard architecture and with its generality.

Chapter Four contains the definition of the CASSANDRA architecture. The chapter describes the main points of the architecture and compares it with the blackboard architecture. The chapter defines the Level Manager concept in detail and describes how inter-Level Manager communications are to be interpreted in the architecture. There are restrictions imposed on Level Managers and on Knowledge Sources because of the potential within the architecture for parallel implementation: the majority of the restrictions are intended to reduce the risk of deadlock or livelock* in an implementation. The main restriction is that

* Livelock is a condition in which two or more processes spend the whole time communicating with each other and never again communicate with the external world or with other processes. When livelock occurs, the processes involved only engage in mutual communication and do not make progress towards a solution because all their resources are spent in performing the communication. The term will be little used in the remainder of this book; instead, *deadlock* will be cited - this is because it is expected that the reader will be more familiar with deadlock than livelock. Whenever deadlock is cited as a problem, the reader should also bear livelock in mind.

Knowledge Sources are not permitted to engage in direct communication with external Level Managers -- they must always forward their messages via the Level Manager in which they reside. In addition, the semantics of Knowledge Sources are modified so that preconditions are able to request information from other Level Managers.

The chapter also discusses in detail the Control Model used in the CASSANDRA architecture. The Control Model requires a separation between local and global control in CASSANDRA systems. The Control Model is compared with other control models (demon systems, production rule interpreters and two forms of procedure call) to establish that it is genuinely distinct. Finally, chapter five describes and motivates the entry deletion model developed during work on the CASSANDRA-II system. The model is a knowledge-based approach to deletion and is applicable to blackboard as well as to CASSANDRA systems. The deletion model was also used in the experiments on WordSys, the second CASSANDRA system developed during this research.

In Chapter Five, I give an overview of the more substantial of the two experimental systems constructed to test the CASSANDRA architecture. The system, CASSANDRA-II, monitors the progress of aircraft through controlled airspace, and, should there be any violations of air traffic separation rules, sends warning messages to the user. The warning messages inform the user of the aircraft involved in rule violations and also include information on the nature of the violation. CASSANDRA-II was designed as a real-time system which would test the Level Manager construct and the local control hypothesis. The system was constructed with the aid of the Civil Aviation Authority in response to a genuine problem.

A detailed account of the CASSANDRA-II controlled airspace monitoring system is given in Chapter Six. The account describes the airspace simulation employed by CASSANDRA-II: it was not possible, for a variety of reasons, to run the system on a real airspace, so a simulation was used instead. The chapter goes into some detail in its description of the functioning of CASSANDRA-II. It is hoped that enough information is provided in this chapter, together with material in Appendix Two, for a rational reconstruction to be possible: that is, it is hoped that the information provided is sufficient to permit replication of this experiment.

The generality of the CASSANDRA architecture is considered in Chapter Seven. Evidence for generality is adduced from the second system constructed using the architecture. The WordSys system recognises English words from a noisy letter input (the input is intended to imitate some features of the human visual system) and is a reconstruction of a system constructed by McClelland and Rumelhart (McClelland, 1981; Rumelhart, 1982). WordSys was constructed to test the viability of the message-passing component of the architecture for this was used only in very rudimentary form in CASSANDRA-II. The description of WordSys is again comparatively detailed and it is compared with a blackboard system which was implemented to solve exactly the same problem. The comparison of the two architectures was considered to be a useful exercise because the CASSANDRA architecture has its origins in the blackboard architecture. Chapter Seven concludes with a review of the CASSANDRA architecture. The review summarises what has been learned during the project.

The final chapter, Chapter Eight, contains a detailed summary of the main points of this research. It also includes suggestions for further work, the most important of which is that the CASSANDRA architecture should be applied to other tasks. Chapter Eight ends with a few concluding remarks.

The book contains three appendices and a glossary. Appendix One is an introduction to Air Traffic Control and is intended to provide background information to assist the reader with the sections dealing with this domain. Appendix One concentrates on information concerning *en route* operations for this is most relevant to CASSANDRA-II's task. Appendix Two contains high-level descriptions of the Knowledge Sources used in the implementation of CASSANDRA-II: in each case, the Knowledge Source is described in English, and, in some cases, a pseudo-code version is provided as well. An annotated trace produced by running CASSANDRA-II is to be found in Appendix Three. The glossary is provided so that readers will find a quick explanation of the Air Traffic Control terms and abbreviations used in the descriptions of CASSANDRA-II.

2. THE BLACKBOARD MODEL OF PROBLEM SOLVING

2.1. INTRODUCTION

This chapter is concerned with the blackboard metaphor and with descriptions of systems which exemplify the blackboard architecture. In the next chapter, I will present a definition of the architecture and examine its consequences. This organisation is prompted by two things:

(i) it follows history. As Nii points out (Nii, 1986a), the blackboard architecture, in its current interpretation, is a result of abstracting features of HEARSAY-II, the original blackboard system; and,

(ii) the architecture is rather complex. Many of the points in the definition can more easily be seen and understood once one has examined a few blackboard systems.

This chapter does, though, provide the reader with enough general information about the architecture to understand the example system descriptions.

2.1.1. The Model

Despite the fact that there have been many implementations of the blackboard model, they have all differed from one another in some respects, or else have been copies of HEARSAY-II (see section 2.2.2 below). What they share is that they have the same common model as a basis for their architectures. This point is important and has been noted by Barbara Hayes-Roth (Hayes-Roth, 1983). In this section, I will present the model in terms of the metaphor of experts and a traditional physical blackboard. Having presented it, I will discuss some of its extensions and implications, again in metaphorical terms.

2.1.2. The Metaphor

Imagine a group of experts trying to solve a complex problem. The experts are competent in different domains which are relevant to the problem. They stand around a blackboard. They communicate ideas for the solution of the problem by word of mouth, by diagrams which they draw on the blackboard, and by formulae and text which they write on the blackboard. This scene is depicted schematically in fig. 2.1.

Each expert makes a contribution to the problem solving process. The experts can put items on the blackboard, they can erase items from the blackboard, or they can refine items which have been

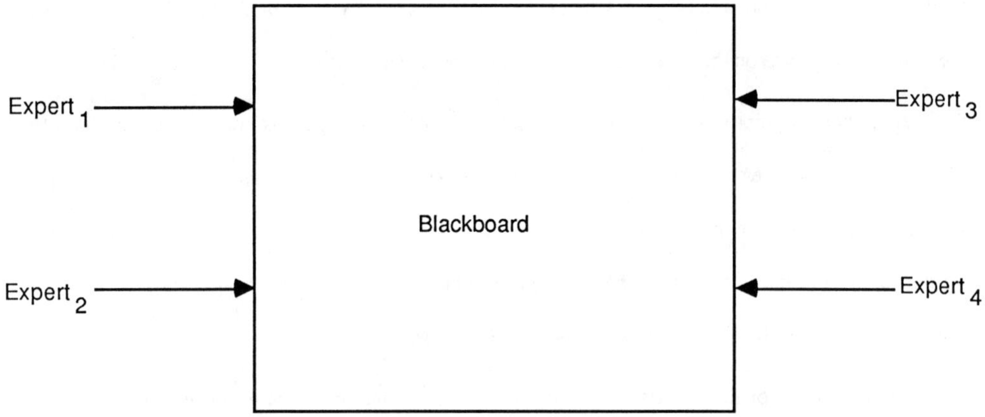

Fig 2.1

The fundamental blackboard model

placed there by someone else. As items are placed on the blackboard, they can begin to form parts of an overall picture which might lead to a solution to the problem (even if they are unable to find one). These collections of parts of the solution are frequently termed "islands". As islands develop they are linked together, perhaps by arrows or some other form of indexing or cross-referencing. Eventually a solution might develop, probably amidst some kind of 'spaghetti' of arrows caused by the fact that the experts put ideas, hypotheses, etc., on the board in the most convenient place.

An important point to note about the metaphor is that each expert is totally independent of the others. Each expert does not rely upon the others for his knowledge, nor for his intervention in the problem solving process. The interventions of an individual expert depend upon what is on the board (at least, for the purposes of the metaphor). When there is something on the board to which at least one expert can respond, then he or she does so, modulo social conventions.

The interaction of the experts described in the last paragraph is an example of opportunism in problem solving. Each expert contributes something to the solution as, and when, the item is needed: the particular item depends upon the state of the solution, and the expert responds to the state of the solution by placing the item on the board. Opportunism can work by the detection of significant patterns in the current solution state and responding to it immediately. A final point to make about the experts' interactions is that they can be either serial or parallel: the experts can put items on the board either one at a time, or two or more experts can put them on the board at the same time.

The account of the experts' problem solving activity given above is, however, somewhat misleading. It is particularly misleading in its implication that the experts merely respond to random events on the blackboard. If this were truly the case, then achieving a coherent solution would be a very hit-and-miss phenomenon. Instead, the experts tend to concentrate on particular aspects of the problem and particular parts of the developing solution. In other words, they focus their attention in an effective manner. In any particular case, the experts will focus on the more promising, or what they perceive to be the more important, features of the problem on the current state of the solution.

Having concentrated on a set of particular features, islands or strategies, it is also possible to see experts relate islands or features which suddenly appear important. This is another example of opportunism, and indicates that problem solving strategies are not adhered to consistently throughout the solution process. This phenomenon has been noted (Hayes-Roth, 1979) and (Hayes-Roth, 1984).

Having discussed the model in metaphorical terms, it is time to look at various implementations and the architectural concepts they employ. For the purposes of the implemented systems, one must consider the experts as being deaf and dumb: they are only able to communicate by placing information on the blackboard and not by talking to each other.

2.2. BLACKBOARD IMPLEMENTATIONS

In this section, the abstract model of the blackboard is transformed into a set of architectural principles shared by the majority of implemented systems. Once the mapping between the model and architecture has been established, a number of example systems are described.

2.2.1. Mapping between Model and Architectures

The model described in the last section contains four main elements:

- a database used by all the experts (the blackboard), and
- the experts themselves;
- items on the blackboard (diagrams, formulae, words, etc.), and
- links between items on the blackboard (arrows, numbers, etc.).

The blackboard represents a database in which records of the steps contributing to the solution are recorded. The database contains items which are placed there by the experts. The records represent states in the solution space which have been explored by the experts. When the problem has been solved, the items on the blackboard represent all the attempts by the experts to converge on that solution.

Although the physical blackboards left behind by human experts seldom show signs of hierarchy, a large proportion of complex problem domains can often be refined on the basis of hierarchies (for example, planning (Sacerdoti, 1974; Sacerdoti, 1977).) The conventional approach to the construction of blackboard systems is to construct a hierarchical organisation for the database based on abstraction, as will be seen in subsequent sub-sections of this chapter. (The reader should note that hierarchical decomposition of the blackboard database is not a necessity.) Within each level in the blackboard hierarchy, items are represented as data structures which are variously termed hypotheses or entries. Each entry (the term preferred in this dissertation) is a complex structure which contains links to other items on the blackboard at the same, or at different, levels of abstraction within the hierarchy.

Entries are placed on the blackboard by Knowledge Sources (KSs) which are the analogues of the experts in the model.

Knowledge Sources are intended to play the role in the architecture which is played by the experts in the model. Knowledge Sources respond to the state of the blackboard by placing new entries on it. Knowledge Sources are activated by some kind of pattern-matching operation (which can be coded predicates which are specific to some application, or can be represented using a pattern-match syntax). If the entries on the blackboard are such that some of the KSs can respond, then they are eligible to make some response. Typical responses for KSs are:

- putting a new entry on the blackboard;
- deleting an entry;
- modifying an entry (by, say, adding a link or set of links connecting it to some other entries); and
- causing an external event (such as requesting some information from a source external to the blackboard system or outputting a result to some other system or to the user).

KSs are normally represented as a pair consisting of triggering-pattern (that which responds to blackboard entries or changes in configuration on the blackboard - the latter is determined by looking for specific links between entries, looking for entries with specific properties or data elements or can be performed on a basis analogous to interrupt processing) and an action-part. The action-part is responsible for performing operations of the kind listed above.

KSs are intended to represent experts. This entails that they should be comprehensive in their function and probably quite large. In HEARSAY-II (see section 2.2.2 below), KSs were very large indeed, but there appears to be a tendency to reduce the size of KSs (e.g. OPM - section 2.3) so that their triggering patterns can be made fuller and their effects on the blackboard reduced in scope.

Although large KSs lead to opaque chunks of code in a blackboard system, they reduce the control overheads just because they are none too specific in their triggering conotations. Small KSs, on the other hand, increase control load (by weight of numbers) and lead to a kind of fragmentation: many KSs may be related to a small set of conditions, but are logically distinct entities which ought to be considered at the same time, but since they are not collected into logical modules, the space of all KSs must be searched for those which can be considered given prevailing circumstances. This point appears to be crucial when considering sophisticated control regimes.

Large KSs also entail that there are possibly many scheduling factors which ought to be taken into account. Smaller KSs tend to lead to fewer parameters just because small KSs are more specific and more easily defined. The reason for this is that large KSs must represent entire classes of solution (as in HEARSAY-II (sect. 2.2.2) whose KSs produced *all* plausible hypotheses on the basis of one input): thus, each of the candidate solutions which *might* be produced by a KS has to be taken into account when scheduling. Also, if a KS has a large grain size, it can, possibly, be activated on a number of regions of the blackboard (one very often finds that what was designed to be a single level on the blackboard, in reality, represents a collection of abstraction levels, each one of which becomes a region for the purposes of side-effects and matching), and, again, these must be taken into account when constructing the scheduler. From these considerations, it can be seen that the number of scheduling parameters tends to increase with the grain size of the KSs in the system.

In the following sub-sections, a number of blackboard systems will be described. Rather than convert the terminology into a neutral form, the terms used in the original papers are used. It is necessary, therefore, to introduce some equivalences between terms. The Hearsay-II term 'hypothesis' is referred to as an 'entry' in OPM and Ariadne-1 (Craig, 1986); the conventional term 'KS' is changed to 'specialist' in the Hayes-Roths' 1979 OPM planning system. The Hayes-Roths also use the term 'partition' where others use the term 'panel'.

2.2.2. HEARSAY-II

The HEARSAY-II continuous speech understanding system (Erman, 1975* and Hayes-Roth, 1977) was

* This description is mostly taken from Erman.

the second and, perhaps the best known implementation of the blackboard model. The task domain of HEARSAY-II was the understanding of continuous speech in approximately real time.** The blackboard model was chosen for HEARSAY-II because of the large problem space and the large amount of knowledge required for the solution of the problem. Furthermore, the knowledge needed for the domain is diverse, including signal analysis, phonology, syntax and semantics. Other factors included the problem that the knowledge provided in the system may contain errors or may be incomplete (either theoretically, or because the implementation is incomplete or erroneous). This problem requires that results must be classified into linguistic structures (such as valid phonemes, words, phrases) as soon as possible using the knowledge possessed by the system (in the form of its Knowedge Sources) and that errors should be reduced: this entails that items of knowledge should co-operate in the solution. Furthermore, the limitations of the researchers' understanding of the domain entailed that a high degree of modularity was required, both in the representation of knowledge and in the strategies used to control the application of that knowledge.

The global database of HEARSAY-II is partitioned into distinct information levels. Each level holds a different representation of the problem space. The levels in the blackboard are organized in a loose hierarchy: the hierarchy is based upon abstraction.*** The lowest level is concerned with digitized signal processing (this is termed the parametric level); the highest level is the conceptual level which deals with the concepts used in the utterance being analysed. Within each level, there are hypotheses. Hypotheses correspond to the 'entries' of the previous sub-section. Each hypothesis is composed of a set of primitive elements associated with a particular level (for example, the lexical level contains words from the lexicon as its primitive entities). Hypotheses exist only at particular levels and are labelled as being some particular element of the set of primitive entities for that level. The level structure of the HEARSAY-II blackboard is shown in fig. 2.2 (from Erman, 1975).

The decomposition of levels in the blackboard represents a natural decomposition of the problem space: it also parallels the decomposition of Knowledge Sources (see below). The loosely hierarch-

** The domain was the language used to extract computer science abstracts from a database.

*** Most implementations have retained the abstraction hierarchy for various reasons -- e.g., see the comments on the SU programs below (sect. 2.2.5).

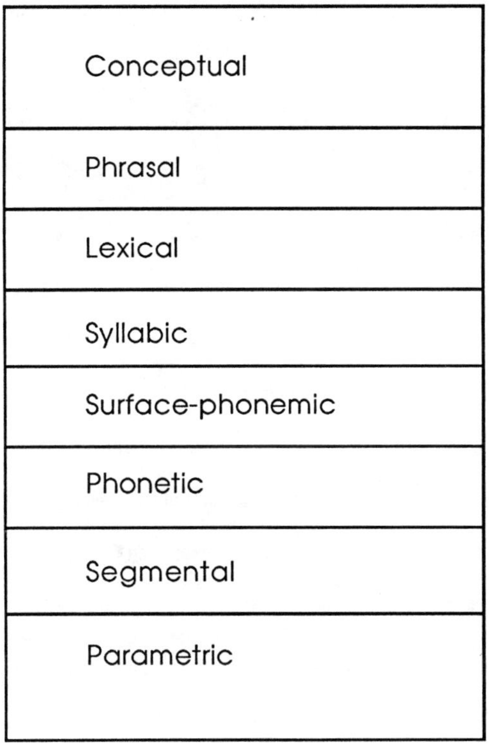

Fig 2.2

Abstraction levels in HEARSAY-II

ical structure of the blackboard leads to the description of a level as being an abstraction of levels lower than it in the hierarchy. The abstraction mechanism can be exemplified as follows: a lexical item (word) is composed of syllables; syllables are composed of phonemes, each of which is composed of acoustic segments.

Hypotheses on the blackboard are connected by numerically weighted links to form a network: the numerical weighting represents the strength (i.e., the plausibility) of that link. The majority of the relationships which exist are between hypotheses at the same level of abstractions. Speech understanding depends upon linear sequences of items (for example the sequence of lexemes is crucial in non-inflected languages such as English): therefore, many links represent the ordering of items with respect to time within a level (for example, at the parametric level, hypotheses are ordered by the arrival time of the signal components). Other kinds of link exist: these usually relate an hypothesis at one level of abstraction with hypotheses at other, typically adjacent levels. The hypotheses and the levels on which they occur, form a context within which knowledge sources can activate. A fragment of the HEARSAY-II blackboard is shown in fig. 2.3 (from Erman, 1975).

Hypotheses, as was noted above, are structured objects. The goal of HEARSAY-II is to form plausible hypotheses from the input signal. Hypotheses contain a field containing the rating of the hypothesis. This is a universal measure of the plausibility of the hypothesis (similar to confidence factors in MYCIN (Shortliffe, 1976)) and is derived from a number of sources such as a priori information about the hypothesis, information derived from hypotheses at a lower level (synthesis) or information derived from hypotheses at a higher level (analysis). There are also fields for recording the amount of computational resources expended on an hypothesis.

The HEARSAY-II system has been described (Erman, 1975) as a "multi-level organization for problem solving using many, diverse, co-operating sources of knowledge". In the system, hypotheses represent short-term memory structures, whereas long-term memory structure is represented as Knowledge Sources (KSs).

Knowledge Sources in HEARSAY-II parallel the decomposition of the blackboard: they partition the problem space into logically distinct areas of expertise in a natural fashion. KSs are usually

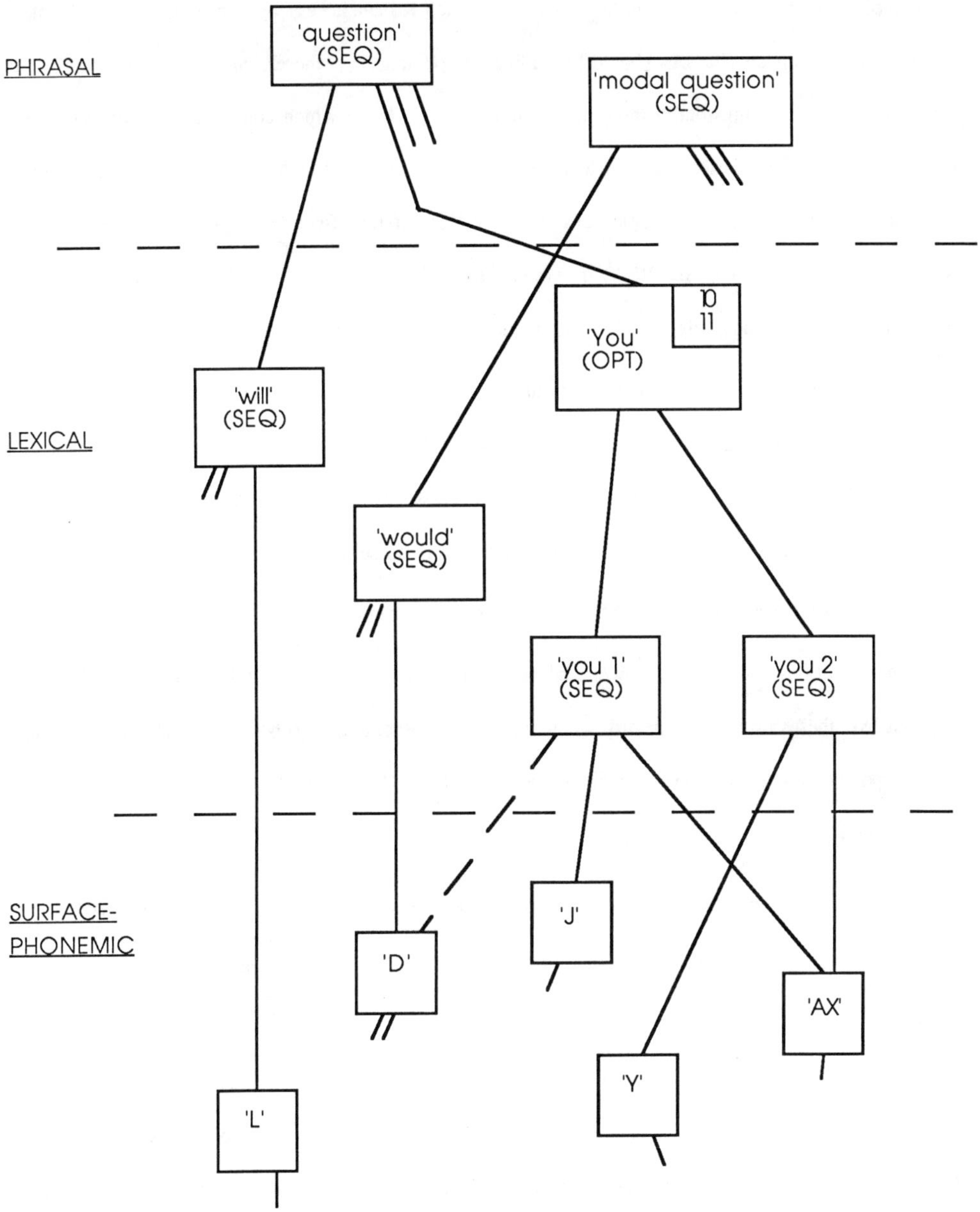

Fig 2.3

A fragment of the HEARSAY-II blackboard

associated with one or two levels on the blackboard. Each KS can access any information on the blackboard and can update the blackboard by adding or updating hypotheses and by adding (etc.) links. KSs are viewed as being totally independent items of knowledge which communicate with each other only through the hypotheses on the blackboard. This constraint entails that each KSs is not aware of the existence of other KSs. The addition or removal of KSs can not affect the other KSs in the system. The Knowledge Sources in the HEARSAY-II system in 1975 are shown in fig. 2.4. The figure shows the interactions between Knowledge Sources and the levels on which they operate.

The high degree of modularity inherent in this approach was one of the design aims of the system. As a strategy for building systems such as HEARSAY-II, the blackboard model requires experimentation with both the knowledge content of the system and the strategies used to control the knowledge in the system. (The control aspects of HEARSAY-II will be described below).

Knowledge Sources in HEARSAY-II have three components:

- the conditions under which they can be activated. This is expressed in terms of the configuration of hypotheses on the blackboard which causes the KS condition to become matched, or the single hypothesis on the blackboard which uniquely matches a KS condition.
- the kinds of changes the KS makes to the blackboard.
- a procedural statement of the algorithm which makes the changes (this is a piece of SAIL code).

KSs possess the computational ability to solve subproblems given appropriate conditions on the blackboard.

KSs are activated and instantiated whenever the blackboard exhibits characteristics which satisfy a precondition of the KS. A KS precondition is a description of a partial state of the blackboard which defines when and where a KS can make a contribution to the problem solving process (the location is specified in the stimulus-response frame associated with each KS). In HEARSAY-II, contributions are made relative to a context: a context is a subset of the previously generated hypotheses already on the blackboard. Modifications caused by a KS are used to trigger further KS activations by creating new conditions to which other KSs can respond. KSs run in data-directed mode: the data which causes activa-

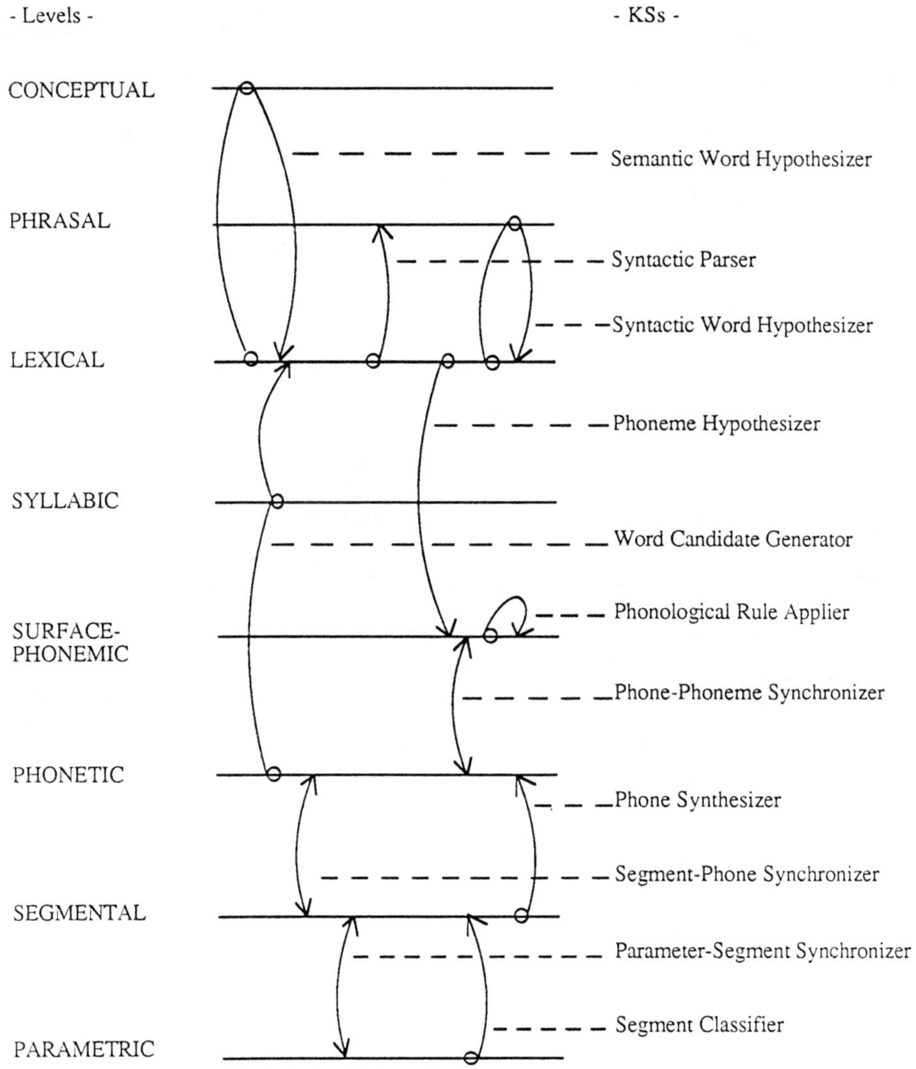

Fig 2.4

HEARSAY-II Knowledge Sources (1975)

tion are the hypotheses on the blackboard. This entails that KSs can also exhibit a high degree of asynchronous activity and potential concurrency.

In HEARSAY-II, KSs are always associated with only a very few abstraction levels, sometimes only one. Given the modularity of the KSs, conceptually KSs need only be aware of the levels with which they interact directly: all other levels are, in effect, invisible to them. Thus, the preconditions of a KS are restricted in the range of objects which can activate them.

The precondition evaluation in HEARSAY-II is made more efficient by placing functions in the routines which update the blackboard. These functions are activated when a KS modifies an attribute of a blackboard hypothesis which some other KS(s) has (have) asked to be monitored. This data is held in a structure called the change set which is specific to the monitored attribute and the KS responsible for the monitoring. KSs can specify either statically or dynamically those attributes they may wish to have monitored. Monitoring can be restricted to individual levels or hypotheses.

Change sets categorize events (blackboard modifications) and are useful in precondition evaluation because they limit the areas of the blackboard which need to be examined in detail.

HEARSAY-II is a goal-directed system and employs a two-stage scheduler to control KS activation. The goal of the system is to produce the most plausible network of hypotheses from the input data. At any stage, there will be incomplete networks of hypotheses which possibly share sub-networks. During processing, networks can be extended or contracted. At any one time, there can be many KSs which can be activated. The HEARSAY-II system uses a goal-directed scheduler to decide which KSs to activate.

The scheduler uses some of the hypothesis attributes in making decisions, for example there are attention attributes which state how much processor time has been used by the system attending to the hypothesis. KSs can also suggest how desirable it is to devote effort to an hypothesis. Processing state attributes are also used by the scheduler.

The scheduler can also use focussing factors which highlight activity in areas of the blackboard in which there are no links between adjacent levels. In such cases, the scheduler should give higher priority to a KS which attempts to make such connections (this is indicated in the KS's external specifications) than to a KS which makes minor alterations to hypotheses. Alternatively, a KS may be selected because it is the only one which can be run. A further factor which determines activation priority is the validity of the hypotheses in the area of the blackboard which satisfied the preconditions of KSs. This last data can be used to implement a best-first strategy.

The implementation of goal-directed scheduling is decoupled from the actions of individual KSs. The decoupling of KSs and scheduling leads to a quick refocussing of KS attention. Rapid refocussing is important to HEARSAY-II because of the errorful nature of KS activity which leads to incomplete and possibly contradictory hypotheses.

Focussing factors are goals (attention attributes) attached to hypotheses. Goals indicate the kind of change desired in a hypothesis attribute and the desirability of the change. HEARSAY-II permits goals to be attached to regions of the blackboard and not just hypotheses. Hayes-Roth and Lesser (Hayes-Roth, 1977) describe in detail a more detailed and general focussing mechanism for HEARSAY-II. I will return to the HEARSAY-II scheduler when discussing OPM (section 2.2.3.2, below).

2.2.3. OPM

The blackboard system described in (Hayes-Roth, 1979) represents a development of the HEARSAY-II implementation. The blackboard develops HEARSAY-II by introducing extra structural partitions into the model, by explicitly representing control information and by simplifying control.

The extra architectural divisions of the blackboard and the explicit representation of control make this system particularly interesting.

The task domain of the system is errand-planning. The knowledge embodied in the system is derived from protocols taken from human subjects who were given a set of tasks to perform (such as 'get medication for the dog') in the context of an imaginary town. The system is presented with the specification of a number of individual tasks that must be performed, but it was not required that the errands be performed in any particular *a priori* order: that is, the errands were presented to the system in no fixed order, although some were clearly more important than others (for example, tasks that involved the well-being of the dog). It was up to the system, just as it had been up to the human subjects, to determine which tasks should be performed and in what order.

The decomposition of the planning problem given by the Hayes-Roths is that it is composed of two primary components: the first is the assembly of planning operators; the second is the execution of the plan. They refer to this paradigm as planning and control. However, unlike Sacerdoti's NOAH system (Sacerdoti, 1974), the approach they advocate is not, basically, hierarchical, but opportunistic. (Opportunism was described in section 2.1 as a motivating factor for the blackboard model). The Hayes-Roths do make the point that opportunism is not incompatible with refinement planning (this is because they are both, basically, control strategies).

In the context of the 1979 system, the Hayes-Roths describe opportunism as follows: "However, we assume that people's activity is largely opportunistic. That is, at each point in the process, the planner's current decisions and observations suggest various opportunities for plan development. The planner's subsequent decisions follow up on selected opportunities. Sometimes, these decision sequences follow an orderly path and produce a neat top-down expansion as described above. However, some decisions and observations might also suggest less orderly opportunities for plan development." (Hayes-Roth, 1979, p.276).

The resulting system uses an opportunistic model of control. The knowledge in the system is derived from the experimentally obtained human protocols. The knowledge derived from the protocols is encoded as knowledge sources which are called specialists (Hayes-Roth, 1979, pp 285,286).

The specialists make tentative decisions for incorporation in a tentative plan. Specialists are differentiated along a number of dimensions, one of which is abstraction - some specialists suggest high-level, abstract additions to the plan; others make detailed sequences of specific actions. Specialists are described in the simulation system as generalised condition-action pairs (similar to the trigger-pattern/action-part description KS in section 2.2.1). Specialists respond either to planning decisions already made, or they can also respond to configurations of decisions, just as HEARSAY-II Knowledge Sources can be activated by the presence or absence of links between hypotheses. The action component of specialists can perform arbitrary amounts of computation, but must result in the creation or modification of decisions on the blackboard.

As with HEARSAY-II, specialists are associated with abstraction levels on the blackboard. The planning system, however, introduces extra structural divisions, called planes, on the blackboard. The planning system has a blackboard with five planes: plan, plan-abstractions, knowledge base, executive and meta-plan. Each plane is concerned with a specific kind of function within the system. The structural divisions are motivated by the need to separate the functions and to provide facilities to perform each of the functions independently of each other. Each plane is divided into abstraction levels: in this respect, each plane operates as a complete HEARSAY-II blackboard, but communication between planes is always possible (by means of specialists).

The plan plane contains items which represent those actions the planner intends to take in the world. In the context of the imaginary town used in the experiment, the planner might want to travel round in a circle or take the shortest route between all the places on the list of errands.

Decisions on the plan-abstraction plane characterise the properties of plan decisions (on the plan plane) which are made by the planner. In other words, the decisions on this plane represent the plan that will eventually be generated at a high level of abstraction. The relationship between the plan-abstraction and plan planes is similar to that between the abstract and concrete levels of plan description in hierarchical planning systems such as NOAH (Sacerdoti, 1974). These decisions indicate the actions the planner wants to take, but without specifying the actions in any kind of detail. Decisions in this plane represent descriptions of sequences of actions. These do not identify particular sequences of actions which need to be taken. Alternatively, the planner may decide to organise the plan around a spatial cluster of errands: this is, again, abstract and does not specify particular actions.

The knowledge-base plane contains observations and computations about relationships in the world of the imaginary town which might have some relevance for the planning process. These items are useful in suggesting plan-abstractions and in initiating them in the resulting plan.

The combination of plan, plan-abstraction and knowledge-base provide a context within which to determine features of the plan. The executive plane determines features of the planning process. The executive plane contains decisions about the allocation of resources. These determine which aspects of the plan are to be developed and which specialists are to be employed at any given point in the planning process. For example, the executive might decide to determine which errands are to be included in the plan before producing any details of the plan, or it might decide to focus on finding routes for previously sequenced errands.

The meta-plan plane contains decisions about how the planning problem should be approached. The decisions made by the meta-plan plane reflect the planner's understanding of the problem, the methods to apply to the planning problem and the criteria to be applied in the evaluation of the various solutions derived by other planes.

As was stated above, the model adopted by the Hayes-Roths divides each plane into levels of abstraction, in a manner very much like the division of the HEARSAY-II blackboard. It is therefore possible to consider the abstraction levels which sub-divide the problem space represented by each plane. The levels in each plane form a potential hierarchy.

In the plan plane, the four levels represent a refinement hierarchy, each level of which represents a more abstract version of the developing plan than the level(s) which is (are) below it. The most abstract level expresses the outcomes that the planner expects from the plan; the most concrete level is the operation level which specifies the sequence of actions which are to be realised in the world. Between these levels are the designs level and the procedure level, in decreasing order of abstraction. The designs level characterises the general approach to be taken by the planner to achieve the desired outcomes. Specific sequences of actions (which are refined by the operations level) are defined by the procedures plane: in the errand planning domain, procedures specify sequences of errands.

The plan-abstraction plane also has four levels. Each level contains characteristics of the type of decisions to be incorporated in the plan. There is a correspondence between the plan-abstraction plane and the plan plane: decisions made on each level of the plan-abstraction plane map directly onto the more concrete decisions made on the corresponding level of the plan plane. Within the plan-abstraction plane, intentions are indicated at the highest level: these map onto the outcomes of the plan plane. Intentions establish all of the initial errands to be performed. Below intentions come schemes which suggest designs featuring spatial clusters of errands in the plan. Next, the planner might develop strategies to schedule errands; below this, come tactics which look for short-cuts between errands.

Tactics determine desirable operation level decisions in the plan plane.

The knowledge base panel has four levels. The knowledge base plane contains problem-specific information. The four levels are errand, layout, neighbour, and route. Each level contains observations and computations required to perform the corresponding operations in the plan and plan-abstraction planes. Information contained in the knowledge base plane is derived from the topography of the town in which the errands are to be performed.

In contrast to the three planes already discussed, the executive plane has only three levels. The inclusion of the executive plane is the second of the interesting points about this system. It performs a hierarchical control task: each level refines the level above it. At the highest level, the plane makes decisions about the priorities of various requests for resources. Priority decisions indicate where resources should be allocated: this acts as a focussing mechanism which directs attention to some areas of the plan plane before attention is directed to others. The next level is the focus level. The focus level makes decisions which indicate the decisions to be made at any specific point in the planning process. Finally, schedule decisions are made to resolve conflicts between scheduling decisions and are made in a manner similar to those used in the later work on HEARSAY-II (Hayes-Roth, 1977). The impact of a separate division of the blackboard will be discussed in greater detail in the next section.

The final plane is the meta-plan plane, which has four levels. Unlike the other planes, the meta-plan plane does not divide into a neat hierarchy: instead, it emphasises different aspects of the human subject's approach to the planning problem. The levels on this plane relate in systematic ways to the other planes of the blackboard. Since this plane is highly-subject specific, no further description will be given.

The layout of the Hayes-Roth's blackboard is shown in fig. 2.5. The figure also shows some illustrative actions of specialists (KSs).

OPM is of considerable interest because of its division of the global database into planes, each of which is concerned with a specific kind of cognitive process. In their paper (Hayes-Roth, 1979) the Hayes-Roths state that the division into planes is somewhat arbitrary, but is justifiable on the basis of subjects' explanations of the kinds of knowledge they apply in the planning process. The importance

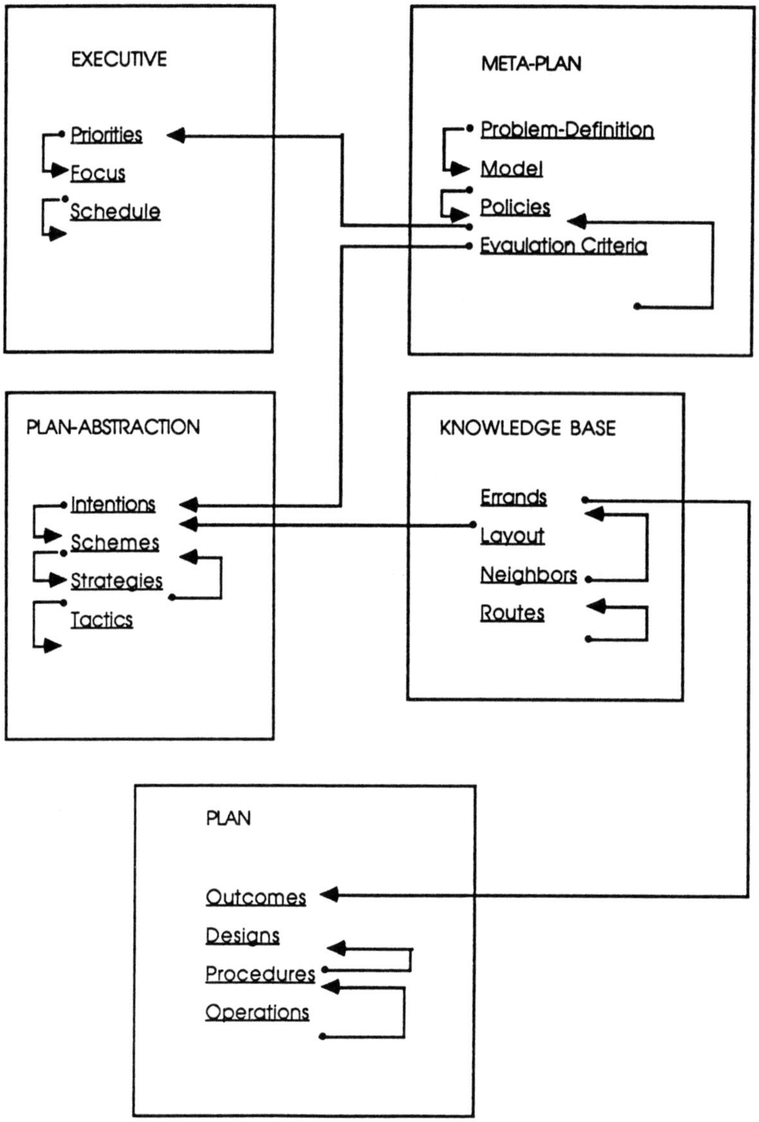

Fig 2.5

The planning blackboard (Hayes-Roth & Hayes-Roth, 1979)
(levels are underlined; KS actions are indicated by arrows)

of the system for this chapter is that it emphasises not only the flexibility of the blackboard model, but also the fact that fine distinctions in the knowledge used to solve problems can be reflected in the structure of the problem solving system. Thus the errand planning system distinguishes plans from plan-abstractions and meta-plans (which have also been investigated by Wilensky (Wilensky, 1983) and Schank (Schank, 1982)): the three planning-specific planes are kept separate from knowledge about the environment in which the errands are to be performed. Finally, the four planes just mentioned are separated from the executive plane which controls the system by means of the explicit representation of control information.

The second point about the system is the executive plane. The executive controls the planning actions of the system. Control decisions are represented explicitly in the executive plane. Explicit representation of control implies that the system can reason about control. Control is thus amenable to intelligent processing, and becomes another domain in which problems can be solved. In the next section, when considering the Blackboard Control Model and Hearsay-III the benefits of explicit control will be examined in greater detail.

2.2.4. Hearsay-III and the Blackboard Control Model

In this section, Hearsay-III (Balzer, 1980; Erman, 1981) and the Blackboard Control Model (Hayes-Roth, 1983a; Hayes-Roth, 1984, Hayes-Roth, 1985) are described. The two systems are grouped together for the following reasons:

1. Both systems basically follow the HEARSAY-II architecture;
2. Both systems contain structural divisions for the explicit control of domain knowledge (as is the case in the Hayes-Roth's system described in the last section).
3. Both systems represent considerable developments of the original HEARSAY-II design.

This section is divided into two parts. The first part describes Hearsay-III. Then the Control Model will be described. The discussion of the Control Model centres on a description of the control structure (rather than on particular implementations) and alternative control regimes for HEARSAY-II and the HASP sonar interpretation system (Feigenbaum, 1982).

2.2.4.1. Hearsay-III

Hearsay-III (Balzer, 1980; Erman, 1981) is designed to be a flexible tool for the construction of knowledge-based or expert systems (it is a shell, devoid of domain-specific knowledge similar in spirit to EMYCIN (van Melle, 1979) -- see also (Kunz, 1983).)

Hearsay-III is implemented on top of a relational database system, called AP3 (Goldman, 1978), from which it inherits strong typing and control facilities. The use of AP3 as a base for Hearsay-III is one of the distinguishing features of Hearsay-III's implementation. AP3 has similarities with the PLANNER-like languages (Hewitt, 1972) and Prolog (Clocksin, 1982; Kowalski, 1979; Warren, 1977; Colmerauer, 1975), but it also provides strong typing for assertions, retrievals and argument transmission in function calls (similar features have been proposed for Prolog by Mycroft (Mycroft, 1984)). All of the publicly accessible data structures in Hearsay-III are represented as structures in the AP3 database. AP3 also provides demons* which are used by Hearsay-III Knowledge Source triggering patterns. Because triggering patterns in knowledge sources are represented as demons, KSs can respond easily to changes in the blackboard.

AP3 also provides a context mechanism similar to that found in CONNIVER (McDermott, 1974). Hearsay-III makes the context mechanism available to user applications, and also makes it an integrated part of the reasoning mechanism. Contexts allow reasoning along independent paths which can be generated by competing knowledge sources and by choices among competing solutions.

Finally, AP3 provides facilities for inference rules and constraints, both of which are available to Hearsay-III users for the representation of global domain-dependent relationships. Inference rules and constraints are also used in the implementation of Hearsay-III (Erman, 1981).

The facilities afforded by the AP3 relational database system were, at the time Hearsay-III was built, unique in a shell.

In Hearsay-III, as in all of the systems described in this chapter, the central communications medium is the blackboard. However, in Hearsay-III, the structures appearing on the blackboard are

* A demon is a procedure which is activated in an asynchronous fashion when some condition obtains in the 'world' which the demon is monitoring.

quite different from those found in other systems.

The Hearsay-III blackboard contains a graph representing partial solutions and pending actions. Partial solutions and pending actions are represented as nodes in the graph. These have internal structure, and are referred to as units: the arcs between nodes are called roles. The blackboard in Hearsay-III is initially divided into two parts, called the domain blackboard (which represents partial results and pending actions specific to the problem domain), and the scheduling blackboard. The scheduling blackboard is used to control domain and control knowledge. Control knowledge is represented in the form of knowledge sources (Hearsay-III Knowledge Sources are slightly different from conventional KSs as will be described below).

The two blackboards mentioned above are the minimum divisions of Hearsay-III. Application builders can further subdivide the blackboard as necessary. This can be achieved by use of the class structure of the system.

The units which represent nodes in the blackboard graph are implemented as typed objects in AP3. The types are referred to as unit-classes. The division of the blackboard into logically distinct spaces is achieved by decomposing the most general class into several, distinct, subclasses. The domain blackboard is composed of the class Domain-Unit and its subclasses; the scheduling blackboard is composed, in the same way, of the class Scheduling Unit. Access is restricted to particular classes by means of the AP3 typing mechanism. User-defined classes can be used to introduce finer divisions of the blackboard.

In addition to their types, units have internal structure. An interesting and important feature of unit structure is that they can represent unresolved decisions. Units of this kind are called choice sets. Choice sets are associated with a set of alternatives which can be static (i.e. declaratively represented), or dynamic (i.e., represented by generators of alternatives). Choice sets can be thought of as the partial elaboration of a decision: the alternatives represent further, potential, elaborations of the decision. Alternatives can, themselves, be choice sets. The choice set permits competing solutions to spread from a single point on the blackboard.

Since choice sets represent ambiguities in the solution space generated by the knowledge in an application system, mechanisms must be provided to resolve the ambiguities. Hearsay-III provides two mechanisms to do this. The first mechanism is called "deduce-mode Choose": this can be used when the application has conclusive evidence that one alternative is the correct solution for the problem represented by the choice set. The deduce-mode Choose is backed up by the fact that the application will not retract the choice it has made when further evidence comes to light. When a deduce-mode choose is made, the choice set is replaced by the selected alternative in the context in which the choice is made (all decisions are made within contexts). When the alternative is selected, all evidence of the choice set is removed from the context in which it occurred (so that no backtracking or retraction can be performed - deduce mode removes non-determinism).

The second choice mechanism is called "assume-mode Choose". An assume-mode Choose replaces the choice set by a unit which represents the merge of the choices, as is the case in deduce-mode. Assume-mode, however, makes changes in the contexts on the blackboard: a new context is created as a child of the context in which the choice was made (and thereby inherits all the units in the parent context, its parent, and so on). The structure in the new context is identical to that produced by deduce-mode. The choice-set still exists in the parent context, but it has one alternative removed: the alternative which is removed is the one which was selected to become part of the new child context. If subsequent inference indicates that the choice was not the best, it can be retracted, and focus can return to the parent context, and another alternative selected. Assume-mode choice permits both backtracking and the removal of assumptions: it permits backtracking in a variety of forms, such as dependency-directed backtracking (Sussman, 1977). Assume-mode choose could be used to build a system using Truth Maintenance (Doyle, 1979); also, it introduces a measure of non-determinism into inference.

Units have a further attribute associated with them: this is called an acceptance. Acceptance is the process of assimilating a unit into a larger structure and verifying that it is appropriate in that structure. Hearsay-III permits the application-builder to associate a LISP predicate with each unit class. This performs the functions of validation, canonicalisation (determining whether the unit is in canonical form for the larger structure), uniqueness-determinination, conflict-determination and integration. Each time a unit is created or is marked as unaccepted by a Knowledge Source, the acceptance routines for the unit's class are executed: if they all return true, the unit is marked accepted, otherwise, it is marked unaccepted, and the unit's context is marked as *poisoned* (see below). Hearsay-III prevents KSs from triggering on unaccepted units, since they are not certain to contribute to the solution of the current problem.

As was stated above, units have arcs which connect them with other units in the graph on the blackboard. The arcs are called roles or component roles. Roles in Hearsay-III are typed relations, and this considerably simplifies the searching of the structure when retrievals are performed. Roles belong to classes, called role sets. Role sets can be used for two purposes. Firstly, role sets define logically distinct component hierarchies in which units can be represented: the hierarchy is defined as the transitive closure of all the roles in the role set. The hierarchies defined over roles act to generate abstractions of the blackboard structure.

The second use of role sets is the description of mutually exclusive units in aggregated structures on the blackboard. Mutual exclusion works by prohibiting structures in which there are two units which are both components of a third unit, both of which have a unique fourth unit in common. This prohibition entails that partial solutions should not be interpreted in different ways in a global solution.

A number of references have been made to the context mechanism in Hearsay-III: it is now time to consider it in more detail.

Choice sets provide a means for representing unmade decisions about alternative interpretations. However, on their own, choice sets are inadequate for they are unable to prohibit interference between investigations into alternatives. The extra structure is provided by the context mechanism. Contexts were invoked when describing deduce- and assume-mode choices, but the relationship between context and the control of inference was not made explicit.

Contexts in Hearsay-III are organised into a hierarchy in a manner similar to units. They are used to present reasoning in logically distinct subspaces of the entire solution space without interference from other, concurrent, reasoning attempts. KSs trigger in the most general context in which its pattern is matched. When the action-part of the KS is executed, it performs actions in the context in which its trigger evaluated to true (unless the KS explicitly changes the context in which it is to act). When actions have been made in a context, the results of those actions are inherited by all sub-contexts of the context in which the action was performed (i.e., all contexts which are closer to the leaves of the tree of contexts which have the context in which the actions were performed as its root).

Contexts can be marked as being unsuitable for executing KSs. This condition is termed poisoned. Poisoned contexts result from the violation of a Hearsay-III constraint, for example trying to aggregate conflicting units. A KS can poison contexts, if, for example, it discovers a violated domain constraint. If a KS has been activated or triggered in a poisoned context, it is put into a wait state until the context is unpoisoned. Hearsay-III permits special KSs, called poison handlers, to run in poisoned contexts. Poison handlers are intended to diagnose and correct the problems which caused the poisoning in the first place.

Knowledge Sources (KSs) in Hearsay-III are another component of the system which is interestingly different from the other systems described in this chapter. As in other blackboard systems, Hearsay-III KSs represent long term memory or the experts in the blackboard model. KSs react to changes on the blackboard and can perform all the functions normally associated with KSs. However, the extra structure of the blackboard and the implementation of Hearsay-III in AP3 entail some significant differences in Hearsay-III KSs.

The structure of Hearsay-III Knowledge Sources differs from the structure of HEARSAY-II KSs. In Hearsay-III, KSs have a triggering-pattern, a piece of immediate code and a body. Whenever the triggering-pattern matches an object on the blackboard, Hearsay-III creates a unit, called an activation record, and runs the immediate code. At some later time, the activation record might be chosen by the scheduler and executed. KS execution means that the body is run: the body is an arbitrary piece of LISP.

The KS activation process, in more detail, is thus:

The triggering pattern is a pattern in AP3. The triggering pattern is a predicate, whose primitives can be AP3 templates and arbitrary LISP predicates composed with the logical operators *and*, *or* and *not* and is modified such that if any AP3 templates in a pattern are satisfied, the entire KS triggering-pattern is evaluated. If the entire pattern matches, then an activation record is created. Activation records contain the name of the triggered KS, the AP3 context in which the KS matched (in AP3, the most general context) and the variables instantiated by the match.

- When the activation record is created, the immediate code is run. Immediate code is composed of arbitrary LISP code: it can associate information with the activation record which may be of some value when selecting an activation record for execution. The immediate code returns, as its value, the name of some unit class on the scheduling blackboard. The activation record is placed on the scheduling blackboard as a unit of the class named by the immediate code. Immediate code is run in the triggering context of the KS and can access the instantiated pattern variables.
- Some time later, the scheduler calls on the Hearsay-III Execute action. The Execute action is applied to the activation record. The usual result of this is to run the body of the KS corresponding to the activation record. The body is run in the triggering context and has access to the instantiated pattern variables. If the triggering context is poisoned when the body is run, and the KS is not a poison handler, the body cannot be run. Instead, the activation record is marked as waiting for the context to become unpoisoned: if the context is ever unpoisoned, the activation record is marked ready (the status of activation records whose contexts are not poisoned).

In Hearsay-III, KS execution is indivisible. KSs run to completion and are not interrupted to allow other KSs to be run. This constraint simplifies the construction of KS bodies and the interactions permitted between KSs and units on the blackboard.

Hearsay-III is intended to be used in domains in which activation record selection (scheduling) is complex. This is why there is a scheduling blackboard in the system. The scheduling blackboard provides a medium for the explicit representation of control; it also allows application builders to experiment with control schemes. Scheduling decisions are represented as units on the scheduling blackboard (these units are activation records, amongst other things), and scheduling knowledge is represented as scheduling KSs.

The second phase of KS operation creates activation records. Activation records contain KS-specific information. Scheduling KSs can make additional changes to the scheduling blackboard: this contributes to the selection of activation records. Scheduling KSs are able to respond to changes on both domain and scheduling blackboards. The actions which scheduling KSs can take include associating information with activation records (for example, assigning and modifying priorities) and creating new units to represent meta-information about the domain blackboard (this might be setting priorities in the currently highest-rated unit in the domain blackboard).

Just as the domain blackboard is the database for domain problem solving, the scheduling blackboard is the database for control decisions.

In order to get the scheduling blackboard and its associated KSs to work, the application-builder must provide a base scheduler. The base scheduler is a LISP procedure which calls the Hearsay-III Execute primitive to run selected KSs. It is called after system startup, and is intended to be as simple as possible since most of the knowledge about scheduling in the system ought to be expressed as KSs. One version of the base scheduler just removes the first element from a queue: should the queue become empty, the base scheduler just terminates - this denotes the end of the run.

Hearsay-III does provide a default base scheduler. It is constructed from two procedures: the outer base scheduler, which repeatedly calls the inner base scheduler. The latter is expected to return a list of activation records. If the returned list is empty, the scheduler terminates. When the outer base scheduler gets a non-empty list, it runs each KS denoted by the activation records in turn. If the KS which is selected is a scheduling KS, its execution returns a list of non-scheduling KSs. The outer base scheduler executes each of these KSs in turn. When the inner base-scheduler is invoked, it selects one ready scheduling KS in a non-deterministic fashion.

The builders of Hearsay-III expect that the default inner base scheduler will be replaced by an application-specific scheduler. The outer base scheduler is expected to be a reasonable skeleton for many applications.

2.2.4.2. The Blackboard Control Model

The work described in (Hayes-Roth, 1984; Hayes-Roth, 1985) grew out of work with the errand planning system (Hayes-Roth, 1979). The Control Model has, by now, been used in a variety of systems (e.g., PROTEAN (Hayes-Roth, 1984b), NBB (Craig, 1987), BB-1 (Hayes-Roth, 1985a) and BB* (Hayes-Roth, 1986)). The points which Hayes-Roth makes in (Hayes-Roth, 1984) are that control knowledge can be represented explicitly and that explicit control can be applied to itself - it can be reflexive. The descriptions of the Control Model in (Hayes-Roth, 1984; Hayes-Roth, 1985) use the OPM system (Hayes-Roth, 1979) as a basis: the explanation of the functioning of the Control Model is given in terms of errand planning: I use the same context in this section.

The blackboard in (Hayes-Roth, 1984) is divided into two non-overlapping sub-regions called panels. Panels correspond to planes in (Hayes-Roth, 1979). There is a panel for domain-specific problem solving; the other panel is for expressing control. Both panels have internal structure. The domain panel is a two dimensional structure: its horizontal dimension represents temporal intervals in the plan, the vertical dimension for the OPM planning system represents abstraction levels in the planning process (outcome, design, procedure and operation). The control panel has problem solving cycles as the horizontal dimension (a problem solving cycle corresponds to the selection and running of a knowledge source); the vertical dimension again represents abstraction levels in the control domain (problem, strategy, focus, policy, agenda, chosen-action). The structure of the two panels which comprise a version of the OPM system using the Control Model blackboard are shown in fig. 2.6 together with their definitions.

In addition to the blackboard, the system has two other structures of primary interest: these are control knowledge sources and the Agenda. The Agenda will be discussed below. Knowledge sources perform the functions which, by now, should be familiar, but, like Hearsay-III, the Control Model requires domain and control KSs. Control KSs respond to events on the control panel of the blackboard and perform control operations. Control operations can refer either to domain Knowledge Sources or to Control KSs: in this way reflexive control is performed. Both kinds of knowledge sources can relate to items on the blackboard (in either panel). As in other systems, KSs are completely independent (and ignorant) of each other: they can communicate only indirectly by modifying the blackboard state.

One interesting observation made in (Hayes-Roth, 1984) is that KSs can embody various inference mechanisms. Top-down KSs refine decisions at one level of abstraction into a set of decisions at lower levels of abstraction. Bottom-up KSs abstract a set of decisions at a lower level of abstraction into a more general decision at a higher level of abstraction. Same-level KSs infer decisions at the same level of abstraction as the decisions upon which they operate. Finally, there are inter-panel KSs which make decisions in one panel of the blackboard based upon decisions already taken in other panels of the blackboard.

Because many KSs may be triggered simultaneously,* an intelligent control mechanism is necessary to determine which KS should execute its action part and modify the blackboard on each cycle. When a KS is triggered by matching its pattern against some decisions (henceforth: *entries*) on the blackboard, a Knowledge Source Activation Record (*KSAR*) is created (KSARs are directly analogous to activation records in Hearsay-III, but the operations defined over them are different). KSARs record the triggering of some particular KS by a blackboard event or combination of events, together with other information, such as contextual information, KS characteristics, triggering event characteristics and so on. The information provided by KSARs is used by the scheduler, together with its knowledge of pattern characteristics, solution state, problem solving strategy, etc., to decide which KSAR to activate on each cycle. When a KSAR is created, it is put into an agenda. The agenda is the primary data structure of the scheduler.

In a serial implementation, the Blackboard Control Model problem solving cycle is composed of three steps:

1. Update the agenda. The most recently executed KSAR is removed from the agenda. All KSARs created by triggering KSs based upon recent blackboard changes are added to the agenda. Finally, KSARs whose conditions are invalidated by recent changes to the blackboard are removed from the agenda (or given a different status in the agenda);
2. The scheduler selects a KSAR to be executed from the updated agenda;
3. The scheduled KSAR is executed: this typically brings about changes to the blackboard.

In (Hayes-Roth, 1984, section 3; Hayes-Roth, 1985, section 3), an alternative to this control mechanism is presented which does away with the 'hard-wired' agenda and scheduler replacing them with KSs in the control panel of the blackboard. The alternative model has three basic knowledge sources:

* A KS is triggered when its condition pattern matches an entry on the blackboard.

Update-To-Do-Set, Choose-KSAR and Interpret-KSAR. All three KSs operate on the two lowest levels of the control panel. The scheduler, in this model, is unlike many other schedulers mentioned in this chapter, because it has no domain-specific knowledge. In order to select a pending KSAR, the scheduler knows only that it must apply some evaluation function to some set of scheduling criteria. Other control KSs which operate at higher levels of the control panel recommend particular evaluation functions and scheduling criteria to apply during particular periods of the problem solving process.

The control model is reflexive. Executed control KSs make recommendations which influence the scheduling of subsequently triggered control KSs as well as the scheduling of domain KSs. The model makes no categorical distinctions between control and domain KSs. The model does not allocate problem solving cycles to control or domain reasoning. Instead KSARs representing all triggered KSs appear on a common agenda: all the KSARs compete for scheduling priority.

These features enable the blackboard control model to reason about the relative priorities of domain and control knowledge sources in exactly the same way in which it reasons about other control issues. The control KSs permit the model to effect an arbitrary number of meta-levels, but without the usual proliferation of architectural levels (Davis, 1980; Genesereth, 1983; Genesereth, 1984; Lenat, 1983).

The Control Model explicitly represents domain and control knowledge while, at the same time, providing an integrated approach to domain and control problem solving. It can adopt high-level strategies and refine them as focus and policy decisions. This process is conducted incrementally and relies upon the activities of individually triggered, top-down KSs; this feature permits incremental strategy formation in the model. The model can also decide to perform actions, on a more opportunistic basis, which do not fall within the current focus or are just part of the current strategy. The model, furthermore, can induce new high-level strategies from useful non strategic series of focus decisions by the actions of bottom-up control KSs. These new strategies can then be refined in a top-down fashion. The model also requires an extremely simple, adaptive scheduler which has no knowledge whatsoever of the problem domain.

The Control Model has been applied to other domains: the HEARSAY-II speech understanding domain and sonar signal understanding as exemplified by HASP (Feigenbaum, 1982), amongst others.

Hearsay-II (See section 2.2.2 above) uses a two-phase strategy. The strategy is implicit, and is buried in the code which implements the scheduler (outlined above, section 2.2.2). The two-phase strategy is bottom-up as far as the lexical level, followed by an opportunistic phase. Higher level opportunism only occurs after the lower level strategy has produced hypotheses with relatively high confidence.

In addition to the three basic control KSs attended to above, the Control Model version of Hearsay-II uses six control KSs. The two phase control strategy is established by a KS called Problem-Triggered-Strategy which notices signal interpretation tasks for which hypotheses at an intermediate abstraction level are substantially more reliable than the input data.

The second control KS, called Strategy-Triggered-Tactic is another top-down KS. It implements a multi-phase strategy as a series of tactics. This KS acts upon a level of the control panel called the Tactic Level (this level is an extra one which is added to the standard levels in the Model; it sits between the Strategy and Focus Levels). Tactics in the Hearsay-II model are refined as a series of foci. The KS which performs tactic refinement is identical in structure to the Strategy-Triggered-Tactic, and they could be combined in a more general KS.

The fourth KS is an inter-panel KS which recommends focussing on areas of the domain blackboard in which there are few or unreliable hypotheses. This KS is called Solution-Triggered-Focus.

Problem Type and Current Tactic determine policies. Policy determination is performed by a KS, called Tactic-Triggered-Policies, which operates top-down. This KS is used for both phases of problem-solving, when the system is in the opportunistic phase, this KS prefers KSARs which use efficient KSs, which are triggered on reliable data, which are likely to produce credible hypotheses, which produce hypotheses which can be linked to reliable hypotheses already on the blackboard and will produce hypotheses which substantially improve the overall solution. When the system is in the bottom-up phase, this KS recommends no scheduling policies which leads to the scheduler relying on only focus decisions.

The final KS, again top-down, recommends a deterministic evaluation function for speech-understanding problems. The evaluation function is computed from the weighted sum of ratings of all foci and policies. This KS is called Task-Triggered-Evaluation-Function.

The HASP system, which developed out of the SU programs (see section 2.2.5) interprets sonar signals in real time. The input signal is analysed by generating hypotheses about different intervals in the signal at different levels of abstraction. The HASP blackboard has as its horizontal dimension time intervals in the signal; the vertical dimension consists of abstraction levels.

HASP generates hypotheses on five abstraction levels. The bottom level is concerned with the sonar signals; the topmost level is the situation board which represents the disposition of signal sources (ships and submarines). Between these levels, there are three other levels: harmonics within the signal, sources of harmonics such as propellers or engines and vessels.

The control strategy employed by HASP is based upon three event-types. The strategy is nested and iterative. The events are clock events, expected events and simple events. Clock events record the times at which KSs can be invoked. Expected events record events which are expected to occur on the blackboard for a given KS: the KS can respond to the events it expects. Simple events correlate additions or changes to hypotheses with a series of KS which can respond to it.

On each cycle the strategy specifies the following actions:

1. For every due clock event in last-in-first-out order, apply the associated KS to the hypotheses to the associated hypotheses;

2. For every expected event which has been verified, apply the associated KS to the verified hypothesis. Expected events are processed last-in-first-out.

3. Select a simple event and apply all associated KSs to it in the prescribed series. (Again, this is a LIFO queue of events);

4. Repeat stages 2 and 3 until all events have been processed;

5. Repeat stages 1 to 4 until all events have been processed.

The OPM implementation of the HASP strategy uses five control KSs in addition to three basic control KSs.

The first KS establishes the nested, iterative strategy. It operates top-down. The KS specifies no criterion for completing the strategy: HASP has no termination condition because it monitors the signals continuously.

The second KS also operates top-down. It implements the current strategy as a series of Tactics. The third control KS is also top-down. It implements the Tactic as a series of foci. HASP's scheduling policies are implemented by a KS, called Task-Triggered-Policies, which allocates preferences to KSs. The preferences are used to select KSs to activate.

The final KS in the HASP model operates top-down. It uses the same evaluation function as the HEARSAY-II model.

Of the three systems discussed in (Hayes-Roth, 1984; Hayes-Roth, 1985), errand-planning, HEARSAY-II and HASP, HASP has the most rigorously defined control scheme and embodies the least opportunitism. The control plan in the model develops in a rigidly top-down fashion, and specifies the ordering of activities down to the level of individual KSARs.

The Control Model is interesting because of its flexibility and for its reflexive properties. The flexibility of the model has been demonstrated in the three domains in which it has been employed: errand planning, speech understanding and signal understanding. The model provides for the explicit representation and intelligent application of control knowledge in a logically separate region of the blackboard. This approach to control (which is similar to the Hearsay-III approach) is different from the control mechanism typically found in AI systems: in the majority of systems, control is embedded in chunks of opaque code.

The model also offers opportunities for a great many control strategies to be employed in one system. Hearsay-II employs two strategies, as was discussed above. It is conceivable that, for complex applications, for example, top-down, bottom-up, best-first and generate-and-test might all be combined in the same system.

However, as Barbara Hayes-Roth states in (Hayes-Roth, 1984, section 7), despite the evidence supporting the blackboard model of control, the version presented in the paper is only a preliminary formulation which has only been verified by the three experiments described in the paper and outlined above, and is in need of further testing. A major problem which faces the model both as a practical proposition and as a theory of knowledge control is the fact that it introduces extra computational load and increases the amount of storage needed by the system. Despite these negative points, the model is very attractive for the reasons given above.

2.2.5. SU/X, SU/P and AGE

All of the systems described so far have contained Knowledge Sources (or specialists in the case of the 1979 planning system of the Hayes-Roths) which have their knowledge expressed mainly as procedures. The triggering patterns of the KSs in these systems have been predicates expressed in the language used to implement the blackboard system (usually LISP). The term *pattern-directed* invocation applies to these systems in a fairly loose sense. Also, the internal structure of the KSs in the systems discussed above has tended to be monolithic: there has been a tendency to construct large, multi-functional KSs, expressed as implementation-language routines. OPM and Hearsay-III offer the opportunity to build small KSs, but these are still in LISP.

The systems described in this and the next section take an alternative approach as their basis. They provide facilities for building KSs which have internal structure. They do this by building KSs out of sets of production rules (Davis, 1980; Waterman, 1978; Newell, 1973; Anderson, 1983).

SU/P (Feigenbaum, 1978) is the direct precursor of CRYSALIS. CRYSALIS adopts an architecture which is slightly different from SU/X as will be described below.

SU/P and SU/X (which later became HASP (Feigenbaum, 1982)) were developed at Stanford during the late 1970s and early 1980s by Nii, Feigenbaum et al. The task domain of SU/P is the interpretation of protein X-ray crystallographic data; that of SU/X is sonar signal interpretation.

Both of the systems are partly concerned with performance issues. SU/P has to cope with an immense search space in which, not only is there comparatively little to learn from human experts, but also the effective choice of operations at an early stage in the problem solving process critically affects the success of the derivation of adequate solutions. SU/X, on the other hand, has to perform in real time; ships and submarines move, and, in a conflict situation, it is imperative to have as comprehensive an analysis as possible - this entails real-time performance.

The same basic design philosophy was followed in both SU/X and SU/P. They also have architectural features in common: both systems are designed to handle large volumes of digitised physical signals. Both systems inherit features from the HEARSAY-II system, but, as has been hinted above, differ in some respects. The main legacy from HEARSAY-II is a multi-level database, which is still called the blackboard. The two systems differ from HEARSAY-II in the following respects:

(i) knowledge is represented as production rules;

(ii) control structure is represented as knowledge sources - knowledge sources encode problem solving methods and strategies;

(iii) both programs can explain their reasoning by tracing the hypotheses on the blackboard, and

(iv) the design is deliberately made as general as possible to facilitate application to other domains.

In SU/X and SU/P, knowledge source function is extended so that, not only can they make inferences, but they can also check the inferences made by other KSs. As in the other systems so far discussed, hypotheses on the blackboard are linked together to form networks. Hypothesis networks can span levels on the blackboard (the blackboard is a hierarchical structure). The hypothesis network is rooted at the lowest level of the blackboard (where the physical signals are received) and is integrated with elements in the highest level. The highest level constitutes a description of the hypothesised problem solution. The network is termed the current best hypothesis.

Within this general framework, the KSs contain a considerable body of domain knowledge, both factual and heuristic. Knowledge sources also represent control knowledge, a fact which establishes a commonality between these systems, OPM, Hearsay-III and the Hayes-Roth's 1979 planning system. A further characteristic of SU/X and SU/P which is common to other systems is the opportunistic process of hypothesis formation. However, the opportunistic paradigm (which, like HEARSAY-II is a hypothesise-

and-test process) is conducted in terms of data-driven and model-driven hypothesis formation techniques. One task which is given to the control component is the determination of the applicable method given current circumstances.

In SU/X and SU/P, the unit of processing activity is the event. Events are divided into three types: knowledge-based events, which are related to changes in the hypothesis; time-based events, which are related to expectations of what will happen at some point in time; problems, which are also expectations based upon the program's model of the situation for which evidence either way has not been found.

The terms *data-driven* and *model-driven* need some explanation before moving on to a more detailed description of the SU programs. By data-driven, Nii and Feigenbaum intended that results are inferred from the input data. By model driven they intend inferences which are based upon expectations inferred from domain-specific knowledge. The choice between the strategies in signal-processing domains is not determined by hard-and-fast criteria, but, rather, from the KSs which are available at any one time or in any particular implementation and upon the strength of the model of the domain. The combination of the two strategies exemplifies the need for multiple knowledge sources which apply to the same aspect of a given problem (Stefik, 1982).

In the SU systems, the blackboard is divided into two planes: the hypothesis plane and the control plane. Both planes are hierarchically organised. In both SU/X and SU/P, control is organised in a hierarchy. The highest level of the hierarchy is concerned with strategies. The middle level is the KS-Activation level. At the bottom of the hierarchy, there is the Hypothesis formation level. The Hypothesis formation level contains KSs which are to make primary inferences in the domain-specific plane. The intermediate level contains KSs which represent meta-knowledge: these KSs comprise the KS-Activation level. KSs on the KS-Activation level know about the capabilities of the KSs on the Hypothesis formation level. KSs at the Activation level represent policies about knowledge utilisation. At the highest level of the control hierarchy is the strategy level: there is only one KS at this level. The single KS analyses the current solution and determines which part of the blackboard to analyse next and it determines what the next strategy to be employed will be.

The control hierarchy in the SU systems is not at all coupled to the domain hierarchy. The domain hierarchy represents an *a priori* plan for the solution (the same point applies to all hierarchically organised blackboards). The control hierarchy (or plane) represents an organisation of the activities necessary to solve any particular instance of the generic problem.

The blackboard structure of the SU programs is somewhat different from that in other systems. The differences (adopted, it would appear, by AGE, see later, and CRYSALIS) are worthy of some attention.

The first point is that Nii and Feigenbaum in (Feigenbaum, 1978) regard it as a control structure and not just a passive database. This alternative view of the blackboard has important implications for its implementation.

It consists of three lists and two global variables, as compared with some complex indexing scheme. In detail, it consists of:

- The current best hypothesis: this is formed by the application of domain and control knowledge;
- The event list. The event list records changes in the hypothesis which have not yet been processed by any KS. An event also contains the name of the KS and the identifier of the rule which caused that change. (Note, that this point, which is taken almost verbatim from (Feigenbaum, 1978), gives a strong hint that KSs in SU/X and SU/P are collections of productions) - this point is not made explicitly in Feigenbaum's chapter.
- The event. This is a global variable which contains the currently 'active' event. The currently active event is an event currently being processed by some KS. The event also represents in a very simple and elegant form the current focus of attention.
- The problems-list. This is a list of unresolved problems which have been encountered by various KSs. Unresolved problems range from expected data, which is not yet available, to detectable errors in the program (such as insufficient knowledge).
- The event history list. The event in conjunction with its predecessor and successor events form a causal chain of reasoning: they also permit a limited amount of scope for temporal reasoning. In signal processing and analysis, the event history list can be used by KSs to analyse a series of events

which have occurred over a period of time. In addition, it can be used for the generation of explanations.

The general features of the SU programs can also be discerned in the AGE system (Nii, 1979).

AGE stands for Attempt to GEneralise. It is a Knowledge-based program for building knowledge-based programs: its shell-like properties are similar to those of Hearsay-III, but it also contains tools and strategies to assist knowledge engineers in building blackboard-based systems.

In their paper on AGE, Nii and Aiello state that their goal is to "demystify and make explicit the art of knowledge engineering". To this end, the AGE system is designed as an extensible set of tools and strategies for building systems based on the blackboard model. The interface provided by AGE is of little concern to the current discussion which is centred on the architecture of the system and its library. The AGE blackboard framework is shown schematically in fig. 2.7.

The version of AGE described in (Nii, 1979) contains a blackboard, facilities for building Knowledge Sources and precompiled control facilities which belong to a control library. In AGE, KSs respond to changes on the blackboard.

The AGE blackboard is, again, hierarchically organised in a fashion reminiscent of the SU programs. AGE permits strict or loose hierarchies, and can support an arbitrary number of planes or panels. The hypothesis formation model adopted by AGE is based upon Hempel's characterisation of hypothesis formation (Hempel, 1966).

An hypothesis can be generated

- deductively using support from above - this support can be (a) theoretical support (or model-based support), (b) support from more inclusive hypotheses that have independent evidential support, or
- inductively, using evidential support from below. (Nii, op.cit. p.546).

Hypotheses are created by KSs. In AGE, the representation of KSs is based on the assumption that there are at least four broad categories of knowledge needed to solve problems. The four categories are:

1 Knowledge of specifics;

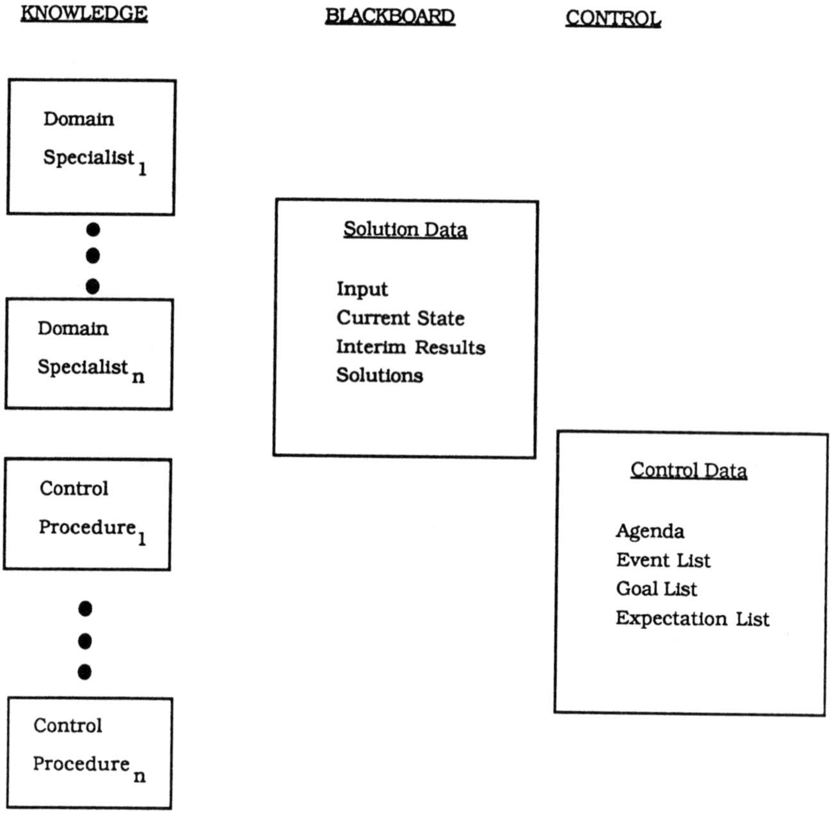

Fig 2.7

AGE - schematic

(from Nii, talk, Insight Workshop on Blackboard Systems, June, 1985)

2 Knowledge of how to deal with the specifics;

3 Knowledge of universals and abstractions in the task domain;

4 Knowledge of problem solving and knowledge utilisation methods in the domain.

This classification is important to the tool-kit aspects of AGE and also informs the representation of knowledge in the system.

Knowledge Sources in AGE have the standard functions which are found in all the systems described in this chapter. They can be model- or event-driven. In the model-driven scheme, KSs are organised around conceptual entities: the conceptual entities represent models. The entities may be unique within a model, or may be arranged in clusters. In the model-driven scheme, KSs operate very much like schemata or frames. In the event-driven scheme, KSs are organised around events: they are clustered around system events such as input or the creation of a new entity. This is another distinction which makes AGE an interesting system: its representational basis makes quite clear the relationship between static and dynamic concepts.

Knowledge Sources in AGE, as in the SU programs and CRYSALIS, are constructed from production rules. KSs serve to collect the production rules in the system according to some logical relationship. Each KSs has five components:

(a) a list of events which act as preconditions for the activation of the KS;

(b) a list of hypothesis levels on the blackboard which the KS spans;

(c) a list of links generated by the KS (note that these are determined on a static and on an a priori basis);

(d) a strategy which is to be used by the rule (either single or multiple hit);

(e) a facility for variable bindings to set local context, to avoid multiple evaluations of the same expression (note: this tells us that KSs are subject to an instantiation process, which is not explicitly stated), and to permit communication between condition and action parts of rules.

Rules within KSs also have credibility values or weight: these reflect the reliability of the rule in a manner akin to certainty factors in MYCIN (Shortliffe, 1976) and PROSPECTOR (Duda, 1978).

The control component in AGE can be user-defined, as in Hearsay-III, but more features are preprogrammed into the system. The system requires a control kernel. The functions of the control kernel are as follows, (Nii, 1979, p.649).

When a KS has been selected for invocation, each rule it contains is evaluated. The condition-part or LHS (Left-Hand Side) of each rule is evaluated in the context of the current blackboard state. When the LHS meets the evaluation criteria (i.e., evaluates to true) the rule is fired. Next, the rules which have fired can generate inferences. Inference generation can be by changing hypotheses, indicating that some event is expected, or indicating that some hypothesis needs to achieve some value.

The third part of the control component is concerned with focus of attention. This mechanism is concerned with the selection of those KSs which might be relevant to the task in hand.

The operations of the kernel are fairly complex, so AGE provides a set of control macros to simplify the construction of kernels. The macros provided in the system are concerned with event- and model-driven strategies.

The event-driven strategy examines entities at a lower level of the blackboard and uses them as evidence for higher-level hypotheses. AGE permits events to be processed by rules on the basis of first-in-first-out, first-in-last-out or best-first: these roughly implement breadth, depth and best-first strategies. When an element is chosen, it becomes the focus of attention. The event-driven strategy is implemented in a manner similar to that in the SU programs.

The expectation-driven macro helps the construction of expectation-driven strategies. As was stated above, expectation-driven strategies are clustered around objects and their attributes. The AGE control model is shown in fig. 2.8 (from Nii, 1979).

Appendix II of the Nii and Aiello paper contains details of the control kernel.

The AGE system differs from many of the other systems in this chapter in its development of the ontological basis of a variant of the blackboard model and in its structuring of the blackboard, which was derived from the SU programs. It also provides the fairly general mechanisms for controlling applications, although the standard facilities are not open to inspection by KSs, as is the case with OPM and

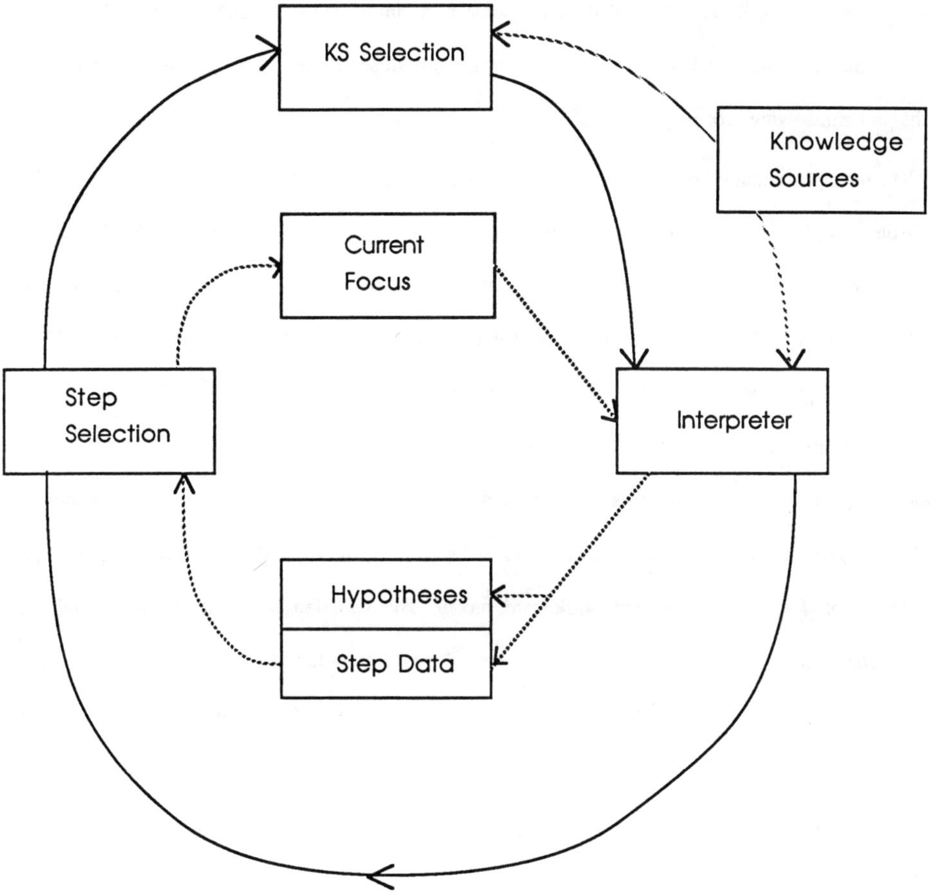

Fig 2.8

AGE Control Model

Hearsay-III.

AGE, despite its basis in signal-processing systems, has been successfully applied to other domains. It has also been used to re-implement PUFF, an expert system for pulmonary function analysis (Aiello, 1983; Kunz, 1978). PUFF has also been re-implemented as CENTAUR (Aikins, 1980; Aikins, 1983), a frame-based production system which introduces contexts and prototypical knowledge into the problem solving process.

The re-implementation of PUFF in AGE is really a case study of three control strategies: it constitutes three implementations, not one. It appears that, given the user-friendly nature of AGE, it did not take very long to perform the implementations. The three strategies were event-driven, model-driven (both familiar from AGE) and backchaining (a new strategy for AGE, and well-known from MYCIN (Shortliffe, 1976)). The point of the re-implementation task was to determine which of the three control strategies is the most appropriate for PUFF's task. The system, called AGEPUFF, used the same domain knowledge (five Knowledge Sources), but varied the control strategies which control the domain knowledge. The fact that the same domain knowledge can be used in different control regimes is a definite plus both for AGE and for the blackboard model. The variation in control structure entails that the configuration of the resulting blackboard structures will be different for each control strategy: that is the concern of the control strategy and not the domain knowledge or the conflict resolution strategy (as it is in OPS-5, (Forgy, 1977)).

For the curious, all the strategies employed in the study were divide-and conquer approaches, but they differ in the way in which domain knowledge is divided. Of the three strategies, the expectation driven strategy won out: it represents a compromise between data- and (implicit) goal-driven strategies. Given a good model of the solution space, an efficient system could be built using the expectation-driven model. One fault with the strategy is that it is possible for some solutions to be missed.

The VM ventilator management system (Fagan, 1980) was also re-implemented in AGE: this, too used an expectation-driven strategy (Aiello, 1983).

The point about mentioning these re-implementations is to show that AGE and the blackboard model are flexible and powerful enough to re-implement systems which were originally constructed using other, very different architectures (PUFF was originally implemented in EMYCIN (van Melle, 1979)). What is not stated in the Aiello paper (Aiello, op.cit.) is the comparative performance of each implementation: this would be most illuminating.

2.2.6. CRYSALIS

CRYSALIS (Terry, 1983), like HASP/SIAP (Feigenbaum, 1982) is a descendant of the SU programs, SU/X and SU/P, described in the last section. HASP developed from SU/P, and CRYSALIS grew out of SU/X.

Just as the SU programs and AGE differ from many other blackboard systems in their use of production rules in KSs, CRYSALIS differs from the other systems in its structure. CRYSALIS has a blackboard as its primary data structure, and its Knowledge Sources are built from production systems. However, CRYSALIS is structured as a Hierarchical Production System. Hierarchical Production Systems introduce extra characteristics into the blackboard architecture. The hierarchical production system was selected because of the way in which it handles the focus of attention problem.

The task domain of CRYSALIS is the same as SU/X: X-ray protein crystallography. A major problem which CRYSALIS faces is that, in addition to the large search space, there are a great many heuristics which can be applied and the widening of the application of the heuristics is then important. Also, as Terry remarks (Terry, op.cit., p.45) "The system's resources are also far too limited (the solution of a small protein currently consumes most of the address space and about ten hours of CPU time on the SUMEX dual PDP KI-10, even with compiled code) and the knowledge is far too weak to permit either exhaustive invocation of rules or leisurely exploration and backtrack. If the system is to find the correct answer it must somehow pick a nearly optimal sequence of rules to apply in response to the specific problem. This is especially true for a production system that does not exhaustively apply the rules in the conflict set. If some rules are not fired when they match, some solutions may be lost. Proper focus is then critical."

Even though CRYSALIS differs in many repects from a conventional blackboard system, it still has a blackboard as its main data structure. The blackboard is divided into two panels: one for hypotheses, the other for representing electron density maps. For a detailed discussion of the blackboard and its relationship to the domain, readers should consult (Terry op. cit): there is insufficient space here to give a detailed description. Suffice it to say that each plane is divided into a hierarchy of abstraction levels. CRYSALIS inherits some of the features of its blackboard from SU/X, but does not have a plane dedicated to control issues. Instead, CRYSALIS relies upon the hierarchical production system to perform control functions: control is expressed as Knowledge Sources which are constructed from production rules (as in SU/X, SU/P and AGE). Within CRYSALIS, the production rules which form the KSs communicate via the blackboard, so the system is properly considered to be an example of the blackboard model. The abstraction levels in the two panels of CRYSALIS are depicted in fig. 2.9

Since CRYSALIS is somewhat different from other blackboard systems, it is worthwhile spending some time describing the architecture of the system in some detail.

The hierarchical production system (HPS) employed in CRYSALIS has a complete production system in each level of the hierarchy. In CRYSALIS, the productions at each level examine the current situation and select actions to perform at the next lower level. The bottom most level (the largest) consists of the object-level rules which construct the solution. The higher levels are composed of control rules which invoke KSs instead of performing object-level computations.

Control within the HPS is top-down. The highest level, as in the SU programs, contains a single control KS. The conceptual unit of control is the KS (a set of production rules) rather than the individual rule. The highest level KS examines the database and selects a KS or a sequence of KSs to execute at the next lower level. This process is repeated until the object-level rules are invoked. When one KS invokes another, control passes to the invoked KS: in other words, there is a procedure-call relationship between invoking and invoked KSs, and control returns to the invoking KS only when the invoked KS has run to completion or has run out of rules to fire.

An HPS, it is argued by Terry, has some advantages over conventional production systems. The first reason is clarity. Traditional production systems require extra context-sensitive elements in their conditions by which control information can be communicated (via 'signals' or items placed in working memory to force certain productions in the production set to be considered). Since rules in the HPS are

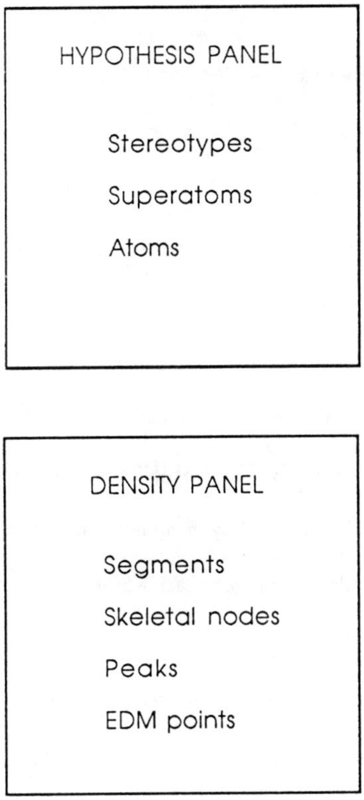

Fig 2.9

CHRYSALIS blackboard hypothesis and data panels
(from Terry, 1983)

collected into Knowledge Sources, the productions they contain need not contain such context-sensitive condition elements: that is handled by the context conditions which determine KS selection.

Representation of control heuristics as rules contributes to the clarity as they are written in a highly constrained representation and tend to be quite small. The same arguments are applied to meta-rules by Davis (Davis, 1980).

The second benefit cited by Terry (p.47) is that the HPS employs a direct control mechanism. If there are specific strategies about what to do and when to do it, there ought to be no good reason to wait for actions to come to the top of the agenda for the right goal to appear (as is the case with OPM). CRYSALIS' HPS permits control rules to fire a KS, which imparts directness of control (as was noted above in connection with the procedure-call relationship between KSs).

Within CRYSALIS, control works top-down. Strategy rules do not examine the hypothesis directly, but, instead, inspect a summary of the blackboard, the FEATURESLIST, which is computed each time control returns to the strategy level (the FEATURESLIST represent parts of the amino acid sequence in the protein). The FEATURESLIST is computed by examining the current best hypothesis (cf., the SU programs). The action of a strategy rule is to invoke a task KS or series of task KSs in response to some pattern it sees in the developing hypothesis.

The middle level of the hierarchy is the task level. Each KS at this level (called a task) is a rule set which directs the activation of object-level KSs to solve a sub-problem identified by the task. Each task has its own area of expertise and a region of the data/solution space (the latter is defined by the pattern of features matched against that region by the invoking KS): these characteristics together define a focus for the task.

As in HEARSAY-II, task rules inspect the blackboard, but only react to changes. CRYSALIS optimises the task of blackboard change detection by packaging changes into events (cf. SU/X). The changes in the blackboard constitute an event-driven control mechanism. Event processing, as in AGE, can operate breadth-, depth- or best-first, depending upon where events are added to the event list.

The bottom level consists of KSs which perform genuine domain-related problem solving actions. KSs at this level are not restricted, but, instead, can examine the entire blackboard. KSs at this level can change data or hypotheses. The bindings for KSs at this level (all KSs have bindings as in AGE) signal that the KS has an action which is cyclic, single or multiple hit. KSs at this level ought to be complex, but quite a lot of the complexity has been delegated to the many access functions which interface the productions to the database and FORTRAN number-crunching routines.

The main point about CRYSALIS is that it employs a different control structure. The conventional blackboard architecture is augmented by a control structure reminiscent of conventional programming languages. CRYSALIS clearly has a lot in common with the SU programs, but employs meta-level reasoning in an effective way to control the inferences possible in the system: in this respect, CRYSALIS represents a development of meta-rules.

2.2.7. Ariadne-1

Ariadne-1 (Craig, 1986) is a derivative of the OPM type of blackboard. Ariadne-1 is a flexible shell to be used in the construction of blackboard systems.

Ariadne-1 is a multiple-panel system and uses an agenda-based scheduler. As with OPM and OPM's successor, BB-1 (Hayes-Roth, 1984b), it is possible to represent control information explicitly in a separate panel on the Ariadne-1 blackboard and to use the system-provided agenda to schedule control KSs and domain KSs.

Ariadne-1's architecture is somewhat more flexible than OPM or BB-1. Ariadne-1 permits applications to create panels and levels dynamically. This is made possible by the fact that the data structures in Ariadne-1 which represent panels and levels are available for inspection and modification by the user. The thinking behind the dynamic creation of panels and levels is that in poorly understood domains, the initial problem decomposition may not be correct and that KSs could be constructed to recognise this fact and introduce extra architectural partitions. The background to Ariadne-1 is made clear by these comments: Ariadne-1 was designed as a shell for learning systems.

Ariadne-1 also permits the user to use meta-operators. Meta-operators in Ariadne-1 can inspect KSs as well as entries in a level. Meta-operators are also provided for the dynamic panel and level creation processes described above.

The final way in which Ariadne-1 is slightly different than the other systems described in this chapter is in the structure of blackboard entries. Entries in Ariadne-1 have predefined slots which contain linkage and history information. The latter slots record the time of creation and the identity of the KS which created the entry. The creation slot also records the identifiers of the entries which caused the KS to execute and, thereby, create the entry. Other history information is recorded: the modifications to an entry are recorded in the entry. Modification data contains the identifier of the modifying KS and details of the modification. The history slots are present so that KSs can reason about the derivations of entries -- again, there is a strong bias towards learning in the existence of these slots.

2.3. SUMMARY

There are a number of points in common between all the systems described above. The similarities are to do with the architecture which acts as a framework for problem-solving. They can be summarised as follows:

- Each system has a central, structured database, called the *blackboard*, on which all intermediate results are placed. The intermediate results are available to all problem-solving processes in each system in the sense that they can be inspected or updated by them. The blackboard is divided in different ways, but there is the common property that there is an abstraction hierarchy which describes the problem to be solved in a variety of different ways.
- Each system has a collection of problem-solving processes called *Knowledge Sources*. Knowledge Sources represent problem-solving knowledge and are applied to objects present on the blackboard. Knowledge Sources usually have two components: a precondition and an action. A Knowledge Source's precondition examines the blackboard for information which is of interest or of use to the Knowledge Source; its action makes changes to the blackboard.
- There is a control mechanism, usually called the scheduler, which selects those Knowledge Sources for execution so that the blackboard state is altered. The scheduler applies one or more problem-solving strategies: for example, the HEARSAY-II scheduler applied a bottom-up strategy and then moved into an opportunistic regime. The Blackboard Control Model differs slightly from other sys-

tems (as does Hearsay-III) insofar as the scheduler it specifies is a complete partition of the blackboard, together with a set of Control Knowledge Sources. In the Blackboard Control Model, control is seen as another problem to solve.

All of these components are clearly seen in each of the systems described in this chapter. There are, it must be stated, ways in which the systems differ from one another: many of these differences are accounted for by the problem each system was to solve. The differences between HASP and HEARSAY-II can be accounted for in this way, but the production rule structure of HASP Knowledge Source actions is a result of experience with production-based systems; the differences between the control mechanisms in HASP and HEARSAY-II are accounted for by different task demands.

There is apparently considerable variation in the domain and task chosen for the application systems I have described. Some systems, like HEARSAY-II and HASP operated in domains in which real-time performance was required; others, such as OPM and CRYSALIS were not so constrained. OPM was an attempt to model the behaviour of human subjects, whereas performance was a key issue for most of the remaining systems. If one looks behind these differences, it is possible to see similarities in the chosen problems, the two most important being complexity and the requirement that different kinds of knowledge be brought to bear in solving problems. Each of the problems tackled by the blackboard systems described above is complex and quite difficult. CRYSALIS was built to solve a problem which was so poorly understood that there were no true domain experts: those crystallographers who attempted the task found it very difficult to reconcile individual items of information to form a solution. The errand planning task selected for OPM derived its complexity from the fact that a number of conflicting requirements was placed on the subject. That is, there was a number of jobs to be done during the hypothetical day and there was insufficient time to complete them all, so a certain amount of choice had to be exercised -- the choices were based upon evaluations of the relative importance of each job.

The complexity of each task is also evidenced by the fact that different kinds of knowledge were required to solve the problems given to the systems. HEARSAY-II contained representations of knowledge about signal processing, about phonology, syntax and semantics. HASP contained knowledge about vessel characteristics, machinery, as well as knowledge about signal properties. OPM contained knowledge about task importance, and knowledge about spatial properties (so that navigation through the hypothetical town would be possible), as well as knowledge about planning. The requirement that there are different kinds of knowledge in OPM is shown in the blackboard structure (the division into levels and planes) and in the different Knowledge Sources and their contents. In many, if not all systems described above, the division in the kinds of knowledge present in the system is reflected in the decomposition of that knowledge into Knowledge Sources: in the OPM system, Knowledge Sources were called *specialists*, a point which emphasises the different tasks which are to be performed by them. Each Knowledge Source represents an expert with a well-defined area of expertise and each can solve a highly constrained set of problems.

It can be said, in summary, that the blackboard architecture has often been chosen to solve complex problems. The source of complexity of each problem may be different -- for example, the real-time needs of HASP imposed a level of complexity over and above that imposed by the task itself -- but the problems tend to require the services of a number of human experts in their solution. The fact that more than one expert is needed indicates that different kinds of knowledge are required and this is reflected in the decomposition into different Knowledge Sources in the implemented systems. The division of knowledge depends very much on the task and the problem to be solved: in Air Traffic Control, one might decompose the domain knowledge into knowledge about vertical and knowledge about horizontal flight control rules.

There are, of course, different perspectives on the blackboard architecture. Many of the systems described above have had the goal of performance: HEARSAY-II was designed to recognise continuous speech in real time, CRYSALIS was designed to produce the best possible structural description which could be derived from the electron density map. OPM, on the other hand, was intended to be a faithful model of human errand planning behaviour: fidelity, in this case, was more important than speed. All the systems so far considered had the goal of accuracy, be it an accurate solution to a problem (in HASP's case, for example, an *inaccurate* solution would be to identify a ship known to be on the other side of the world as being in the sea area under surveillance) or a faithful replication of some observed, human behaviour.

Another perspective, perhaps one which can often be overlooked is that the blackboard architecture constitutes a method for building complex systems in a modular fashion. Because of the fact that the blackboard database is a structured object and because the knowledge in blackboard systems is in the form of independent Knowledge Sources, one can see a way in which a team can be employed to construct these systems. The team could be divided so that individuals concentrate on abstraction levels, with each team member being allocated an abstraction level to work on. Each team member would interview the human expert most closely associated with the kinds of reasoning performed on that abstraction level and generate Knowledge Sources from the interviews. This view of the construction of large AI systems differs from the usual one in which a single Knowledge Engineer works with a single expert in its way of catering for different experts. It also provides a structure within which to manage the project and allocate work -- this contrasts with the usual 'iterative design' method which says very little about how to manage the construction of a system.

A significant problem with the blackboard architecture is that it is a basically informal construct. In the next chapter, a definition of the architecture is given and some of its implications are drawn out.

3. THE BLACKBOARD ARCHITECTURE: DEFINITION AND IMPLICATIONS

3.1. INTRODUCTION

In the last chapter, the basic blackboard metaphor and some example implementations were presented. In this chapter, I will attempt a more or less rigorous definition of the blackboard architecture. Such an exercise is quite obviously required, for there is no adequate definition in the publicly available literature of what constitutes a blackboard system, although there is a brief published definition by Nii (Nii, 1986a), there is a Stanford Technical Report by Hayes-Roth (Hayes-Roth, 1983) devoted to the subject and there is a brief definition in Hayes-Roth's 1985 paper (Hayes-Roth, 1985b). The comments by Nii are very brief and, perhaps, rather biased towards the demands of signal processing applications; the Hayes-Roth paper is not generally available, although it discusses the architecture in considerably more detail than (Nii, 1986a). The definition proposed by Nii suffers from some significant problems, as I will argue below.

The blackboard architecture is considered to be a general model for problem solving. As such, it cannot be described or defined purely in terms dependent upon one particular class of problem. In this chapter, I will attempt a definition which is completely independent of application domain needs. It will be seen that some implementations of the blackboard architecture violate some of the constraints which I will require; others will add features that I do not see as being central. As Barbara Hayes-Roth notes (Hayes-Roth, 1983, p. 2), the blackboard architecture is, basically, an informal construct which is frequently adapted to the needs of a specific application. Without a standard against which to compare systems and models, there is very little sense in which one can present a system as being a blackboard system, nor is there much meaningfully to be gained in comparing and contrasting other problem solving architectures with the blackboard architecture. The point of this exercise is to provide a 'gold standard' against which to compare the CASSANDRA and blackboard architectures. The availability of a definition of the blackboard architecture will also facilitate discussion of the ways in which the CASSANDRA architecture develops from and improves upon the more established model.

The definition proposed by Barbara Hayes-Roth is very similar to the one I shall present here. The definition presented here differs in one major respect from the one proposed by Penny Nii. That difference is the emphasis which Nii places on opportunism. Nii cites opportunism as a defining characteristic of blackboard systems. Indeed, she claims it as *the* fundamental property of the architecture. I do not agree with Nii's claim, so I will briefly consider her remarks and will argue that her analysis is faulty.

The structure of this chapter is as follows. I will begin by giving a a general definition of the blackboard architecture. This definition will serve for the remainder of the chapter, although it might be seen to exclude some systems (notably CRYSALIS (Terry, 1983)). During the presentation of the definition, I will contrast blackboard systems with other architectures such as production systems: this will be done by pointing out those features of blackboard systems which are radically different from other architectures. I will then move on to the question of opportunism: Nii cites opportunism as being one of the key defining features of the architecture. I will argue against the position taken by Nii and will suggest:

(i) that opportunism is only *one* aspect of the control behaviour and that it is not crucial to the definition of the architecture,

(ii) that Nii's interpretation of opportunism has unfortunate implications, and

(iii) that opportunism is really not one but many related control phenomena.

The discussion of opportunism is one of the novel aspects of this chapter. From this discussion of opportunism, I will consider the methodological implications of the blackboard architecture. Again, there is little discussion of methodology in the literature, so I hope to make some small contribution to this area. The methodological discussion will indicate some substantial problems with the blackboard architecture. These problems are concerned with the separation of knowledge into neatly encapsulated chunks and the relationships between them. The discussion will also indicate that the complexity of the blackboard architecture can sometimes be overwhelming, a fact which seems to suggest limitations to the claim that blackboard is a *general* model of problem solving. This fault is already evidenced, I believe, by the fact that one would not normally consider the blackboard architecture for some classes of problem (although if one's focus is cognitive modelling, one might consider something similar).

In contrast to the blackboard architecture, the architecture which I will refer to throughout this document as the CASSANDRA architecture will be presented as an alternative without the majority of the theoretical and methodological problems associated with blackboard architecture.

3.2. BASIC DEFINITION

In this section, I will present the basic definition of the blackboard architecture. Readers familiar with the blackboard architecture will see that it is a fairly conventional definition which concentrates on the usual features.

For my purposes, the blackboard architecture has four defining elements:

(i) entries, which are intermediate results generated during problem solving;

(ii) knowledge sources, which are independent, event-driven, processes which produce entries;

(iii) the blackboard, which is a structured global database which mediates knowledge source interactions and organises entries, and

(iv) an intelligent control mechanism which decides if and when particular knowledge sources should generate entries and record them on the blackboard.

These elements interact to produce a problem solving style which is "incremental and opportunistic" (Hayes-Roth, 1983, p. 4) in character. Partial solution islands emerge in different structural partitions of the blackboard, one entry at a time (in a serial implementation). New islands appear and existing ones grow as a result of the addition of entries. Eventually, mutually supportive partial solutions merge to form a complete solution.

I will describe each of the architectural elements in more detail.

3.2.1. Entries

Entries are intermediate results generated during problem solving. Entries may include both elements of the problem solution and information considered important for generating solution elements. Depending upon the problem domain, entries may include perceptions, goals, judgements, beliefs, hypotheses, decisions, expectations and so on. In HEARSAY-II, the domain was continuous speech understanding, so its entries represented hypothetical interpretations of the speech signal. For OPM, the task was to generate an errand plan, so its entries were decisions about the entries and the organisation of the plan. For PROTEAN (Hayes-Roth, 1984b; Hayes-Roth, 1985a), the task is the determination of protein structure: its entries represent hypothesised atom configurations and constraints between hypotheses.*

* The development of PROTEAN continues as I write. This accounts for the tense change over the last three sentences: HEARSAY-II and OPM are completed projects.

Entries may contain representations of relationships with any other structures found useful or beneficial by the user. The relationships (frequently referred to as *links*) connect entries together into solution islands. In HEARSAY-II, the hypothesis "The first word in the utterance is 'get'" might have a *supports* relationship to another hypothesis, "The first phrase in the utterance is 'get me'". In OPM, the decision "From Stanford, travel east on University Boulevard" may have an *elaborates* relationship to another decision "Go from Stanford to The Good Earth". PROTEAN entries are related by relationships expressing constraints between structural entities: an entry on the Secondary-Anchor level has constraints indicating the position of the secondary anchor (part of a protein structure) relative to atoms in other pieces of protein secondary structure.

Entries are represented as structures of arbitrary complexity. They are frequently represented as sets of attribute/value pairs which describe an entry's semantic content and its relationships to other entries. Sometimes, entry history (in terms of the time it was created, and by whom, and its subsequent modifications) is recorded (as it is in, for example, (Craig, 1986)), as well as other information considered useful by the user.

To make the typical structure of an entry clear, I now give an example entry from the blackboard control model (Hayes-Roth, 1985). The entry is generated by the PROTEAN system (Hayes-Roth, 1984a) and resides on the Focus level of the control blackboard. The entry is first described in tabular English form and then in symbolic form (the latter was printed from a runtime blackboard display). I will then explain some of the details of the entry so that the reader may gain a better understanding of the role of the entry and the range and type of information it contains.

Name "Focus" + number
Goal Predicate or function to rate potential actions
(result in range 0 - 100)
Criterion Predicate to evaluate an expiration condition
Weight Goal importance (value in range 0 - 1)
Rationale Reason for Goal
Creator Action that created this decision
Source Information that triggered the Creator
Type Role in the control plan, e.g., "Strategic", "Solution-Based"
Status Function in control plan, e.g., "Operative", "Inoperative"
First-Cycle First operative cycle number
Last-Cycle Last operative cycle number

The entry actually appears as the following. This will give the reader an idea of the genuine structure of entries on the PROTEAN control blackboard.

```
Name        Focus1
Goal     (Eq KS-Type 'Anchor)
Criterion  (for Element in ($Level 'Secondary-Anchor)
            always
            ($Find-One ((Level-Is 'Secondary)(Copies Element))))
Weight      0.8
Rationale  "Develop a comprehensive set of partial solutions
         before deciding which ones to refine at the blob level"
Creator     Chosen-Action5
Source      Strategy1
Type    Strategic
Status      Operative
First-Cycle 6
Last-Cycle  20
```

The interpretation of Focus1 is as follows.

The Goal of this entry, Focus1, contains a predicate which finds all triggered anchoring KSs: i.e., KSs which perform an anchoring operation -- anchoring, in PROTEAN, is the process of attaching one piece of protein structure to another via the establishment of constraints between the structures. Focus1's Criterion says that a mapping should be established between entries on the domain blackboard levels Secondary-Anchor and Secondary (Secondary-Anchor is the highest abstraction level; Secondary comes immediately below it): the mapping is establishes a correspondence between Secondary-Anchor entries and Secondary entries such that the lower entry is a copy of the higher (in simpler terms, the entry at the Secondary-Anchor level has been dicovered to be a piece of secondary structure which has been incorporated into a partial solution). When such a correspondence has been derived, Focus1 may expire -- that is, change its Status to *Inoperative*: it will no longer take part in control reasoning. Focus1's Rationale requires that partial solutions generated at the Secondary level should be preferred for refinement down to blob and atomic levels: effectively, this requires that the partial solutions chosen for refinement should be properly constrained. The Weight of Focus1 is used to determine the priority assigned to KSARs considered for execution during problem solving cycles 6 through 20: the Weight is used by the blackboard control model in determining priority. During cycles 6 through 20, the control regime partially defined by Focus1 is *Operative*. Focus1 was created as a result of a control decision at the Strategy level of the control blackboard. The Creator was the fifth KSAR to be executed during the execution of the system.*

Despite the implementation specificity and detail of this example, it can be seen that entries contain large quantities of information. Focus1 contains information about the kind of decision it represents (the Goal and Criterion slots), about its history (Creator and Source slots) and about its role in the solution process (Rationale and Weight). Focus1 also contains relationships to other entries: in particular, the Creator slot refers to a Chosen-Action (an entry recording the KSAR selected for execution on any cycle) and to a Strategy decision (the value *Strategy1* in the Source slot). This example entry also shows the variety of information which may legally be contained by entries: the attribute values range from single symbols to pieces of implementation-language code. The interpretations of these items is performed by Knowledge Sources which trigger on entries and by users of the system (the Rationale value is used during explanation, for example).

3.2.2. Knowledge Sources

Knowledge Sources are the processes which generate or modify blackboard entries. Hayes-Roth describes them as "cognitive processes". Knowledge Sources are the procedural representation of the knowledge used by a system to solve problems. They also contain information which assists the system's control component in making decisions about which KS to execute.

* The information in the Creator, Source and Type slots is explained only with reference to the blackboard control model. This is an example of how information contained in entries depends, for its interpretation, on a global understanding of the system, its architecture and the details of the application domain. A similar point can be made about the slots which refer to the PROTEAN problem solving blackboard.

The structure of a KS is usually described as being in two parts: a condition and an action. The condition describes the circumstances under which a Knowledge Source can contribute to the problem solving process. Usually, the condition requires the existence of previously generated entries and can be viewed as a predicate which can be applied to those entries to determine whether they contain particular information. The action of a Knowledge Source generates new entries to be posted on the blackboard or else modifies the contents of existing entries. The two-part structure or condition-action format corresponds to the two stages of KS operation:

(i) triggering, during which a KS's condition is evaluated, and

(ii) execution, during which a KS's action is performed.

Knowledge Sources are basically event-driven because only those KSs whose conditions have evaluated to *true* can execute their actions.

Knowledge Sources represent independent knowledge-possessing entities. They are permitted to interact *only* by the generation or modification of entries. That is, communication between KSs must always be via the blackboard and not, say, via shared variables. KSs influence each other indirectly whenever the execution of a KS's action generates or modifies entries which satisfy the condition of another Knowledge Source.

These points are illustrated by the HEARSAY-II KS, MOW, and the OPM Knowledge Source, FIRST-LEG.

MOW can be described as follows.

KS-NAME: MOW
CONDITION:
There are previously generated syllable hypotheses
ACTION
Hypothesise words that comprise sequential subsets of the syllable hypothesis. Adjust their beginning and end times. Rate their credibilities.

MOW is invoked when other HEARSAY-II KSs hypothesise sequences of syllables likely to be present in the speech signal. When executed, MOW first hypothesises all words in its vocabulary which contain subsequences of the hypothesised syllables. Because of noise in the speech signal and because of ambiguity in the interpretation of syllables, MOW usually hypothesises more than one word for any given syllable sequence. MOW then adjusts the beginning and end times in the speech signal of each hypothesised word and rates each word's credibility against the syllable data.

FIRST-LEG can be summarised as follows.

KS-NAME: FIRST-LEG
CONDITION:
Two tasks, t1 and t2, have been planned in temporal order t1, t2.
ACTION:
Plan the first leg of the route t1-t2 as:
start = t1.
leg1 = the direction-on-street from t1 which minimises the angular disparity from the straight line connecting t1 and t2.
end-of-leg1 = the first intersection encountered on leg1.

FIRST-LEG is invoked when other OPM KSs decide to perform two tasks, t1 and t2, in the temporal order <t1, t2>. When executed, FIRST-LEG establishes t1 as the starting point for the route from t1 to t2. The KS then enumerates the paths starting from t1 in all directions on all streets in the town. This set of paths usually includes at least two paths in each of two directions on t1's street; it will include additional paths if t1 is on a street intersection. FIRST-LEG determines which of these paths minimises the angular disparity from the straight line connecting t1 and t2** and plans that path as the first leg of the route. It then identifies the first street intersection encountered on the planned route and makes that intersection the end of the first leg (this is because another choice will usually have to be made to connect the intersection to t2).

These examples illustrate the general point that Knowledge Sources typically transform entries at one level of abstraction into entries at another level. Some KSs, MOW is an example, operate in a basically bottom-up manner. Bottom-up KSs aggregate several lower-level entries into a smaller number of higher-level entries: MOW aggregates syllables into words. FIRST-LEG exemplifies top-down KSs. Top-down KSs expand higher-level entries into a larger number of lower-level entries: FIRST-LEG expands task sequences into route segments. Other Knowledge Sources operate within a single level of the

** OPM represents the town as a two-dimensional coordinate array. Each object in the town (building, park, etc.) is represented as a coordinate in the array. Street are represented as a sequence of points, each point representing the streets which intersect the given street.

blackboard (for example, KSs which attempt to find a temporal ordering over entries representing plan segments), or between different blackboard panels (OPM contains many such KSs, as does CRYSALIS). The blackboard architecture can combine Knowledge Sources embodying different general inference mechanisms in a single problem solving system. It should be noted that by 'general inference mechanisms', I mean *only* characterisations of the type just given: I do not intend characterisations such as model-driven, data-driven, and so on. These terms apply to descriptions of individual systems and not to the blackboard architecture in general: what I am attempting to do here is to give a *general* characterisation.

The representation of Knowledge Sources is basically that of condition-action pairs. The condition component requires that there be at least one previously generated entry with particular attributes and values and that the evaluation of the condition yield exactly one of *true* or *false*. (One may assume that there is some process external to the blackboard system which creates and posts one or more entries to start problem solving.) The action component generates one or more new entries or modifies existing entries already on the blackboard: the action component may also combine new entry generation with existing entry modification. Beyond these specifications, KSs may be viewed as 'black boxes' of arbitrary internal complexity which are applied to the user-defined entry structures on the blackboard.

3.2.3. Blackboard

The blackboard is a global database which contains all entries generated by all Knowledge Sources applied during the problem solving process. The blackboard serves two purposes. Firstly, it mediates all Knowledge Source interactions in the following sense. Although Knowledge Sources may not communicate directly with each other, they influence each other indirectly by placing and responding to entries on the blackboard. An entry posted by the execution of one Knowledge Source may satisfy the condition of another KS. Second, the blackboard organises and collects all partial and complete solutions generated for the solution of the problem under attack. The solutions on the blackboard comprise configurations of related entries on the blackboard. The contents of the blackboard are at least notionally inspectable by any KS: the blackboard makes entries public.

The blackboard may have a user-determined structure which defines important relationships between entries.* The relationships might be, for example, generalisation, aggregation, support, or temporal

* It is a matter of fact that most, if not all, blackboard implementations impose internal blackboard structure.

sequencing. The relationships may be combined in various ways. The blackboard focusses Knowledge Source activity. It is usual for a Knowledge Source condition to refer to previously generated entries in a particular region of the blackboard, while its action may alter another blackboard region. A Knowledge Source need not consider entries in regions of the blackboard which are of no concern to its condition or which are not mentioned in its action. Viewed this way, the blackboard is a framework for organising, interrogating and generating entries.

The blackboard may have additional structure: in fact, it may have any additional structure desired by the user. There are, however, two dimensions of particular importance to the structure of the blackboard: these are the vertical and horizontal dimensions. The vertical dimension separates and distinguishes entries at different levels of abstraction. Entries at a given abstraction level may elaborate or support entries at the next level or at some other level in the hierarchy. The horizontal dimension represents intervals in the solution. Horizontal intervals may represent temporal, spatial, conceptual or other groupings: indeed, in some cases, the horizontal dimension may be extended to cover many interacting groupings. It is usual, though, for the horizontal dimension to represent some form of temporal ordering of the solution process. Together, these dimensions define an aggregation structure (a hierarchy).

The structure of the OPM blackboard is thus:

Outcomes
Designs
Procedures
Operations

The vertical dimension represents tentative decision types collected into an abstraction hierarchy. The abstraction relation may be described as generating a *refines-to* relationship between adjacent abstraction levels. The horizontal dimension of OPM's blackboard represents time points in the emerging plan. Each level of abstraction offers a different specification of the plan. The highest level represents the outcomes the plan should achieve; the **Designs** level represents designs for the general spatial/temporal layout of the plan (e.g., do tasks in the S.W. corner of the town); procedures represent the sequencing of individual tasks (e.g., pick up the medicine for the dog before buying a newspaper); operations represent the performance of individual tasks and make inter-task transitions. Operations are aggregated into procedures, procedures into designs and designs into outcomes. Because the errand planning problem requires the linearisation of plan components with time, the blackboard structure distinguishes temporal intervals within the plan.

3.2.4. Control Mechanism

During problem solving, many different Knowledge Sources may be triggered simultaneously by entries on the blackboard. In a serial implementation of the blackboard architecture, only one Knowledge Source may execute at any one time (in a problem solving cycle, that is). In parallel implementations, more than one KS may execute. In both cases, an intelligent control mechanism determines which of the currently triggered KSs is allowed to execute at any time.

In HEARSAY-II, OPM, BB1, HEARSAY-III and NBB (Craig, 1987), control is implemented in terms of an agenda-based scheduler. On each problem solving cycle, the agenda lists all pending Knowledge Sources (that is, KSs whose conditions are satisfied by entries or entry configurations on the blackboard). The scheduler rates these pending KSs and selects one (or more, in the case of HEARSAY-III) for execution. Control can be implemented in other ways: for example, HASP/SIAP represents control in terms of stack-like event lists which are used by an algorithmic control mechanism; CRYSALIS makes control decisions in terms of hierarchically organised control rules and uses a control model that is very similar to a procedure call. The fundamental differences between the various implementation approaches to the control mechanism are none too important for it can be shown (e.g., Hayes-Roth, 1985b) that that the agenda-based mechanism can be used to implement other mechanisms.*

The control mechanism's level of intelligence reflects its understanding of the system's Knowledge Sources and their applicability to particular aspects of the the current problem; it also depends on its understanding of the development of a solution. The scheduler can exhibit a range of behaviours based upon its level of understanding. At one extreme, the scheduler may adopt one, well-defined, strategy. It might, for example, adopt a strategy to proceed top-down through the abstraction levels, executing KSs which are known to produce entries at the next abstraction level lower in the hierarchy from the current one. Alternatively, the scheduler can integrate multiple strategies: for example, a mixed strategy might execute both

* There are reasons other than those mentioned by Hayes-Roth in (Hayes-Roth, 1985b) for prefering agenda-based scheduling. The reasons are made clear when I discuss opportunism in the next section (sect. 3.3).

bottom-up and top-down KSs, preferring that strategy which prescribes the smaller number of triggered Knowledge Sources -- that is, preferring the strategy which more effectively reduces the search space. The scheduler can also deviate from the prescriptions of the current strategy, adopting arbitrary criteria -- that is, behaving in an opportunistic fashion. Some opportunistic strategies (it is quite possible to have opportunistic *strategies*: indeed, more than one may be active at any time) might prescribe the execution of KSs which have recently triggered, or might prescribe the execution of KSs known to generate particularly important entries. Intelligent schedulers are able also to alter the control strategies adopted as a dynamic response to progress in problem solving. It is a characteristic of the blackboard architecture that there is a capacity for opportunistic behaviour (a stronger claim is that opportunistic behaviour is, somehow, predisposed, but I intend to argue against this stronger claim as being based only upon empirical and not upon conceptual issues).

A clear example of multiple strategy scheduling is implemented by the HEARSAY-II scheduler. The HEARSAY-II scheduler operates a two-phase strategy. In the first phase, a bottom-up strategy is employed. Signal parameters are progressively aggregated into lexical items. The scheduler begins by executing all KSs which have triggered on the Parameter level, then schedules all KSs triggering on the Segment level. Next it schedules all Knowledge Sources which have triggered on the Syllable level and which generate word hypotheses on the Word or Lexical level of the blackboard.

During the second phase of HEARSAY-II's activity, the scheduler engages in a more opportunistic mode of operation. On each cycle, the scheduler calculates a priority for each pending KSAR. A KSAR is a Knowledge Source Activation Record. KSARs record information about the conditions which caused a KS to trigger. KSARs are the unit of control in HEARSAY-II and other blackboard systems. The scheduler rates each KSAR against three criteria:

(i) the local effects of the proposed activity. This includes the nature of the hypotheses which would be generated, the cumulative credibility of the generated hypotheses and of their predecessors;

(ii) the global effects of the activity in terms of co-operative and competitive relationships between the hypotheses it would generate if executed and the existing hypotheses on the blackboard; and,

(iii) the computational resources which would be required by the proposed activity.

On each cycle, the scheduler executes the KSAR with the highest priority.

3.2.5. Summary

The blackboard architecture can be summarised as a list of eleven points. These points are similar to those cited by Hayes-Roth (Hayes-Roth, 1983).

1. Problem solving activity generates a set of intermediate results which are represented as objects with attributes and values. The objects are called entries.
2. Entries may have user-specified relationships with other entries.
3. All entries have the relational attributes: abstracts/refines and adjacent-to. These attributes define the vertical and horizontal structure of the blackboard.
4. All entries are recorded in a global database called the blackboard.
5. The blackboard structure includes partitions for different levels of abstraction and solution intervals.
6. The blackboard may have additional, user-specified, structure.
7. Independent knowledge-representing processes, called Knowledge Sources, generate, modify and record entries on the blackboard.
8. Each Knowledge Source has a condition and an action. The condition matches a hypothetical configuration of entries on the blackboard, performs computation and is a predicate. The action performs computation and generates blackboard modifications.
9. Only triggered Knowledge Sources (those KSs whose conditions evaluate to *true*) can be executed.
10. An intelligent scheduler determines which triggered KS(s) should execute its (their) action(s).
11. The scheduler can base its decisions on user-determined criteria such as the characteristics of the triggered KS, the utility of the proposed action, information about the general blackboard state, characteristics of the problem, or information about previous control decisions.

It is generally believed that the criteria listed above exhaustively define the blackboard architecture. It is possible to extend the properties of a system and still correctly refer to it as a blackboard system. For example, the BB1 (Hayes-Roth, 1984b; Hayes-Roth, 1985b; Hayes-Roth, 1986) and NBB (Craig, 1987) systems introduce extra KS components. The two major introductions are obviation conditions and a distinction between trigger and precondition predicates.

Obviation conditions are designed to be an additional relevance check: if any obviation condition evaluates to *true*, the KS is not permitted to execute. Obviation conditions are permitted to examine any part of the blackboard state (any configuration of entries in the simplest case) in an attempt to preserve consistency and to ensure that the execution of the KS will genuinely contribute to the solution of the problem currently under attack.

The division of the KS condition into a trigger and a precondition is designed to separate the event-based triggering mechanism from the state-based matching processes typical of many KS conditions. According to the definition stated above, KSs trigger as the result of changes to the blackboard state. However, there are often circumstances in which the condition should also examine the blackboard state to determine if the KS should execute. KS trigger conditions are intended to respond to events and preconditions to blackboard states: they represent a refinement of Knowledge Source semantics in the sense that what was originally represented as one test can be separated into two tests, each of which has a different functionality.

Although these two features are not included in the definition of the blackboard architecture, their inclusion in a system does not preclude that system from being a blackboard system. These additions are implied by the definition given above and in no way contradict the terms of that definition.

The definition given above clearly differentiates the blackboard architecture from other problem solving models. Let us consider the production system architecture for comparison.

Production rules are frequently assumed to be like black boxes for they represent small pieces of information and have internal behaviours (albeit very simple internal behaviours) which are not open to inspection by an external observer. Production rules are often explained as generating working memory items represented as attribute/value pairs. Working memory serves the production architecture in the same way that the blackboard serves its architecture: it represents a single, global, database through which all inter-production communication should pass (indeed, Rychener (Rychener, 1978) describes IPS's working memory *as* a blackboard). The contents of working memory are generated or updated by the execution (firing) of production rule actions, and firing may only take place when the situation-fluent (condition part) of a production has been satisfied.

These properties are common between the blackboard and production rule architectures: this fact is a result of the structure required for pattern-directed knowledge processing -- both architectures fall into this class, of course. It is also a result of the psychological theories from which they are both derived. In both architectures, there is a procedural representation of the knowledge base (KB) and KB elements operate on a declarative representation of Working Memory (WM). In the blackboard architecture, WM is represented by the blackboard.

The differences between the architecture really become clear when one considers the structure of the Working Memory representation and the model of control each presupposes. In the blackboard architecture, WM is represented as a structured database; in the production rule architecture, WM is a collection of items with no imposed external structure. The blackboard architecture states that WM elements have arbitrary internal structure and that elements are related to each other in various ways. That is, the blackboard architecture imposes different structuring and organisational constraints upon WM elements. The production rule architecture goes no further than to require working memory to contain intermediate results. When considering control, it is apparent that the blackboard architecture makes many more assumptions than the production rule architecture. It is also clear that blackboard systems can exhibit far greater ranges of behaviour than can production systems. Control in production systems is usually based upon syntactic notions of match and of the number of clauses in the condition-part of the rule: control can also be based on the concept of counting the number of rule firings or of counting the number of rule action components executed per cycle. The blackboard architecture, on the other hand, permits very much more sophisticated and semantically or epistemologically based control regimes. This additional control capability extends the functionality of the blackboard architecture beyond that of the production rule architecture, and it allows blackboard systems to make decisions in a far more reasoned and rational manner than can production systems -- for one thing, the scheduling mechanisms of a blackboard system can take a global view of solution development.

These points serve, I believe, to distinguish the blackboard from all other architectures. They also indicate, I think, that the blackboard is very much more powerful than other architectures. This is not to suggest that I believe that the blackboard is the *ultimate* answer, for, as I will argue, there are severe problems with it and these problems are not just those cited by Anderson (Anderson, 1983, p.130) which are concerned with the computational and memory loads imposed by blackboard systems.* It is to these wider issues that I now turn.

3.3. OPPORTUNISM

It is often said that opportunism is *the* feature which distingushes the blackboard architecture from all others. The claim is that opportunism is really "what blackboard is all about", for no other architecture accommodates it as readily. In this section, I will argue that the concentration on opportunism is a fundamental misconception of the architecture and that suggestions that the blackboard architecture should be considered for some problems "because they are opportunistic" is based on too superficial an analysis of the assumptions and consequences of the architecture. The main proponent of the 'blackboard = opportunism' movement is Penny Nii, so I will concentrate on her remarks.

I wish to examine opportunism in detail because I want to establish a view of the blackboard architecture which puts opportunism in what I consider to be its correct place -- as one control regime among many. The longer term reason is that I need to have this correct view of opportunism accepted in order that I may make fair comparison between the blackboard architecture and my own CASSANDRA architecture. Specifically: because it is not immediately clear that a CASSANDRA system exhibits opportunism in as obvious a fashion as a blackboard system (although it is possible and may be as natural in some cases as it is in blackboard systems), objections may be raised about the functionality of CASSANDRA systems. I have stated that one of my aims in developing the CASSANDRA architecture was to equal, if not exceed, the functionality of blackboard systems. Without a correct account of opportunism, the objection may be raised that CASSANDRA systems do not permit it, and are therefore not as versatile as blackboard systems. Equally, without an adequate account of opportunism, it may be objected that many of the similarities

* In any case, hardware costs are dropping so what is computationally expensive today is cheap tomorrow. Anderson does not make it clear whether he is considering absolute measures or measures relative to the currently available computational power.

between CASSANDRA and blackboard systems are purely illusory.

In order to examine Nii's account of opportunism, I will concentrate on the remarks she makes in the first part of her survey papers (Nii, 1986a; Nii, 1986b). I will present two quotations taken from (Nii, 1986a), both on page 39.

The first quotation appears on the top right of the page: "In an *opportunistic reasoning model,* pieces of knowledge are applied either backward or forward at the most "opportune" time. Put another way, the central issue of problem solving deals with the question "What pieces of knowledge should be applied when and how?" A problem-solving model provides a conceptual framework for organizing knowledge and a strategy for applying that knowledge. ... The blackboard model of problem solving is a highly structured special case of opportunistic problem solving. In addition to opportunistic reasoning as a knowledge-application strategy, the blackboard model prescribes the organization of the domain knowledge and all the input and intermediate and partial solutions needed to solve the problem." (Italics and spelling as in original.) This quotation appears at the end of a definition of the term 'problem solving model' which includes descriptions of forward and backward chaining rule-based reasoning models.

The second quotation is taken from the definition of the control component of the blackboard model (page 39, bottom right): "**Control.** The knowledge sources respond opportunistically to changes in the blackboard." (Bold face as in original.) Quite clearly, KSs have to respond to entry configurations on the blackboard. Opportunism can be viewed as responding to beneficial items and events in one's environment. What is at issue, really, is the use of the word **respond**? -- it suggests and is implied by control processes of one form or another.

The contrasting view is exemplified by Hayes-Roth (Hayes-Roth, 1983, p. 9): "The capacity for and disposition toward opportunistic behavior are characteristic of the blackboard architecture."

The view espoused by Hayes-Roth and by me is that opportunism is typical of the architecture and that the architecture easily supports opportunistic control: this contrasts strongly with Nii's claim that opportunism is a fundamental property of the architecture and must be argued for.

The definition of opportunism given by Nii states that knowledge must be applied at the 'most "opportune" time'. This suggests that knowledge must be applied at the 'best' time, with 'best' being defined according to some criteria. In other words, the choice of words made by Nii is not the 'best'. It does not appear to be correct, for one can imagine other problem solving architectures which apply knowledge at the best time according to the search strategy being applied. That is to say, the search strategy will select that problem solving operator which it has determined to generate a next state which appears to lead most quickly to the solution state.

Now, a characteristic of the blackboard architecture is that it retains Knowledge Source instantiations between problem solving cycles. Thus, it is possible for a blackboard system's scheduler to examine instantiations which were created on cycles previous to the current one. It is possible, therefore, in blackboard systems to examine previous Knowledge Source instantiations as well as those created on the current cycle in order to determine which instantiation will most directly lead to some desired state. It is possible, therefore, for a blackboard system to hold instantiations in memory until they represent the best of the current set of choices. However, unless it is possible to determine exactly how the solution is to be derived, the scheduler cannot know beforehand which of the instantiations in control memory is to be preferred at which particular times: given the search space size of most blackboard systems, it is highly unlikely that a scheduler *could* be created with this property. One could, in any case, construct a problem solving system not using the blackboard architecture which recorded operator instantiations in a database and applied them at a later time. What this amounts to is that the blackboard architecture is able to record instantiations just in case they might turn out to be useful on a later cycle.

In summary, Nii's account of opportunism is, I believe, deficient and does not capture an adequate definition. It does not appear to provide grounds for singling the blackboard architecture out for its use of opportunism, apart, perhaps, from historical grounds. I wish to suggest that any strategy will apply the best knowledge at the best time, but there does appear to be some property which differentiates opportunism from other strategies. Nii's account of opportunism begs the question of what is meant by the best time to apply an item of knowledge.

There is an alternative account of opportunism which I consider to be of greater utility. The alternative account is suggested by the descriptions of the behaviours of subjects in the experiments which preceeded the construction of OPM (Hayes-Roth, 1979). The Hayes-Roths state: "However, we assume that people's planning activity is largely *opportunistic*. That is, at each point in the process, the planner's current decisions and observations suggest various opportunities for plan development. The planner's subsequent decisions follow up on selected opportunities."* One could paraphrase this quotation by saying that opportunism consists of making the best possible use of what appears in the environment by accident or of what has been overlooked. This seems to be an outline for a species of control strategy. Indeed, in control terms, one can say that the effect of applying one or more strategies may be to produce a state in which there is little or no benefit from continuing with those strategies, and in which the accumulated effects of previously applied strategies provide a better foundation for making progress towards a goal than does the continued application of the strategy. In other words, control strategies generate situations in which there are opportunities to make faster progress towards a goal by deviating from any strategies currently in force. Opportunism is a species of control strategy and not a consequence of the blackboard architecture.

If the above be accepted, one must ask what constitutes an 'opportunity'. This appears already to have been covered, for any control decision creates an opportunity for continuing with the current strategy or for deviating from it and making decisions on the basis of what appear to be the best scheduling parameter values: this is the usual way in which opportunism is implemented in blackboard systems. The presence of a control database (which encapsulates the state of a system) facilitates opportunistic control strategies, for it allows the retention of previous Knowledge Source instantiations together with their scheduling parameters. Because these values are available at any time, they can be compared against the values generated by the current strategy: the instantiations with the best values are usually selected for execution, so this is one very clear mechanism by which opportunism can enter a system. I suggest that this property is not necessarily confined to blackboard systems, but is general to all systems which maintain a control database: it seems to me that opportunism has been so closely identified with the blackboard architecture because few other architectures or systems maintain such a database.

It also seems to me that opportunism is a kind of default behaviour for blackboard systems and that this is the property which Nii has emphasised. I suggest that opportunism be considered a separate control strategy (or, perhaps a class of strategy) which can be included in or excluded from a system at the

* As far as I am aware, this is the first time the term 'opportunistic' appears in the literature.

implementer's discretion. Opportunism may appear when the current strategy is detected to be sub-optimal and a transition to an alternative has to be made. Such a transition requires the establishment of specific states and the path from the current state to a state in which a new strategy can be applied may not be directly detectable: opportunism can be employed to select the best possible operators, perhaps from previous cycles, in order to make progress.

There is, I believe, a risk in accepting Nii's definition at face value. She requires blackboard systems to exhibit opportunistic behaviour as an architectural principle. In the limit, this is equivalent to requiring that a system make control decisions based entirely upon what is already present in the environment; that is, a system will *only* examine the environment and not, say, explicitly create subgoals. This is the same as requiring that there be no controlled behaviour and leads to the danger that a solution may never appear. The reader should note that this is the limit case, and I doubt anyone would ever construct a system in this way: yet, I suggest that it is a direct consequence of requiring that opportunism be present in a system to conform to the definition of the architecture. If, on the other hand, one considers opportunism to be another species of control strategy, this risk is no longer present and one can choose whether or not to apply an opportunistic strategy, and one is able to maintain control of the system at all times.

In summary, I consider opportunism not to be a fundamental aspect of the blackboard architecture. It appears to be central because of the way systems have been constructed. Instead, I suggest that opportunism be considered to be only another strategy.

3.4. MODULARITY

One of the claims made for the blackboard architecture is that it is highly modular. The architecture is usually claimed to be modular on the basis of the independence of Knowledge Sources. Other claims could be made about the relative independence of the abstraction levels which typically form the vertical structure of the blackboard database: relative independence because the blackboard architecture is commonly taken to be a representative of models which exploit near-decomposability (Simon, 1969).

The conventional method for building blackboard systems emphasises the relative independence of abstraction levels. Knowledge Sources are constructed for one particular level of the blackboard at a time.

The Knowledge Sources are tested on entries at the chosen abstraction level: the results of executing the KSs are just placed in a nameless space during the earliest stages of development. When one level's KSs have been shown to operate properly, another level (frequently one that is adjacent) is then developed. The process iterates until all levels have been covered. This method relies upon an assumption that it is possible to decouple a particular abstraction level from the overall structure and operate upon it. It is also a way of managing complexity during development which relies upon the modular structure of the architecture. The method uses the fact that the effects of KSs can be separated out. Depending upon task, first the KSs which trigger on the chosen level and then those which modify that level are introduced into the system; next, KSs which trigger on the chosen level and modify other regions of the blackboard are introduced and tested. The effects of this second kind of Knowledge Source are collected in an effectively unnamed space which represents 'the rest of the blackboard'.

The reason for introducing an aspect of the development methodology is to show that the blackboard architecture is considered to be highly modular by application builders and to show that it can be considered to be so, to an approximation. The caveat is important for I wish to show that the architecture is not quite as modular as one might think.

It is usual to cite Knowledge Sources as the basic source of modularity in blackboard systems. Knowledge Sources are independent knowledge structures which cause changes to the solution state recorded on the blackboard. They are not permitted to interact with each other directly, but must communicate only indirectly by posting entries on the blackboard. One KS may not share variables or other data with another KS unless that data is represented as a blackboard entry. Because of this modularity, it is possible to add or remove KSs from a system without causing configuration problems. By adding or removing a KS, only the quality of the emerging solution can be effected. The emerging solution is represented as a configuration of entries on the blackboard, so the addition of new Knowledge Sources will either allow new entries to appear in the solution, will allow new relationships to come into being between entries, or will alter the range of modifications to existing entries. The removal of KSs is directly analogous, but operates in the reverse direction (e.g., the removal of a KS will reduce the number of possible entries which can be posted on the blackboard). Since there is no direct interaction between KSs, the addition or removal of a KS cannot impact upon the internal workings of any other KS.

Since Knowledge Sources are independent modules, any alterations to their internal structure or to their content, equally, cannot cause changes to anything other than the quality of the emerging solution. By making a particular KS more specific, for example, the entries it generates will also be more specific -- this is observable externally only as a property of the solution.

The case for KS modularity is, I think, quite sound. Knowledge Sources, however, communicate by posting and inspecting entries on the blackboard. As has been pointed out, a KS may inspect one region of the blackboard and record an entry in quite another region. This prompts the question of how the various regions are related to each other. The simplest case of this (and the one with the most general theoretical importance) is the relationship between the constituents of the blackboard structure's vertical dimension; that is, its abstraction levels.

The hierarchy of abstraction levels on the blackboard is one of the most commonly cited structural details in descriptions of blackboard systems. Feigenbaum (Feigenbaum, 1978) describes the hierarchy as defining a prototypical control plan. The hierarchy represents views of the problem at varying levels of abstraction. The structure and interpretation of the blackboard may be considered as being analogous to the abstractions in hierarchical planning (Sacerdoti, 1974; Sacerdoti, 1977): a problem is solved by considering its properties at a variety of levels of abstraction, the highest of which should provide the most concise description of the problem. This view of blackboard structure actually ignores other structural information as I will now argue.

At any abstraction level of a blackboard, there is usually one Knowledge Source which triggers on the entries there. It is usual for a KS only to trigger on one abstraction level because entries are allowed to reside on only one level. Triggering events are caused by the addition or modification of entries and so are each related to only one particular abstraction level. When a triggered KS is executed, it causes modifications to the blackboard at the same abstraction level as it was triggered or to another level.

The generic Blackboard Control Model KS, Implement-Strategy, for example, is triggered on the Strategy level of the control blackboard and makes modifications to that level *as well as* to the Focus level (the abstraction level immediately below it in the control blackboard hierarchy). Implement-Strategy changes the status of the current Focus entry (similar to Focus1, above) to "Inoperative" and proposes a new focus entry. A consequence of this action is the introduction of a new problem solving strategy created by posting an entry on the Strategy level: the appearance of the new entry on the Strategy level of the control blackboard will cause other KSs to be triggered.

This example clearly shows that the relationships between abstraction levels on the blackboard is rather more complex than is apparent from the definition given above. The example shows, in particular, that entries may, in theory, be recorded on a particular abstraction level by any Knowledge Source in a system. The interface between abstraction levels depends upon the Knowledge Sources which trigger on one level and cause modifications to another. The inter-level interface is hidden in the actions of all Knowledge Sources in a system and is, what is more, *distributed* across KSs. In other words, there is no central interface between abstraction levels. The interface between blackboard events and KSs is described in systems like BB1 and NBB as a causal connection which is locally defined for each KS. The definition is the trigger condition associated with each Knowledge Source. The interface describing the more global relationship between Knowledge Sources and the locus of their effects (the levels at which they alter the blackboard state) is not made explicit, but remains implicitly defined by individual KS actions.

The structure of an abstraction level may be considered to consist of a set of entries and a set of Knowledge Sources which trigger there. The KSs themselves may be thought of as being relations between abstraction levels. Two levels are related if at least one Knowledge Source triggers on one level and alters the contents of the second. This makes clear the fact that the information held in entries at any particular level of the abstraction hierarchy depends upon information held at other levels, not just adjacent levels. It also makes clear the idea that KSs may post or modify entries on levels which are not adjacent in the abstraction hierarchy.

The second of these points is the important point: abstraction levels are related otherwise than simply by the abstraction hierarchy which defines the blackboard. Entries are created as a result of executing KS actions; KS actions are permitted to execute as a result of KS triggering. The entry which causes a KS to trigger determines some, if not all, of the information the action uses to make changes to the blackboard. Thus, there is a relationship defined by information flow across the blackboard. This relationship is defined in terms of the relationships represented by KSs and is additional to the generator relationship for the abstraction hierarchy. Quite obviously, the information flow across the blackboard (in the sense of the general order in which entries are added to database) is important, yet it seldom receives attention: it has never, to my knowledge, been expressed in these terms before, but has always been submerged in descriptions of the abstraction hierarchy.

These considerations show that the blackboard database is not an encapsulated (or modular) construct. The interfaces presented by the abstraction levels in the abstraction hierarchy are related by means other than by the abstraction relationship. The ways in which levels are related are hidden in KS actions, so there is no explicit statement of how an arbitrary pair of levels is related. What is more, there is no explicit statement of how information on any particular level is, in general, produced -- to obtain this information, one must examine the individual entries to determine which KSs have created and modified them, then examine the KSs mentioned by the entries to see where they trigger. The second step of this process may involve going through historical information to find entries on the KS's triggering level.

The modularity of the blackboard architecture rests *entirely* with Knowledge Sources. KSs have well-defined interfaces with regard to their areas of competence. The levels at which a KS triggers and at which it executes its action are well-defined inside the KS. The larger issue of interfaces *across* the blackboard is far less clear. The argument above has shown that information from a variety of sources may contribute in the creation of entries at any given abstraction level. One of the justifications for the abstraction hierarchy is that it separates the structure of the blackboard into distinct and distinguishable regions. This justification appears to be defeated in the face of the evidence that information on a particular level may be composed of information from practically everywhere else without any statement (other than in each individual KS) of how it got there.

If abstraction levels are genuinely independent in the way that it seems they should, it becomes important to be able to define their relationships to other levels, just so that one can give a definition of what it means for an entry to appear at any given abstraction level. One way to do this is to define cleaner interfaces between abstraction levels. This permits an abstract description of the boundaries between levels. It also allows constraints to be imposed upon information flows across the blackboard. One interpretation of this is that it defines the kinds of information which can legally be used to construct an entry at a given level. At present, any Knowledge Source at any level may, in theory, post information on any other level without constraint -- in the limit, this leads, of course, to chaos.

Fodor (Fodor, 1983), makes the distinction between vertical and horizontal organisations in cognitive systems. Vertical organisations are domain-specific and encapsulated; horizontal organisations, on the other hand, are non-specific and unencapsulated. Perceptual and linguistic processes are examples of vertical processes; central cognitive processes are cited by Fodor as examples of horizontal processes. In the blackboard architecture, vertical structure is represented by Knowledge Sources. There appears to be a tacit claim that, because the blackboard is organised into abstraction levels, there is an encapsulation mechanism here, too. The claim rests upon the usual interpretation of 'abstraction' which implies that objects at different levels of abstraction do not strongly interact. From the way the blackboard is treated and described in implemented systems, it would appear that it has a horizontal structure, but its definition suggests a combination of vertical and horizontal structure. The very fact that the blackboard is organised into abstraction levels implies that each level is specialised and has special-purpose processes operating upon it: this is precisely equivalent to the definition of *vertical process* given by Fodor. The blackboard database *as a whole* may be regarded as a general-purpose process (a horizontal process, that is), but its components are specialised. This indicates that there is scope for re-examining the blackboard architecture from the viewpoint of modularity to see if it is possible to derive a model with clearer structure.

3.5. GENERALITY

Finally, we must examine the claim that the blackboard architecture is a *general* model of problem solving: that is, that it provides a general framework within which to express and develop theories of problem solving. Nii (Nii, 1986a) states that "HASP, as the second example of a blackboard system, not only added credibility to the claim that a blackboard approach to problem solving was general, but it also demonstrated that it could be abstracted into a general model of problem solving." Hayes-Roth (Hayes-Roth, 1983) specifically asks if the architecture is general. After examining the computational advantages and psychological plausibility of the model, she concludes (p. 23): "In summary, I would answer the question posed in the title of this paper: "The Blackboard Architecture: A General Framework for Problem Solving?" in a single word: Perhaps."

Although it seems inuitively plausible that the blackboard architecture *is* a general model of problem solving, this has not been conclusively shown.

Anderson (Anderson, 1983) argues that it cannot be an adequate model because it makes great demands of memory and requires considerable computational power. For Anderson, production rule architectures are the most plausible general model because they make fewer demands on computational resources. Although I take the point, I am disinclined to accept that this is valid for it is not easily possible to express all that one can express within the blackboard architecture within the confines of productions, complex control being an obvious case.*

One of the major generality claims for the blackboard architecture is that it is general because it is so flexible and so powerful. The blackboard has been used, it should be remembered, to tackle high complexity problems. It has been argued that the blackboard is the *only* architecture capable of operating in these domains (this argument is implicit in the selection of the architecture for the task). This seems to suggest that, were the task not so complex, the blackboard would not have been the chosen architecture. We have to be a little careful, here, because there are, effectively, two claims to generality: one is a *psychological* claim, the other rather more pragmatic. The argument that the architecture was chosen because it can handle the complexities of a given domain is a pragmatic one and depends only upon the flexibility of the architecture and upon the architecture's native power. One can see, practically immediately, that the blackboard architecture is not suited to some tasks: resolution theorem proving is one example -- one would not use the full power of the blackboard to do what Prolog does, although one might want to include a lush resolution theorem prover (a theorem prover which employs the same strategy as Prolog, that is) in a KS. The counter to this is that the blackboard provides a methodology within which it is possible to make problem solving and control knowledge more explicit.**

* It has to be admitted that I feel somewhat uneasy about Anderson's ACT* work. In particular, he has presented tasks which appear to support his theory of top-down goal-directed control. Although Means End Analysis and its relatives are attractive, I wonder if they capture the entire story: that is, work on MYCIN, for example, indicates that there are alternatives to sub-goaling strategies.

** I have heard a rumour that MYCIN and some of its derivatives are to be re-implemented as blackboard systems. The rationale is precisely the one which I have given.

The claim for generality for the blackboard architecture is based on the claims that

(i) it produces a general model of problem solving; and,

(ii) it is powerful and flexible enough to be employed as the architecture for any problem solving system.

The second point is wholly empirical and depends upon a sufficient number of implemented systems, operating in different domains, performing to satisfactory levels. The first claim is more difficult to assess, but there are pointers. The fact that there have been a number of completed and successful blackboard systems indicates that point (ii) has some truth: indeed, recently the general level of interest in the blackboard architecture has increased and it is being applied to many, different, problems.

If the architecture can be applied to different problems and, what is more, produces a *natural* solution (i.e., one which is aesthetically, theoretically and computationally satisfying), one would be inclined to assert that the architecture can be generally applied. This is said despite the fact that it is very difficult to apply the architecture to some domains and that systems which look highly counter-intuitive can result.

In particular, consider some of the tasks Anderson chooses for his work on ACT* -- elementary geometry and LISP programming. The reason ACT* seems to be such a plausible account of these domains is that there is a good fit between his architecture and the complexity of the problem. As a paper exercise some time ago, I took the geometry experiment and attempted to re-cast it as a blackboard system. The result was unspectacular. One consequence of adopting the blackboard architecture was that the concept of abstraction levels had to be taken on board and the result of that was that abstractions had to be found where there were none in the experimental data. The geometry production set shown on page 222 of (Anderson, 1983), reveals, on close examination, three abstraction levels: Goal, Sub-Goal and Operation. The solution is retrieved from the Operation level. This analysis appears to be less attractive than the one suggested by Anderson in which there are goals and results which are distinguished, basically, by the role each plays in the problem solving process. The control model one would have to adopt to cater for Anderson's results is simply a variation on recursive sub-goaling: each rule in the set on page 222 is sensitive to the presence of a goal and merely expands that goal. This suggests that most of the power of the blackboard architecture is not used, and it also suggests that a blackboard implementation of these productions would be computationally wasteful.

It could be argued that it is comforting to know that the blackboard architecture *could* be applied to simple problems. This argument, though, continues with the suggestion that the full power of the blackboard is not needed for such a simple problem, but it is there in case it is needed. My point is, however, that the power of the blackboard is always there and that it is being wasted in solving problems of this level of simplicity.

A second argument concerns abstraction levels. For many tasks, it is extremely difficult to discover a natural abstraction hierarchy -- oft times, the hierarchy looks highly artificial and contrived (the controlled airspace monitoring problem is such a problem, as is the interpretation of visual images). The Hayes-Roths found this a difficulty with parts of OPM and imply this in (Hayes-Roth, 1979). One could say that the system builders simply have not done their analysis correctly, but this will not do, for this problem is encountered by experienced and careful application builders.

Many of the more successful applications of the blackboard architecture have been in domains in which there is a fairly obvious decomposition which can serve as the prototype for the blackboard: the speech processing domain is an example. Even when it is possible to find abstractions (it is usually possible to invent abstractions, at least in the domains I have considered), it is not always possible to form them into a coherent hierarchy. There is a further problem: abstraction hierarchies tend, very often, to be problem-specific. That is, it is not usually the case that an abstraction hierarchy can be used for another problem, let alone another domain. One must ask the question as to whether an architecture is general if it posits structures which cannot readily be generalised, assuming that they are not already adequate: in the present context, it would appear that the evidence can be taken to indicate that the architecture is not fully general. This point could be expressed by saying that the abstraction hierarchies are problem-specific. A partial counter-example is afforded by the BB* environment (Hayes-Roth, 1986). A number of assembly tasks are being implemented using the BB1 blackboard interpreter: the tasks use a more-or-less similar abstraction hierarchy. Even if hierarchies can be found for entire domains (and I am doubtful, though willing to be convinced), it is hard to see how anything but very general organisations could be used: this would make, I suppose, the hierarchy fairly useless for specific problems and would, consequently, reduce the power of a system using these general hierarchies. Basically, an abstraction hierarchy is a knowledge-organising device and is domain- and/or problem-specific. The *capacity* of the blackboard architecture to represent abstractions is not in question: that is a matter of fact. What I am really questioning is the methodological assumption that everything must exhibit hierarchy in this way. Even in her paper on the generality of the architecture, Barbara Hayes-Roth equivocates on the status of abstractions (Hayes-Roth, 1983, section 3.2.7, p. 18).

In summary, these are my points. Firstly, the blackboard architecture is powerful and flexible, but when applied to simple problems much of the power and flexibility is just not required. Second, abstraction levels are in many ways problematic and only apply within particular domains or within particular parts of a domain. The blackboard methodology requires one to find abstractions in order to build working models, even when this might not appear necessary or advisable. It may be the case that non-hierarchical organisations are more appropriate, in which case, the blackboard becomes a set of panels with little or no internal structure. This last point sounds to me very much like a trick to force the architecture to cater for every case.

Methodologically, there are problems with the blackboard architecture. Specifically, its methodology is under-specified. It is under-specified in the following sense. The methodology basically states that problem solving systems should be constructed from modular Knowledge Sources which operate on a hierarchically organised database called the blackboard. Insofar as it is suggested that Knowledge Sources trigger on entries at particular abstraction levels of the blackboard, it specifies the relationship between KSs and abstraction levels. The methodology says a little about control, but not much, for the architecture does not really specify its control mechanisms. The methodology for building blackboard systems emphasises the fact that a system can be considered as a collection of black boxes. A major assumption of the methodology is that the entire power of the architecture is always needed.

If a problem solving architecture is to be a candidate for the title *General Problem Solving Architecture,* it must do a number of things. Firstly, it must be sufficiently flexible that any instance of problem solving activity from the simplest to the most complex can be covered. Second, it must not project unwanted constructs on descriptions of problem solving activity. Third, it must supply a general methodology which can be applied to every case of problem solving: when the architecture or its methodology fall down, the architecture must be revised. In some of these respects, the blackboard architecture is inadequate and cannot qualify for the generality title.

The subject of this book, CASSANDRA, is an attempt to rectify some of these perceived faults with the blackboard architecture. It provides definite and enforceable interfaces between its counterpart to abstraction levels -- this, I suggest, gives a clearer idea of the structure of the working memory of any system built using the architecture. The architecture also provides for modular control: one problem with the blackboard architecture is that a full and complex control component is always required. The CASSANDRA architecture offers a model of problem solving which is additive in the sense that the full power of the architecture is only invoked when necessary, and is not, as in the case of blackboard systems, present at all times. If a model of problem solving is to be called general, it must provide for simple as well as complex cases: that, I claim, is true of the CASSANDRA architecture. The architecture has similar functionality to the blackboard model: it is possible, for example, to introduce opportunistic control strategies, and it is possible to employ knowledge-based control, just as in blackboard systems. The strong claim is that the CASSANDRA architecture, because of its better encapsulation, has the advantage that for smaller and/or simpler problems, a more nearly optimal system is produced because the architecture is additive, and that where more complex systems are needed, the architecture provides a clearer and more modular environment for problem solving. The architecture also makes clearer methodological points than does the blackboard.

All the same, the CASSANDRA architecture is, I suggest, a development of the blackboard architecture and shares the same functionality with its antecedent. Indeed, one implementation of the architecture is as a modularity-enforcing pre-processor which converts a system expressed in the CASSANDRA architecture into a conventional blackboard system. Such an implementation might be used in circumstances in which a centralised blackboard system is required, but in which the benefits of modularity provided by the CASSANDRA architecture are desired.

4. THE CASSANDRA ARCHITECTURE

4.1. INTRODUCTION

This chapter is concerned with the general properties of and the rationale for the CASSANDRA architecture. In chapters two and three, the blackboard architecture was first introduced via a set of example systems and then was defined in fairly rigorous terms. The definition suggested some problems with the architecture: consideration of these problems led to the development of the CASSANDRA architecture described in this chapter. The CASSANDRA architecture attempts to make the relationship between blackboard abstraction levels clearer and it is aimed at repairing modularity faults in the blackboard architecture. As a consequence of these fixes, a new architecture with structural similarities to the blackboard has emerged. The new architecture is arguably more modular and cleaner than the original architecture and has a message-passing basis.

In the new architecture, the central database is divided into a system of autonomous agents, called *Level Managers*. They communicate via message-passing and have local control components. Message-passing and local control facilitate both modularity and enforced distinctions between significant structural divisions of the global database. The basic communication model in the CASSANDRA architecture is *asynchronous*. Asynchronous communication is a specialisation of synchronous communication (in the sense that it can be simulated or implemented by synchronous processes): it is a weaker assumption and thus permits a greater variety of implementation. These factors lead to the development of a methodology which does not have the faults identified with blackboard systems.

In this chapter, I will describe and illustrate the CASSANDRA architecture, and I will compare it with other architectures in an attempt to show that it is genuinely different. In addition, I will argue for the differences between the new architecture and older ones.

4.2. THE STRUCTURE OF A CASSANDRA SYSTEM

A system built using the CASSANDRA architecture retains the concepts of knowledge source and blackboard level. The blackboard level retains its status as a working memory which contains entries of a given class or set of classes. In CASSANDRA systems each level is, however, considered to be a wholly independent unit and is contained in a *Level Manager*. Level Managers are active structures which contain a local working memory or database (the level database) and Knowledge Sources which trigger on the entries held in the level database; they also contain local control mechanisms. Level Managers communicate with each other so that information may be transferred between levels as in the conventional blackboard architecture.

Level Managers are composed of the following structures:

- a local database. This represents the blackboard level. It is a working memory purely local to the Level Manager. No other Level Manager and no Knowledge Source which does not belong the Level Manager owning the database may directly inspect or update its contents. The local database is completely private (as far as the local working memory is concerned, one might view the Level Manager construct as being related to the object manager concept in operating systems (Lagally, 1978)).
- a collection of Knowledge Sources. Knowledge Sources have the structure usually associated with KSs (they contain a precondition composed of a trigger and a condition, and they contain an action). The KSs held within a Level Manager belong to the Level Manager and have their trigger and condition evaluated on data held in the Level Manager's local database. Knowledge Sources may engage in indirect communication with other Level Managers via the port and channel mechanisms described below.
- a local scheduler. Each Level Manager in a CASSANDRA system is considered to be an autonomous module with local control. Local control is effected by the local scheduler. The local scheduler operates on instances only of the Knowledge Sources belonging to the Level Manager in which it resides.
- a control database. The control database contains information useful to the local scheduler in making control decisions. The control database is private to the Level Manager in which it resides, but may contain information with a more global extent.
- a matcher and action interpreter. These components are responsible for matching KS preconditions and for executing KS actions. The presence of separate matchers and action interpreters allows different Level Managers to use different knowledge representations if the domain requires.

- a set of ports. Communication between Level Managers is achieved via ports and channels. Messages are sent via ports along channels to destination Level Managers. Ports can be used either for input or for output with the restriction that a particular port may only have one type (no input-output ports are permitted) and that port types are statically assigned (it is not permitted to change an input port to an output port, or vice-versa, at runtime). Communication via ports may be buffered or unbuffered: this is an implementation decision.

Level Managers exist within envelopes.* The envelope is concerned with implementing the basic match-schedule-execute loop and with handling communications. Below, the envelope will be ignored. It is worth remembering, though, that when discussing message-passing, the operations on ports are handled by envelopes. The envelope is present to support the Level Manager abstraction and to provide an interface to the message-passing system. In implementations of the architecture, the envelope performs the actual interfacing tasks to the communication medium being used in the implementation: in this respect, it is close to Hoare's original concept.

The most significant architectural detail after the provision of local control (which will be discussed more fully below) is that inter-level communication is regularised by the use of uni-directional communication channels (these will be called simply 'channels' below). The channels which convey information from one Level Manager to another must be statically defined with the Level Manager.

4.3. CHANNELS

Level Managers are connected via channels. They are used to convey information between one Level Manager and another. Channels are used to describe the configuration of a CASSANDRA system and to render the information flows between Level Managers explicit. They also serve to limit the possible communication paths between Level Managers so that Knowledge Sources cannot post entries to arbitrary

* The term is due to C.A.R. Hoare. However, I am unable to find any references to this concept in the literature. Hoare used the concept during lectures given during the late 1970s at P.R.G., Oxford. Envelopes were used extensively in programs constructed using Pascal Plus, particularly those written by Hoare's colleagues at Queen's University, Belfast. The idea was that a process is represented by a collection of procedures and that these procedures should not need to interface directly to operating system services: all such interfaces were provided by the envelope. The process envelope provided a higher level interface to the operating system than that afforded by the operating system primitives. The motivation behind the envelope concept was the isolation of user programs from the details of the interfaces with the operating system. In effect, envelopes provided environments within which processes operated: the environment was constructed from an abstraction of the underlying operating system.

places in the system but only to those Level Managers which have been declared to be the recipients of information from the Level Manager in which a particular KS resides. That is, the potential recipients of information from the KSs in a particular Level Manager, say, LM1, must be declared when LM1 is defined: it is not possible for any of LM1's KSs to send information to any other part of the system.

Each channel has a start point and an end point: information flows from the start to the end. The channels between Level Managers serve to make the relationships between abstraction levels clearer. This is because a Level Manager must have a distinct channel for each Level Manager with which it communicates.

Channels may be used either for input or for output. A particular channel may only be used in one direction at any time -- they are uni-directional, it should be remembered. Channels are connected to Level Managers via ports. An input and an output port when connected together form a uni-directional channel.

The notational convention which will be adopted here for writing inter-Level Manager communication is that input ports will be denoted by the suffix **in** and output ports will be denoted by the suffix **out**. Each suffix can have an optional integer subscript so that ports can be uniquely identified. The identifier of the Level Manager in question is used as a prefix so that the Level Manager to which a port belongs can be uniquely determined. The identification of a channel is rendered easier because a pair of Level Managers can only be related by at most two channels.

If two Level Managers, LM1 and LM2, wish to communicate bi-directionally, there must be the following ports defined for each Level Manager: LM1.out, LM1.in, LM2.out and LM2.in. The ports LM1.in and LM2.out are connected to a channel which conveys information from LM2 to LM1. Similarly, the ports LM1.out and LM2.in are connected to a channel which conveys information in the reverse direction. The connections can be written as

LM1.out → LM2.in
LM2.out → LM1.in.

If, on the other hand, LM1 also communicated with LM3 by accepting information from LM3 via a port, there would be an ambiguity as to which port was connected to which channel. Assuming that LM3 has a unique output port LM3.out, the connections between LM1, LM2 and LM3 can be described as follows:

LM3.out → LM1.in0
LM1.out → LM2.in
LM2.out → LM1.in1.

Note that LM1 can only receive information from LM3: it cannot send messages to LM3. If information were sent from LM1 to LM3, LM1 would need another output port, say LM1.out1.

Connections between ports will always be written with the output port on the left and information flowing in the direction of the arrow.

It is possible for a particular Level Manager to be connected to many channels. There can be at most two channels between each pair of Level Managers. The reason for this is that there are only two operations which may be performed via channels: messages may be received or messages may be sent. When there are two channels connecting a pair of Level Managers, one may think of them as comprising a bi-directional channel: information is transferred in both directions between the Level Managers.

In order that channels be easier to recognise, they are given names. In the last example above, the channel names Chan1, Chan2 and Chan3 are assigned to the port configurations. Channel names precede the port connections and are separated by a colon. Thus:

Chan1 : LM3.out → LM1.in0
Chan2 : LM1.out → LM2.in
Chan3 : LM2.out → LM1.in1

The existence of channels and ports connecting Level Managers solves one of the modularity problems of the conventional blackboard architecture. It is now possible to define the relationships between levels and to constrain Knowledge Sources to write information only to a few blackboard levels. If there is no 'official' path between two levels, there will be no channels connecting them; if there is no channel connecting two Level Managers, there can be no direct communication whatsoever between them. If, on the other hand, there is information flow between two levels, there will be at least one channel connecting them. The direction of the connection in the channel specification determines the direction of information flow between levels. From the example, it can be seen that LM1 and LM2 have bi-directional information transfer, whereas LM1 and LM3 only have uni-directional transfer in the direction LM3 to LM1.

The explicit connection of ports to channels entails that the information flow between levels can be regularised and made clearer to the system builder, verifier and, if explanation is important, to the user.

Together, channels and the Level Manager construct serve to build 'fire walls' around local databases and Knowledge Sources. If two Level Managers are not connected by a channel, there can be no communication between them, and there is no possibility that information can be exchanged. The structure of channels and ports serves to act as a kind of protection mechanism. In its simplest form, the protection mechanism is similar to the non-hierarchical scheme proposed by Graham and Denning for use in operating systems (Graham, 1972).

Graham and Denning's proposal is to allow a non-hierarchical protection mechanism based on capabilities. The central construct in their proposal is the *access matrix*, a two-dimensional matrix which represents the capabilities of various *subjects* for all system *objects*. A capability is a representation of the operations which may be performed on a resource by a process: a file might be read-only to some processes, but read-write to others -- the ability of a process to perform an operation (such as writing to a file) is called a *capablity*. Subjects are represented as the rows of the matrix and each has the form *(process, domain)*: each row indicates the capability list for each process executing in any particular domain. The columns of the matrix represent the system resources, or *objects*. Each object is associated with a *controller* which is entered whenever the object is accessed. The controller is responsible for allocating capabilities to the subjects accessing the object.

Level Managers can be connected by one or more uni-directional channels. If one Level Manager has an output port connected to an input port in another Level Manager, the first Level Manager has what approximates to a write capability with respect to the second. That is, the first Level Manager may send information to the second. The second, though, has only a read capability with respect to the first Level Manager. If two Level Managers are connected via two channels, they both have what approximates to a read-write capability with respect to the other. The existence of a channel connecting two Level Managers amounts to the possession of a pair of capabilities by the Level Managers concerned: where there is no channel between two Level Managers, there are no capabilities of any sort and one may not perform any operation on the other. Capabilities were introduced into operating systems to improve the level of protection afforded by the system from malicious or incorrect processes and to allow processes access to only those resources which are strictly necessary to perform some operation. In the CASSANDRA architecture, the encapsulation provided by the Level Manager construct and the capabilities implicitly assigned by the presence or absence of channels performs an analogous role.

Channels connect Level Managers and allow information to flow between them. What is the nature of the information? The most obvious form for this information is that of the blackboard entry, and this is, indeed, true. When a Knowledge Source action sends an entry to a Level Manager other than the one to which it is bound (the one to which it 'belongs'), the entry is sent along the appropriate channel to the destination Level Manager. So, in the example, if LM1 contains a Knowledge Source which has to send an entry to LM2, the Knowledge Source will send the entry along Chan2 (the channel connecting LM1.out to LM2.in). In addition, control information may be sent along channels (this point will be addressed below when discussing control in the CASSANDRA architecture).

4.4. KNOWLEDGE SOURCES AND COMMUNICATION

As in the blackboard architecture, problem-solving behaviour is produced by Knowledge Sources in the CASSANDRA architecture. The CASSANDRA architecture adds the problem of inter-Level Manager communication to the more conventional triggering and entry posting or modifying actions. KSs in CASSANDRA systems must be involved in communication because they must occasionally access non-local information. Level Managers are not intended to be complete encapsulations of the entire solution state, but record only that portion of the global state which locally concerns them. Knowledge Sources, on the other hand, produce Level Manager local states by transforming entries which are either local to a Level Manager or which are held elsewhere in some completely distinct Level Manager. It is the latter case which requires KSs in CASSANDRA systems to engage in communication with Level Managers other than those in which they reside. In the blackboard architecture, there is a single global state: in the CASSANDRA architecture the global state is, at least notionally, distributed among Level Managers.

Because of these considerations, KSs in the CASSANDRA architecture must engage in communication acts with other Level Managers. This entails that they be able to access the communication mechanisms provided by the architecture: this is where problems set in. KSs are intentional: they perform certain actions in order to satisfy some goal -- the goal is sometimes explicit but is, more often, implicit in the tasks they perform. When a KS transforms one set of entries into another, it is doing so in order to satisfy its goal or to fulfill its purpose. Level Managers, on the other hand, are intended to be encapsulating mechanisms: they collect related knowledge and information into identifiable modules. Since the transformation performed by each KS depends upon its purpose and intensional description, there seems to be no good reason for requiring that inter-Level Manager communication acts be taken by Level Managers. The point of an inter-Level Manager communication is, by and large, to give a KS access to certain information. KSs, therefore, must be able to initiate communications and process their results.

The problem with making KSs the initiators and processors of information derived from inter-Level Manager communications is that there is the risk of introducing deadlock or livelock into a CASSANDRA system. The CASSANDRA architecture restricts communications in a number of ways so that problems with concurrency are reduced. This is done by restricting the behaviours of KSs which engage in non-local communications and by requiring Level Managers to handle the inter-Level Manager transactions. If such constraints are too strict, the functionality of the architecture will be reduced; if the constraints are not strict enough, concurrent *chaos** results. Since the CASSANDRA architecture is intended to be general purpose, the constraints imposed on its inter-Level Manager communications are intended to be just strict enough to avoid *chaos*, but not strict enough to reduce its functionality below that of the blackboard architecture. In short, any behaviour permitted by the blackboard architecture should be possible within a CASSANDRA system. The communication constraints imposed on the architecture were chosen very much with this in mind.

4.4.1. Deadlock and Livelock

Deadlock and livelock are insidious problems with concurrent, non-deterministic and distributed systems. When a system enters a deadlocked or livelocked state, it will eventually cease to operate: deadlock and livelock spread across it like a disease destroying behaviour as they progress. They are an issue in the CASSANDRA architecture because it is *notionally* distributed and capable of parallel execution. Deadlock

* cf. (Hoare, 1985, p. 127).

and livelock are immediate consequences of the Level Manager encapsulation and of the general principles which support Level Managers. Since the architecture can be *implemented* as a distributed parallel system, the properties of deadlock and livelock must be discussed.

Deadlock is a system state in which processes cannot gain access to the shared resources they need to make progress. The typical characterisation of a deadlock is that all processes wishing to access a shared resource are perpetually locked out of the resource or are unable to make progress because the process currently accessing the shared resource depends upon the results of another process before it can release it.

A very simple example of deadlock is that of two processes sharing two buffers. A process can gain access to a buffer only by gaining the semaphore for the buffer ('gaining' or 'holding' the semaphore is meant to indicate that the value of the semaphore is such that the process is given access to the buffer). Imagine that process one gains access to buffer one, and then, while in possession, gains access to buffer two. Now process two tries to access buffer one, but finds that it cannot hold the semaphore, so it waits. It then tries to access buffer two, but cannot gain the semaphore there, either. However, to make progress, process one requires processs two to place information in buffer one. This is not possible because process one is holding the semaphore, so process two cannot place its information in buffer one. Process two, though, needs information from process one which should be in buffer two. Process two cannot access that information because it cannot gain the semaphore to read the contents of buffer two. Since the semaphore is needed both for reads and for writes, neither process can progress because they are *deadlocked.* Process one cannot release buffer one because it needs information from process two to release the semaphore. Process two wishes to access buffer two but cannot because it is held by process one. Neither process can do anything other than wait for the other.

The example given above is based upon the allocation of resources solely on their availability. Since the example assumes that the resources (the buffers) are unshareable and neither process can release its buffer, deadlock is ensured. In general, there are four necessary and sufficient conditions for deadlock (Coffman, 1971). These conditions are:

(i) the resources required by the concurrent processes are unshareable;

(ii) processes hold the resources which they have already been allocated while waiting for more resources;

(iii) while a resource is being used, it cannot be pre-empted, and

(iv) a circular chain of processes exists such that each process holds resources which are currently being requested by the next process in the chain.

Here, note, a process is said to 'hold' a resource if it has been given sole access to it. Also note that the fourth condition, the circular request condition is important in showing that the CASSANDRA-II airspace monitoring system is deadlock-free: CASSANDRA-II contains no circular dependencies between its resources and so the fact that one Level Manager is waiting for a message from another cannot cause the system to deadlock.

There are three basic strategies for solving the problem of deadlock. They are

(i) prevent deadlock by ensuring that at least one of the four necessary and sufficient conditions does not hold in the system;

(ii) detect deadlock as soon as it occurs and try to recover from it, and

(iii) avoid the possibility of deadlock by some suitable anticipatory action.

The three strategies will now be discussed briefly.

The first strategy is to prevent deadlock by ensuring that at least one of the four necessary and sufficient conditions does not obtain. The first condition involves unshareable resources. It is frequently difficult to make resources unshareable. Line printers, for example, by their very nature are unshareable. In a similar fashion, ports are, basically, unshareable because every Knowledge Source in each Level Manager must, at least notionally, have access to them. Ports are also shared between Level Managers. The constraint imposed on the KSs in a Level Manager (see below) is that they may not *directly* access ports either for reading or for writing. This solution is similar to spooling and to the creation of virtual devices in operating systems: both of these techniques reduce, if not totally eliminate, the possibility of deadlock. The contents of Level Managers' local databases are private as far as all Level Managers other than the owners are concerned, so they are not, by definition, shareable resources in CASSANDRA systems.

The second condition can be obviated by requiring that all processes in a concurrent system declare their interest in the resources they will require as soon as they are created. This is not a particularly viable option in most operating systems because it requires that resources which are to be used only for a short period of time must be allocated for the entire life of a process. Similarly, in the CASSANDRA architecture, it is not possible for all KSs to declare their interest in using ports: the use of a port is a dynamic decision made by each KS on the basis of the information it possesses when executed. There is no need to consider the contents of local databases in this connection, for they are, in any case, private. The channels which connect Level Managers are created at system start-up time and are statically allocated, so they are covered by this strategy.

Condition (iii) can be denied by requiring that each process which is refused access to a resource must give up all of the resources it currently possesses. This move tends not to be very convenient in practice because the pre-emption of (say) a physical line-printer would involve the interleaving of output from several processes. In the CASSANDRA architecture, as will be seen, it would not be possible for a KS instantiation to hold more than one port at any one time. Consequently, if a KS instantiation is refused, it simply cannot be deadlocked by this condition.

The final condition requires that there be circular dependencies between processes. In the normal case, the denial of this condition can be achieved by insisting that the resources be allocated in some order. That is, if a process has been allocated resources of type t, then it may only request resources which follow t in the ordering. This move ensures that circular wait conditions never arise. The problem with this approach is that it imposes an ordering on resources, so processes have to wait to be allocated resources which might be commonly requested (the way out of this is to place commonly requested resources, memory, for example, early in the ordering).

The fourth condition is, though, wholly irrelevant to the CASSANDRA architecture. A primary constraint on Knowledge Sources is that they may only communicate by adding or modifying entries in the entry database local to the Level Manager in which they reside. This entails that there is never any direct communication between KSs. Because there is no direct communication, it is not possible for one KS to depend upon the use of a port by another KS: thus, there can be no circular dependencies generated by KSs within a Level Manager. There may be circular dependencies between entire Level Managers within a system, but this is concerns the configuration of individual systems, a matter not covered by the definition of the architecture.

As will be seen below, the CASSANDRA architecture denies two of the necessary and sufficient conditions for deadlock.

Within the definition of the CASSANDRA architecture, it is not possible to entertain deadlock detection and recovery and deadlock avoidance strategies. These strategies depend upon the nature of the system in which they are applied. In any case, deadlock detection techniques depend upon the detection of circular wait states between processes: if one assumes a CASSANDRA system which is implemented as a physically distributed system, there would have to be at least one node which was responsible for performing the detection process, and because of saturation or bandwidth constraints in the communications medium, such a node may, in fact, never, detect circularities in the worst case. In any case, the architecture is neutral as to whether a particular system is implemented as a distributed, concurrent (and centralised) or a serial system. Furthermore, the communications patterns between Level Managers in any particular system cannot be anticipated at the architectural level, and this would appear to be a pre-requisite of the specification of techniques such as these. It seems better,therefore, to allow any detection, recovery or avoidance strategies which the builder of any particular system sees as appropriate to the problem under attack.

Livelock has similar effects to deadlock, but works in a slightly different way. Imagine two processes, P and Q. The processes are connected by a single communication channel. In the CASSANDRA channel notation, one might write

$$P.out \rightarrow Q.in$$

(the input to P and the output from Q are of no interest, here). There is no risk of deadlock. If neither process stops to engage in communication with any other process, then the process represented by P.out → Q.in does not stop, either. The risk, here, is that P and Q will spend all their time communicating with each other so that the processes will never communicate with any other process or processes and will, therefore, never make progress towards a solution. This situation is called *livelock*.

Although I will concentrate on deadlock in this section, the reader should be aware that livelock is also a possibility in CASSANDRA systems. The reason for concentrating on deadlock is that I suspect that it will be more familiar than livelock.

Deadlock can appear in a variety of ways in CASSANDRA systems. One particularly dramatic context is the case of link traversal or link chasing. This case shows the problems in a concrete and graphic way. Link traversing or chasing is an operation performed by a KS (typically a KS action) when it attempts to gather information not stored directly in an entry. Link traversal is required, for example, when it is necessary to find an entry with particular information which is related to a KS's triggering entry.

The HEARSAY-II Knowledge Sources, MOW (introduced in the last chapter, section 3.2.2) and RPOL can be used as examples. Hypotheses on the HEARSAY-II blackboard are related by a variety of links (cf. fig. 2.3). Links from a given entry allow a KS triggered on it access to the entries pointed to by the links. MOW triggers when there are new syllable hypotheses: it hypothesises words from the syllables and rates their credibilities. When a word is hypothesised, it is represented as an entry on the Lexical (or Word) level of the blackboard. The syllable entries contain *supports* links which point to the newly generated word hypothesis. The word hypothesis will contain a *supported-by* link which points to all of the syllables which together suggest that the newly hypothesised word is plausible (*supported-by* is an inverse of *supports*). Each syllable has a start and end time in the speech signal and a credibility (which represents the confidence the system has in the hypothesis). MOW's task is to create word hypotheses, to adjust each word's start and end time and to assign it a credibility. When MOW's action executes, it is dealing with a set of syllable hypotheses and only a subset of these will suggest any particular word hypothesis. When MOW creates a new word hypothesis, it examines the information in the syllable hypotheses to assign values to word hypothesis attributes: this involves examining the syllable hypothesis data to derive values. MOW, of course, does all of this locally: that is, it need not actually engage in link traversal. However, once MOW has done its job, RPOL, another KS, is executed to evaluate the quality of the emerging solution (RPOL is the rating KS used during the opportunistic phase of HEARSAY-II's control strategy). When there are hypotheses on the higher levels of the blackboard with higher levels of confidence than average, all the links which point to those hypotheses are given boosts in their credibilities. In order to do this, RPOL has to follow links from high level lower level hypotheses, increasing credibility ratings as it goes. RPOL actually traverses links, whereas MOW holds link information in KS-local variables.

If HEARSAY-II were implemented as a CASSANDRA system, matters would be different. In a CASSANDRA implementation, RPOL would still engage in link traversal, but *so would MOW.*** To see this, consider the natural structure of HEARSAY-II viewed as a CASSANDRA system: each abstraction level is represented as a Level Manager. MOW triggers on the Syllable level and produces new hypotheses on the Word level of the HEARSAY-II blackboard. In a CASSANDRA implementation, MOW would most naturally be a KS local to the Syllable Level Manager, but would post entries to the Word Level Manager. When new syllable hypotheses appear, MOW would trigger as usual.

Now, let us assume the worst case and assume that the medium used to communicate between Level Managers is such that it makes better sense for MOW to generate word hypotheses and then post them to the Word Level Manager and that the Word Level Manager contains a KS, say, MOW1, which does the rating and adjusting operations. This assumption might be warranted if, for example, the medium were unreliable and the system had to maximise its throughput for some reason.*

In the Word Level Manager, MOW1 responds to the appearance of new word hypotheses. They appear as a result of MOW's sending them to the Word Level Manager. MOW1 has to adjust the start and end times of each word in the speech signal and to rate the credibility of each word hypothesis. The information it needs to perform this task is not held locally, but remotely in the Syllable Level Manager. MOW1 has to send a request to the Syllable Level Manager for the start and end times of all the syllables which comprise the new word and for the credibility rating of each syllable hypothesis needed to support the new word. If the Syllable Level Manager responds with the requested information, all well and good: MOW1 is able to update the new word hypothesis. MOW1 might have to wait some considerable time for the information to become available, but the information will become available.

If the Syllable Level Manager, for some reason, is unable to respond to the request, MOW1 cannot update the word hypothesis and, presumably, no further action can be taken by the Word Level Manager.

** This is the point of describing MOW's actions in detail.

* Assuming the worst case appears, anyhow, to be the best strategy for arguments like this.

The latter might be the case because all Word Level Manager KSs require credibilities and start and stop times to be assigned (rather unlikely, but possible). The result of the failure to respond by the Syllable Level Manager is that the Word Level Manager becomes, effectively, deadlocked: it cannot make progress for it does not have access to the information it needs to progress. (It is, actually, more reasonable for the Word Level Manager to make some default assumption just so that progress can be made: this is an application-specific, not an architectural, decision.)

A further problem occurs if the action of MOW1 is allowed to make the information request to the Syllable Level Manager. If it is assumed that Level Managers schedule KSs in a serial fashion (i.e., that only one KS is ever executed at any given time), the fact that MOW1's action waits indefinitely for information from the Syllable Level Manager entails that the Word Level Manager cannot execute another KS while MOW1 is waiting for a response. Internally, the Word Level Manager would enter a wait state from which, in the worst case, it would never exit.

The hypothetical (and rather extreme) example of MOW and MOW1 shows that inter-communicating Level Managers can deadlock internally or externally. In the first case, MOW1 waits for a response: a response never comes, so MOW1 waits for ever. In the third case, since the Level Manager can only execute one KS at a time, it is unable to execute any other KSs and grinds to a halt. In the second case, the information needed by the KSs in a Level Manager never arrives. The KSs have nothing to work on and can produce no new solution elements. There may be some internal activity (for example, some KSs might perform actions which improve the internal solution state but which do not result in the transmission of new information to other Level Managers), but there is no external activity, so to the external observer, the Level Manager has stopped. The second case is, I think, always a risk in systems with architectures like the CASSANDRA architecture. The first, I will argue, can be resolved by the imposition of constraints on communication.

There are two basic sets of constraints imposed on communication in the CASSANDRA architecture: those on Knowledge Sources and those on Level Managers. I will describe each in turn.

4.4.2. Constraints on Knowledge Sources

KSs have a tri-partite structure composed of a trigger, a precondition and an action. Triggers respond to database events (the addition of a new entry to or the modification of information of an entry in a Level Manager's local database): they can be regarded, in general, as event-based predicates.* Preconditions examine the state of a Level Manager's local database. Preconditions are state-based predicates. Actions are executed to make changes to the local database. Because KSs may engage in communication acts, this definition needs to be slightly extended to permit communication. In particular, the fact that deadlock can occur when engaging in communication while executing a KS action needs to be taken into account.

If the components of a KS are considered, the possible sites for communication within a KS become clear: in the precondition and in the action. Triggers can never engage in communication because they are interested only in local events. It is in preconditions and in actions that communication occurs.

Actions transform entries in one Level Manager into entries in the same or in another Level Manager. It is clear that actions should be able to send information to other Level Managers. The fact that the execution of actions making requests can lead to deadlock indicates most strongly that actions should not be permitted to make requests to Level Managers other than the one in which they reside. This restriction immediately rules out the case in which a KS action requests information from a Level Manager and then sends that information elsewhere.

If **request(LM1, info)** represents a request to Level Manager, **LM1**, for information described (in some way) by **info**, and **send(LM1, item)** represents the sending of an item of information, **item**, to the Level Manager **LM1**, the restriction forbids the construction of a KS with an action of the form:

request (LM1, info);
send (LM1, info).

In fact, it forbids actions of the more general form

request (LM1, info);
S;
send (LM1, info),

where S is an arbitrary sequence of sub-actions or of programming language statements. If either of these

* The architecture does not actually *require* that triggers be event-based. CASSANDRA-II, in fact, does not exploit event-based triggering.

forms were permitted in KS actions, the risk of deadlock would be immediately obvious (as it would be in the case in which a KS action makes a request to a Level Manager, LM1, and then sends information back to LM1).

The architecture requires that actions which perform communication acts may only execute *send* operations. That is, they may only send information to another Level Manager. When the constraints on Level Manager communications are described, the reader will see that send operations immediately return control to the sending Knowledge Source: this allows KSs to treat the send operation as if it had the semantics of a normal (local) procedure call.

If triggers and actions are not permitted to request information from outside a Level Manager, then conditions must be so permitted. This is, indeed, the case. Only KS conditions may request information from sources other than the database local to a Level Manager. Because of the possibility that a request may never elicit a response, thus causing the requesting KS to enter an infinitely long wait state, KS conditions must have rather special semantics. A KS action may not be executed until its condition is satisfied: this is stated in the definition of the blackboard architecture and represents a general statement of KS semantics.*

Usually, the truth value of a precondition (viewing it as a state-based predicate) can be determined just by examining the blackboard: in CASSANDRA systems, this is not possible because a KS may request information from another Level Manager and be forced to wait for information. If a precondition is waiting for information, it cannot be assigned a meaningful truth value. This is because the information actually supplied in the response is not known until it becomes available. It may be the case that the response is such that the precondition is not satisfied, in which case it can be assigned a truth value of *false*; if the response is such that the precondition is satisfied, it may be assigned the value *true*. Until the information is actually available to allow the evaluation of the precondition, no decisions can be made about the overall truth value. It would be possible to assign a value of *false* to the proposition that the precondition has

* It is, in any case, very similar to the semantics of production rules. Since CASSANDRA KSs are stimulus-response models of long term procedural memory, this definition of their semantics is reasonable. Fundamentally, they are stimulus-response because they are stimulated by changes to the local database and respond by making changes to it based on the information which stimulated them into action.

insufficient information available to permit evaluation, but this confuses the availability of information with the value to be assigned to the precondition predicate.

As a consequence, preconditions are evaluated in a *three-valued* logic. The precise formulation I have in mind is a *strict* three-valued logic with truth-values *true*, *false*, and *undefined*, with implication considered to be a derived operator. In this logic, any binary operator (**and** or **or**) which has one operand evaluating to *undefined* evaluates to undefined. That is, letting $\wedge$ be 3-valued conjunction and $\vee$ be 3-valued disjunction,

$$X \; cnj \; undefined = undefined,$$

and

$$X \; orr \; undefined = undefined,$$

where X denotes a value from the set *{true, false, undefined}*. The negation of *undefined* is *undefined*.

This interpretation of 3-valued logic is adequate to express KS preconditions as logical terms. In addition, it is necessary to add an evaluation rule for preconditions. The rule is as follows.

If a precondition issues a non-local request for information, it must be evaluated against the state of the local database. The precondition is then placed in a waiting state until all of its non-local requests have been satisfied. The precondition is then evaluated against the information derived remotely in order to determine its overall truth value. Note that local information must be derived: it is possible that a request is issued which mentions information currently held in the local database. Also, the evaluation of the precondition against local information may be necessary to determine whether or not it is worth making the non-local request: clearly, if the local state is such that the precondition is not going to be satisfied, there is no point in making the request at least for the present.* While in the waiting state, the truth value assigned to a precondition is *undefined*.

This rule specifies the behaviour which the precondition matcher must exhibit. The architecture does not specify any mechanisms to match preconditions. Some implementations might opt to evaluate precondition clauses sequentially, or to issue requests as soon as there is enough information to instantiate the

* Some implementations might opt to check the preconditions of all KSs which have triggered on each cycle until they are satisfied. In such a scheme, if the precondition is not satisfied on a cycle, there is the possibility that it may be satisfied by local data at some later time.

request (this considers requests to be, effectively, pattern expressions). A particular implementation might provide operators which assist the user in specifying the combination of local and remote information-gathering tasks in a manner similar to optimised and unoptimised **and** and **or** in Ada (**andthen** vs. **and**, and **orelse** vs. **or**). These are matters for the implementation of a CASSANDRA system: the architecture specifies only the semantics.

The restrictions imposed upon the communication behaviours of KSs in CASSANDRA systems are natural extensions of the semantics of KSs in general. The trigger and precondition are devices which gather information upon which the action is to operate. Requesting information from other Level Managers is a form of information-gathering. Actions alter the blackboard state in the blackboard architecture; actions alter the local or a non-local state in the CASSANDRA architecture. The restrictions on KSs can be enforced in implementations of the architecture: a simple syntactic check is all that is needed.

4.4.3. Constraints on Level Managers

Level Managers are responsible for managing all communications. Thus, when a Knowledge Source in Level Manager LM1 requests information from Level Manager LM2, the request will actually be made by LM1 on behalf of the KS. Similarly, if a KS in LM1 sends information to LM2, LM1 will perform the send operation.

There are a number of reasons for this. The most immediately obvious reason it that communications are performed via ports and ports belong to Level Managers, not to KSs. If there are many KSs all requesting non-local information, the Level Manager to which they belong will have the job of managing the requests: it has to schedule port operations so that communication does not interfere with its internal operations (assuming that Level Managers are considered to be serial processes). Port operations of any kind require computational activity from Level Managers. In the case of requests, a message must be sent to the destination and one must be received; the Level Manager must also route the response to the correct KS if it arrives. The manipulation of ports and the scheduling of port operations belongs, I consider, to the Level Manager rather than to the problem solving processes it contains.

The second reason for making port operations part of the Level Manager's responsibility is concerned with the risks inherent in parallel computation (deadlock and livelock). If access to ports were not regulated by Level Managers, KSs would have to perform state manipulations: that is, each KS would have to remember to wait for the response to a request and it would have to ensure that any messages it sends are sent on the correct port.

If KSs can directly inspect ports, it becomes possible for them to engage in explicit waits for information. An example of this is a KS which just listens directly to an input port in its precondition and performs an action whenever information of the right kind just *happens* to arrive. This KS could wait an indefinite amount of time for relevant information, but would require the evaluation of its precondition on every cycle. A KS such as the one just described could cause deadlock quite easily: it would wait for information which never comes, thus preventing the Level Manager's problem-solving processes from making progress. If Level Managers handle the communications machanisms as recommended, such problems do not arise. Also, the implementation of the special waiting states required by KS preconditions can be supported and, perhaps, more importantly, enforced.

The third reason for banning explicit KS access to ports and for making basic communication the responsibility of Level Managers is that communication becomes encapsulated: KSs do not need to know anything about the communication mechanisms, but can rely upon them as part of the basic services provided by each Level Manager. This also implies that the communication mechanisms can be verified once and for all (and not for every KS in every Level Manager), resulting in a system in which there is more confidence and which is more reliable. Some communication mechanisms might require buffering routines: these should be provided by Level Managers. Buffering is a low-level operation provided only to make communication possible or more efficient: it should not exist as far as KSs are concerned (they have no need to know, in other words).

As a result of making low-level communications and all port operations invisible to KSs, the view KSs have of communication acts can be more abstract. In particular, the encapsulation of send operations allows KS actions to perform a send operation as if it were some variety of procedure call. Control is returned to KS actions immediately after the send operation's internal activities have completed (say, after the send operation has put the message on an output queue). By making this ruling on communications,

KSs can send information and immediately continue with executing their actions.

4.5. MESSAGES

This section describes message contents and general mechanisms required by the architecture for processing them.

There are two distinct types of message provided for by the CASSANDRA architecture: problem solving and control messages. Problem solving messages contain information relevant to the solution of the problem currently under attack. Control messages contain information relevant to the control of problem solving process. Messages of either type may be sent to enquire if something in the recipient is the case: for example, "do you have any solutions to problem P yet?" Messages may also be sent to provide information or to give an instruction.

In the CASSANDRA-II airspace monitoring program, a problem solving message is sent from the Vertical Separation Upper to the Vertical Separation Lower Level Manager. The message contains references to two aircraft and contains the latest value for the vertical distance which separates them.* The Lower Level Manager creates an entry containing the vertical separation distance and the aircraft references and places it in its local database: Knowledge Sources local to the Vertical Separation Lower Level Manager are then able to trigger on the new entry.

In a CASSANDRA implementation of HEARSAY-II, the MOW Knowledge Source takes a set of syllable hypotheses, forms word hypotheses from them and then sends them to the Word Level Manager. (This is the type of communication behaviour I consider the 'sensible' way to implement MOW: it corresponds to the first description I gave in the last section. The second version was extreme: it was introduced only to make a point, not to suggest that I approve of that approach.) The message sent by MOW from the Syllable to the Word Level Manager contains one or more word hypotheses. When the Word Level Manager receives the message, it adds the word hypotheses to its local database.

Similar behaviour is expected when information with a grain size less than that of a whole entry is

* The aircraft are assumed by the Lower Level Manager to be separated by no more than five miles in the horizontal: this is a precondition for any kind of vertical separation conflict. This fact is knowledge common to both Level Managers -- common knowledge does not usually need to be sent in messages.

transmitted from one Level Manager to another. If, for example, a message is sent from one Level Manager to another, instructing the recipient to change the value of an attribute present in its entries (some variety of hypothesis credibility, for example), the receiver will, upon receipt of the message perform the alteration on behalf of the sender (examples of this kind of behaviour on receipt of messages is described when WordSys is presented in Chapter 7). The alteration constitutes a local event, so KS triggering will occur.

Control messages are required to ensure that Level Managers are making the kinds of decision considered correct or necessary by other Level Managers in a system: the relationships between Level Managers can be arbitrary and time-varying -- they may be peer-peer, master/slave and so on. Control messages can be divided into two fundamental sub-types: instructions and enquiries. An instruction message tells the recipient that it must or should do something. An enquiry asks the recipient if something is the case or asks it for a value. A global control strategy might issue a control request for the maximum value stored in the attribute A in KSARs held in the receiver's control database. This information could be used to determine a threshold value for a control message of the form "Prefer all your KSARs which have a value greater than the value V in their A attribute." When a Level Manager receives this message, it will institute a control strategy preferring high values in the A attribute of KSARs.*

Control messages representing requests can be handled directly by the receiving Level Manager (this is similar to the case in which entries are sent from one Level Manager to another). The Level Manager examines its state, forms a reply and sends a message back to the initiator of the control request. Control instructions, similarly, can be handled directly by the Level Manager. In the case of the opportunistic strategy mentioned in the last paragraph, the receiving Level Manager will install the attribute-preferring strategy as its current strategy.

The reponses to messages have so far been considered as Level Manager actions. It is, of course, possible that KSs respond to messages. The case of the KS which requests information from another Level Manager is a case in point. Although the receiving Level Manager may be able to respond directly to the

* This example is taken from a generic control KS in the Blackboard Control Model (Hayes-Roth, 1985b). The generic KS looks, for example, at the triggering time attribute of KSARs and prefers more recently triggered KSs.

request, it is also the case that some amount of inference will be necessary to provide as complete an answer as possible. A similar situation holds in the case of control messages: KSs may be needed to provide a correct or adequate response. In the case of the opportunistic strategy, the decision is actually a focus decision: it focusses attention on KSARs with high values on the A attribute. In such cases, the CASSANDRA architecture is neutral as to how such knowledge-based communication should be handled -- it is considered to be highly application-specific. One possibility is to extend Level Manager structure by the addition of a communications database: this plays a role directly analogous to the control and local databases. A communications database would act as a working memory which stores entries containing information about communications with other Level Managers. Specialist KSs would act on this information and provide for interactions with control and problem solving. This possibility is attractive for it allows Level Managers to reason about the communication acts in which they are involved -- they might, for example, consider communication acts as varieties of speech acts (Austin, 1962; Searle, 1965; Searle, 1969) -- and to reason about the responses they can or should make. The introduction of a separate reasoning space in Level Managers is perfectly legal within the context of the architecture for it provides only a basic definition of what constitutes a CASSANDRA system. The suggestions that Level Managers *reason* about their communication acts and that communication acts can be viewed as speech acts requires more attention: it appears to be too large a topic to examine in the present context.

The transmission of attribute and entry information between Level Managers is complex and seems to present problems of description and identification. It is clear that such transmissions are necessary, but the details have not so far been worked out. For example, how does Level Manager LM1 send a message to Level Manager LM2 instructing it to change the value in the A attribute of some entries without knowledge of the structure of and relationships between entries in LM2's local database? Similarly, how can one Level Manager supply an entry *description* so that the recipient of a message is able to find the subset of its entries which are to be updated with the information from the sender? In part, of course, this is down to common knowledge: Level Managers, in the general case, must know something about the tasks performed by other Level Managers in the system and send messages on this basis. The problem is reminiscent of the other minds problem in philosophy, an area of hot debate. This is left as a major area of research in distributed problem solving systems.

In a problem solving architecture which is at least notionally distributed, such as CASSANDRA, inter-agent communication is performed by message-passing because there is no system-wide memory to represent the global state. Message-passing in such systems is used to convey problem solving information as well as control information. The precise semantics of message-passing may vary from implementation to implementation, but a specification of an architecture must provide some guidelines on how messages are to be interpreted. This section has done just that and has indicated some extensions which may be adopted by an implementation. In an architecture like CASSANDRA, control may be decentralised, so it has to be implemented by message-passing.

4.6. HIERARCHY AND COMMUNICATION

In this section, I will briefly compare the general organisation of CASSANDRA systems with that of blackboard systems. In particular, this will be concerned with the abstraction hierarchy which is at the centre of the blackboard architecture.

The blackboard database, in blackboard systems, is arranged as a linear hierarchy of abstraction levels. In the case in which the blackboard is divided into panels or planes, the database is arranged as a set of linear hierarchies with one hierarchy per plane/panel. If one wanted to be strict and logically correct about things, one would insist that the action of a Knowledge Source always acted on one of the abstraction levels immediately adjacent to the abstraction level upon which the KS triggers. Such strictness would ensure that data (entries) would be passed along the abstraction hierarchy in a strictly linear fashion, obeying the generator relation for the hierarchy as it progresses. Naturally enough, such strictness is not usually tolerable in practice: Knowledge Sources are permitted to post information to any abstraction level in the hierarchy which seems appropriate. The practical approach to constructing KSs does two things: firstly, it violates the abstraction relation with respect to the passage of information, and second it makes the operation of the system a little harder to understand. I will return to the second point below (in chapter seven). The first point is really only a minor sin for it makes the realisation of the blackboard architecture easier and it also makes for more efficient and less redundant passage of information.

The point, though, is that the blackboard architecture *enforces* a linear hierarchy upon problem-solving. Sometimes this imposition is unfortunate and causes the system designer to invent *ad hoc* abstractions just so that they fit the architecture.

The CASSANDRA architecture, on the other hand, does not enforce any hierarchies at all. The CASSANDRA-II airspace monitoring system (the subject of the next two chapters) contains a set of pairs of Level Managers and each pair bears no hierarchical relationship to any other pair. On the other hand, the WordSys word-hypothesising system (to be described in chapter seven) contains a strict linear hierarchy. In the airspace monitoring task, there is no need to construct an abstraction hierarchy: indeed, when the system was designed, a number of hierarchies was considered and each hierarchy was rejected as being unnatural. By using the CASSANDRA architecture, the fact that a linearly hierarchical organisation was unnatural was not an issue: the architecture allows free inter-connection of Level Managers. The WordSys task, by contrast (and, I suspect, in common with many other perceptually-oriented tasks) does admit of an analysis which requires a linear hierarchy. In the case of the system described in chapter seven, the hierarchy is strict in the sense outlined above: KSs only alter information on their triggering level (in their triggering Level Manager) or on a level immediately adjacent (in an immediately adjacent Level Manager modulo the hierarchy generator relation). WordSys is just as much of a CASSANDRA system as CASSANDRA-II.

The moral is that the CASSANDRA architecture permits Level Managers to be connected in linear hierarchies, in directed acyclic graphs or even as cyclic networks (in a physically distributed implementation of the architecture, cyclic networks can lead to deadlock, as has already been mentioned -- this is a case of *caveat emptor*). In other words, the Level Managers in CASSANDRA systems can be related via an arbitrary connection graph, with the connections being realised by inter-Level Manager channels. There is no loss of modularity in CASSANDRA systems, even with this property, and the relationships between Level Managers are more explicit than are the relationships between abstraction levels in the conventional blackboard architecture (a point to which I will return in chapter seven). Thus, the CASSANDRA architecture removes a potential source of problems with the blackboard architecture: the problems created by the linear hierarchy requirement.

4.7. THE CASSANDRA CONTROL MODEL

The most important aspect of the CASSANDRA architecture is its model of control. In this section, the model is described in detail. The model is an immediate consequence of turning conventional blackboard abstraction levels into independent Level Managers.

Level Managers have definite and pre-determined communications channels by which they transfer information between each other. The control model is based upon the needs of the Level Managers and upon the fact that Level Managers may contain internal symbolic processing tasks which may proceed independently of all other tasks in the system. Level Managers contain a purely local control component which is charged with scheduling Knowledge Source activations. All Knowledge Sources operate within the environment provided by the Level Manager in which they reside: Knowledge Sources may not directly engage in any activities outside of their containing Level Manager. Local control is concerned with scheduling these activities. I will frequently use the expression that a Knowledge Source 'belongs' to a Level Manager when it resides in that Level Manager.

In order for a collection of Level Managers to contribute effectively to the solution of a problem, it can often be necessary to provide a global control component. The global controller is concerned with guiding Knowledge Sources by suggesting or demanding that certain decisions be made. For example, a global controller might instruct a Level Manager to concentrate on KS instances which refer to some parameter. Since the global control component cannot directly intervene with Level Managers' internal state, it operates by sending messages. Control messages are sent either in response to state information transmitted by individual Level Managers or on some other basis.

Global control in completely distributed problem solving systems is a difficult and open problem, so the reader is warned not to expect any solutions.

4.7.1. Local Control

A major justification of the CASSANDRA architecture is that it enhances the modularity of the blackboard architecture. The CASSANDRA architecture requires the explicit declaration of inter-level communication paths in the form of port and channel definitions. It seems to be but a short logical step from the situation in which levels have their external communications stated explicitly to the position that levels should be totally independent entities with their own control component. The reasons for this step are concerned with modularity and with the fact that during processing there will be scheduling decisions which impact upon a level and not the system as a whole: precisely, the choice of the best KS instance to execute next on this blackboard level. This choice depends upon conditions prevailing on the level and upon global considerations (e.g., the current focus of attention). It is, furthermore, the case that in conventional blackboard systems, all scheduling decisions, at whatever level, and with whatever intent reduce to decisions about which Knowledge Source on which level to execute.

The criteria upon which scheduling decisions within a blackboard level are made may vary from one level to another, for it is reasonable to assume that different attributes are employed at different levels in the representation of entries. The attributes of the entries found at any particular level on the blackboard, together with the set of values to which they may legally be bound define the knowledge representation for that level and, consequently, serve to differentiate one level from another. One might almost consider each blackboard level as containing objects of a unique type (I shall return to this point below when discussing ways of assisting control), even though it will commonly be a sum type.

Since the attributes of the entries at a particular level of the blackboard are the defining properties of that level, it is logical to infer that the scheduling mechanisms must take them into account when deciding what next to do. This is not to suggest that all previous schedulers have had a detailed knowledge of the attributes on each and every level, but it is meant to suggest that some classes of attributes are more important than others and contribute to the meaning of the scheduling function (most particularly in the priority assignment mechanism). This is because the priority assignment mechanism and the scheduling function both have to know what the relative merits of a given attribute are when compared to some other attribute. Also, they have to make decisions on whether an attribute on one level of the blackboard is more or less important than the same attribute on another level. Thus, unless Knowledge Sources are able to set priorities, which sometimes they are able to do (Ariadne-1, (Craig, 1986), is a case in point) and Knowledge Sources have the most immediate contact with attributes, the scheduler must make decisions based on attribute-value pairs and therefore have a knowledge of them in some form. An example of this is a PRO-

TEAN control Knowledge Source which states that KSs triggered on protein components representing long anchorees should be preferred for execution (Hayes-Roth, 1986).*

This last point clearly indicates a problem with attributes in conventional blackboard systems. Are instances of attributes occurring on different levels of the blackboard the same or different? For example, in her paper on the Blackboard Control Model (Hayes-Roth, 1985b), Barbara Hayes-Roth refers to an attribute with the name *goal*. The goal attribute appears on many of the control blackboard's levels, but frequently with a different intuitive interpretation: sometimes it contains a statement of a goal, sometimes it contains an evaluation function and sometimes it contains a reference to a KSAR (Knowledge Source Activation Record). It is only in a very abstract sense that the goal attribute has a uniform interpretation across the system.

In CASSANDRA systems, this ambiguity does not arise because each attribute is considered to be part of the definition of a unique type localised within a particular Level Manager.

This point is emphasised in the CASSANDRA architecture which requires each Level Manager to have its own scheduler or controller. Because local controllers in CASSANDRA deal only with the entries found in the local database of the Level Manager being controlled, it is possible for a local scheduler to make finer-grained decisions on what should be done next than is the case in the more conventional centralised scheduler. That is to say, in CASSANDRA systems, although a global view of the solution process is not possible in any Level Manager, each Level Manager has a representation of its own, local state, and, because of this, each Level Manager can make control decisions based upon intimate knowledge of its own state and the possible actions it can take. It is this last aspect of control which is referred to above as being fine-grained.

In other words, the level of explicitness in a CASSANDRA system is potentially greater than in more conventional blackboard systems because it is possible to isolate information in fairly narrowly confined parts of the system.

* An anchoree is a piece of protein fragment which can be anchored (attached) to an anchor point in the molecule. An anchor is a segment of the protein (not always the backbone) which may have other structures attached.

The CASSANDRA architecture provides independent scheduling or control mechanisms for each Level Manager so that the scheduling or control function which is most suited to that Level Manager can be provided. Level Managers which require specialised control regimes simply have that regime encoded as their local control component. This permits specialised control to be employed at the place where it is needed (in the CASSANDRA-II system, there are three fundamentally different control regimes -- sequence, LIFO discipline and agenda-based -- and each is used where it is most appropriate). An argument concerning the types of entries on the blackboard and the scheduling requirements imposed by them is given below (section 3.5.2): this argument is finer-grained than the one just given and is backed up with evidence from the current implementation of the architecture.

Local control also allows special-purpose control structures to be separated from more global concerns. In the CASSANDRA-II system, the specialised control regimes are wholly independent of the global regime (as they are in WordSys -- see chapter 7). If one were to discover that a particular regime were inappropriate, it could be replaced without disturbing the rest of the system. The CASSANDRA approach also avoids the complexities resulting from a change of regime in the intelligent scheduler (such as the one used by HEARSAY-II). This is because the intelligent scheduler contains special-purpose control (what in CASSANDRA terms, is Level Manager-specific control) mixed with global control regimes. Any change to a special-purpose and localised control component can involve major alterations to the intelligent scheduler. An example of the mixture of global and local control in conventional blackboard systems is exemplified by the OPM control KS which requires the execution of KSs at successive levels of the domain blackboard (Hayes-Roth, 1985b, p. 273): this strategy begins by executing KSs at the highest level of the OPM planning blackboard and ends by executing them at the lowest level -- what the criteria are for selecting particular KS execution orders at each level are not specified by the KS (it is left to other control KSs to decide). In the CASSANDRA architecture, local and global control are decoupled to a great extent, thus enhancing the modularity of the control component of an implemented system.

In CASSANDRA systems, it is also considerably easier to add or remove Level Managers because the local control component resides entirely with each Level Manager. When a Level Manager is to be added or removed, only the global control component needs to be modified. This, it is suggested, is easier to modify because it does not contain detailed information on how each Level Manager is to be controlled.

There is a methodological corollary to this decision: the separation of global and local control into two interacting but logically separate components, each simpler than if there were only one control component.

Within a CASSANDRA system, the control regimes adopted are implemented by considering global and local needs independently. This suggests quite strongly that the control components in a system constructed using the CASSANDRA architecture can be built on a more-or-less independent basis* with global control decisions implemented separately as a form of glue. In other words, the methodology is to describe a global behaviour or set of behaviours and to refine that into behaviours for each Level Manager, then add the interactions between global and local control components so that the global policies are enforced.

Control decisions are made within a Level Manager. Control decisions are concerned with the scheduling of the most appropriate Knowledge Source which belongs to the Level Manager. The control decisions are made locally so that a Level Manager may contain a scheduler which is specifically tailored to the tasks to be performed in that Level Manager. Such level-specific control may pay more attention to the details of the representation employed for entries in the Level Manager and permits the local scheduler to respect purely local constraints such as processing time or available memory. In a more conventional blackboard system, the execution of Knowledge Source instances across levels is interleaved. In the present scheme, the activations of Knowledge Source instances within a Level Manager are *not* interrupted by the need to schedule activations elsewhere in the system.

In some cases, for example, the lowest level of the HEARSAY-II blackboard, the CASSANDRA approach can bring immediate benefits: as the signal train enters the system, the Level Manager can process elements as soon as they arrive, thus parameterising the signal as it arrives at the Level Manager. There is no delay in scheduling activations relating to other levels of the blackboard, so the Level Manager stands a better chance of keeping pace with the signal. The lower levels of the HEARSAY-II system

* 'More-or-less' is an important qualification: it is not possible to state *a priori* that all domains will permit the construction of global and local scheduling components in such an idealised and interaction-free manner. To do so would be analogous to the demand that stepwise refinement be followed to the letter.

operate a bottom-up regime in which parametric data is made available and causes triggering of the Segmental Analysis KS when hypotheses are added to the Parametric abstraction level of the blackboard. When segmental data is available, there is the opportunity for other KSs to be scheduled. However, there is the need to keep up with the acoustic signal if the system is to process it in real time. In a CASSANDRA version of HEARSAY-II, it appears to be easier to do this than in the original system.

4.7.2. Global Control

A CASSANDRA system can contain local and global control. Global control of some sort is required in order that the system of Level Managers converge upon a solution as a collection of problem solving entities. This property is often referred to as *coherence* (Davis, 1983). Coherence is the most difficult aspect of distributed problem solving systems: there is no generally agreed solution to the problem, and, indeed, none is suggested here. Coherence is a property of systems in which all problem solving components operate in a directed and 'harmonious' fashion: in any system in which there are many agents, there is the possibility that their actions are somehow mutually interfering and not mutually supportive. In order for a CASSANDRA system to solve problems, it must exhibit coherent behaviour. Coherence depends upon the amount of state information available and upon the nature of that information: is it centralised and complete, or distributed and partial? The CASSANDRA architecture is neutral with respect to this division. It is possible to build systems using the architecture which have one centralised working memory to hold state information, and it is possible to build a system using the architecture which has one global scheduler or controller. Equally, it is possible to build completely distributed systems with no centralised control or state memory and which rely wholly upon message-passing to communicate information of all kinds.

Even when there is a centralised, global controller, there are problems. One particular problem is that, if a great deal of control information is sent across the system, those messages will absorb much of the bandwidth available in the communications medium. If the components of a problem solving system are distributed, if only logically, the job of assembling global state information becomes considerably harder. One reason why such information-gathering becomes harder is that the information held by the global controller may be out of date by the time the global controller can act upon it: it is not possible for it to access the latest state information simply by pointing to a data structure in local memory.

It is usual to require each node in a distributed problem solving system to be capable of performing global control tasks. This is because of the risk to the solution of the removal of the control node. When the control node is removed from the system for whatever reason, the other nodes in the system are unable to achieve coherent behaviour, and can engage in unsupervised activity which may endanger the whole problem solving process (two nodes might become obsessed with some aspect of the solution and concentrate on discussing the issue, thereby entering a livelock; nodes might decide to focus on mutually disjoint parameters, causing divergence, and so on).

However global control is performed, the modularity constraints imposed by the CASSANDRA architecture imply some form of message-passing. Control messages are sent between Level Managers. This scheme may be implemented as a virtual system (i.e., one in which messages become pointers to shared memory) or as the transmission and reception of actual messages.

The details of global control are highly domain specific. Each task will impose its own constraints upon solutions to the global control problem. One of the example systems discussed below employs domain-specific global control mechanisms; both exploit the message-passing system provided by the CASSANDRA architecture.

4.7.3. Sensitivity

What of the issue of sensitivity? Sensitivity concerns the ability of a system to respond to changes in its environment. Do the constraints imposed on Knowledge Sources in CASSANDRA imply any reduction in sensitivity and responsiveness compared, say, to the blackboard architecture?

When entries are sent to a Level Manager, it is the Level Manager which is responsible for placing them in the local database. There may be some delay in performing the addition because the Level Manager may be engaged in some other activity (for example, scheduling KS activations). An entry may have been in the input queue for some time because the Level Manager was otherwise occupied. This suggests that some KSs may not have been instantiated as soon as would have been the case if they could respond to incoming messages at the time of arrival. The answer to this is in the affirmative if all KS instantiations selected for execution are actually executed at the same time (as is the default case in

HEARSAY-III): if there were KSs which could have triggered on the new entries, they could have been executed on the cycle after the message's arrival. In the case of the more normal execution method in which only one instance is executed per cycle, it is hard to give an answer one way or the other because the instance created by the newly arrived message may have had the highest priority on that cycle. However, it is more likely (in the abstract and given the assumption that most priorities will occur in a band somewhere in the middle of the range defined by the highest and lowest possible priorities) that some other instance would have been scheduled anyway. All that has been lost is a few cycles which have intervened between the arrival of the message and the scheduling decision: most instantiations remain in the control database for at least one cycle on average, so, again, nothing much has been lost.

In order to minimise delays, the Level Manager must inspect its input ports on every cycle. If there are entries to be added to the local database, they are added immediately so that matches can be performed as soon as possible after the arrival of the messages. The input ports are, most sensibly, inspected between matching and scheduling, and again after scheduling. Thus, there are two points in every cycle at which the ports are examined: this clearly reduces the average waiting time for each message. The point of inspecting the input ports between matching and scheduling is that it averages out the amount of time required to process incoming messages (the delay incurred by adding new entries to the local database is shared between the two inspections and not incurred by the inspection between execution and matching). Since the precise nature of the triggering process is not defined for CASSANDRA, it is possible that KS instances are created *every time* an entry is added to the local database: this would be the case in an event-based triggering system such as that employed by BB1 and NBB. If event-based triggering were employed, the time required to create the set of triggered KSs for any cycle would be evened out across three parts of the Level Manager cycle: the first port inspection, the second port inspection and the execution of the chosen instantiation's action.

The sensitivity arguments for events internal to each Level Manager are the same as for the conventional blackboard architecture. The problem amounts to the same thing as asking about the efficacy of the scheduling regime employed by the system. In the context of Level Managers in a CASSANDRA system, this reduces to the effectiveness of the chosen local control regime. Once entries have been received from sources outside the Level Manager, they become subject to local constraints and are identical to all internally generated entries. Thus, once an entry has been placed in the local database, it generates KS instantiations in the same way as internally generated entries.

The argument for more global sensitivity is not so clear-cut. In part, the sensitivity of any implemented system will depend upon the communications medium chosen to connect Level Managers. The choice of communications medium has effects upon the bandwidth available for communication and upon response times. Since the architecture does not specify any inter-Level Manager control protocols, this issue depends crucially upon the choice and design of inter-Level control protocol and upon the need to exchange control information.

4.8. COMPARISON WITH OTHER CONTROL MODELS

In this section, the CASSANDRA control model will be compared with other models. In particular, it will be compared with production systems (conflict resolution), demon systems (frame systems in particular) and procedural control mechanisms. The intelligent scheduler found in many conventional blackboard systems is not considered here: it has often been used for contrast above.

4.8.1. Production Systems

This sub-section is concerned with the relationship between the CASSANDRA control model and the control model employed in the neo-classical production rule architecture. The information on production systems* is derived from OPS5 (Forgy, 1977; Forgy, 1979; Forgy, 1980; Forgy, 1981; McDermott, 1978). The information on conflict resolution is derived from work by the OPS team. The sub-section is concerned entirely with the so-called *neo-classical* production rule interpreters as exemplified by OPS.

In production rule interpreters, control is performed by a Conflict Resolution (CR) module. The Conflict Resolution module implements one or more conflict resolution strategies. The module is applied to all productions which have been matched on a cycle of the interpreter. The conflict resolution module operates only on those productions which have just been matched, and does not record all productions

* The term 'production system' properly refers to a collection of production rules. It does not, in proper usage, refer to the interpreter.

which have matched and have been fired (executed) to date unless a loop-avoidance strategy is used. Even when refractoriness (loop-avoidance) is used as a strategy, the CR module only performs fairly superficial tests on the previous bindings for each rule. CR modules do not retain instantiations of rules which have been matched on previous cycles but which were not chosen for firing.

Conflict resolution strategies vary enormously, but many consider productions as black boxes. Some strategies are based upon the recency of the addition of working memory elements and prefer productions which refer to recent additions. Other strategies work on the basis of the specificity of the productions in the conflict set with the aim of firing the most specific.

The specificity-based conflict resolution strategies do not consider productions to be black boxes, for they examine the contents of each rule to build a generalisation tree. Specificity is determined by the number of clauses in the production's condition and by the ordering of clauses. A rule which has an antecedent longer than any other is considered to be potentially less general. However, in order fully to determine the specificity of a rule, it must be compared with other rules with the same initial segment in their situation-fluent. The rule with the longest initial segment in common with other rules is the most specific of that set. Although specificity strategies examine the contents of rules, they are not usually given access to detailed information about the attributes of condition elements. The condition elements are considered to be black boxes of smaller size than entire production rules.

Recency and refractoriness strategies (the latter try to avoid firing the same instantiation of a rule on adjacent or nearly adjacent cycles so that looping behaviour can be avoided as far as possible) only examine information such as the time of arrival in working memory of an element, or the time since an identical or nearly identical production instance was fired. Neither class of strategy has access to information on the importance of working memory elements, nor to their internal structure, and neither has access to any information pertaining to the rationale for the creation of a working memory element. Loop avoidance strategies, similarly, are not usually able to use any information about production rule reliability or importance.

These points on the general mechanisms employed by CR strategies indicate that they work on the basis of information only of a general, and fairly superficial nature. The information is purely syntactic in the case of specificity-based strategies. Other information used by CR strategies is derived from measures of time. In a blackboard system scheduler, very much more information is made available, some of it semantic. That is, a blackboard scheduler has information about the structure of the blackboard (as is displayed by the OPM control KS which installs a strategy specifying that successive abstraction levels should be the focus of attention, or by control KSs which prefer KSARs whose actions are executed at a specified abstraction level), the importance of attributes (as is exemplified by control KSs which states that KSARs with high values on an attribute, A, say, should be preferred for execution -- the attribute A can be a KSAR or entry attribute) or which are sensitive to the presence, or absence, of attributes (an example, here, being the control KS which prefers KSARs which have triggered on entries containing instances of an attribute A). This kind of information can be introduced into the production rule architecture, but it requires an additional layer of meta-rules to be implemented: this is basically Davis' proposal (Davis, 1980).

Conflict resolution is performed by one fixed module in the production interpreter. This module is comparatively hard to modify to specific cases (the OPS5 system tries to ease this problem by supplying two strategies MEA and LEX). Production system interpreters rely upon fixed strategies which are in force throughout an entire problem solving episode. The CR strategies employed by production interpreters are fixed and are unable to respond to changes in the environment. The latter suggests that CR strategies are, by and large, inflexible.

This argument is very similar to that given by Aikens (Aikens, 1983) in her description of the CENTAUR medical diagnosis system. Aikens argues that the structure of production rules is such that it leaves control information implicit in clause orderings. She argues that control information should be factored out and given explicit representation. By leaving control information in an implicit form, the control of inference becomes very much more opaque and depends, to an extent, upon incidental syntactic features. Implicit representation of control also makes the intepreter's job very much harder, especially when there are modifications to some part of the system's knowledge. The proposal which Aikens makes is that control information and knowledge should receive an explicit representation. Such explicit representation allows the system to consider control as another problem to solve and one which requires its own vocabulary (in CENTAUR, this is based on disease prototypes). The explicit representation of control information allows for a more flexible interpreter and for problem solving behaviours which can be altered by changing the amount and quality of control information. Interpreter flexibility is ensured by the fact that it is concerned only with the interpretation of a general control vocabulary and not with a control vocabulary embedded in problem solving knowledge.** In production systems, there is only one global control mechanism which is not able to respond to detailed changes in the environment: it must be augmented by rules to manipulate working memory in various ways if higher level strategies are to be employed. These additional rules complicate the structure of the production set in production memory and compete with other rules for CR. Additional control rules can perform operations such as signaling (placing special markers, called *signals*, in working memory with the intention that only one or two other rules will respond to the signals) which is *ad hoc* and renders the production system harder to understand and debug. The combination of a global and inflexible CR strategy and the need to construct special purpose productions entails that production systems are less modular and that it is more difficult to build an effective control structure in a modular fashion.

In summary, the arguments against the control mechanisms in production rule interpreters are:

- The control mechanism is coded into the rule interpreter. It is, therefore, difficult to modify (even though some options may be provided, as is the case in OPS5).
- The strategic knowledge encoded in the conflict resolution module is nowhere made explicit in the production system. This entails that other parts of the program cannot reason about control and strategic knowledge.

The CASSANDRA architecture improves on the production system control regime by permitting schedulers to have access to a variety of information. Scheduling in a CASSANDRA system is based on two levels of control: local and global.

The CASSANDRA control model makes control and debugging tasks easier because of its distinction between local and global control.

The CASSANDRA control model also allows control components to have access to historical and semantic information (examples of semantic information are attribute importance and attribute definitions)

** Similar remarks apply to Barbara Hayes-Roth's control model for the blackboard architecture (Hayes-Roth, 1985b).

as and when required. In production systems, it is possible to access attribute information and to process rules and working memory element structures only if meta-rules are present. The addition of meta-rules adds an architectural level to the production system and forces meta-rules to compete with object-level rules for interpreter cycles. In the CASSANDRA control model, meta-rules are not required, for control based on the CASSANDRA model can be performed in ways which do not suggest architectural proliferation (i.e., the addition of extra layers to the system) and in ways which do not require the control component to compete for KS interpreter cycles. It is, of course, possible in the CASSANDRA model to make control a problem domain in its own right in a fashion similar to the Blackboard Control Model (Hayes-Roth, 1985b). If that were done, the control component would compete for cycles. However, since control in CASSANDRA systems is at least notionally distributed, the effects of control operations need not be felt to any significant extent at the global level. The CASSANDRA control model has one other advantage over the neo-classical production rule model. Since control is distributed, it is possible to supply different control regimes to different Level Managers. This, in production rule terms, amounts to the provision of different interpreters in the system. In conventional production interpreters, this is simply not possible.

4.8.2. Demon systems

This sub-section is concerned with the relationship between the CASSANDRA control model and demon-based systems. The most common form of demon-based control is to be found in frame systems such as FRL-0 (Roberts, 1977) and KRL (Bobrow, 1977)

The first thing to note about demon systems is that control may be situated in one of two places. It may have its locus in the program which accesses the frame system as its database or it may be in the frame system itself. Frame systems usually act as databases to enclosing programs and the enclosing programs usually perform inferences not included in the frame database. Only the case of control within a frame system is considered here.

In frame systems, demons can be activated whenever a slot is accessed. In FRL-0, demons are activated whenever a value is needed but not supplied and whenever values are added to or removed from slots. A demon may cause other demons to be activated because it may perform operations associated with demon activation. For example, an **if-needed** demon (one which supplies a value when none is specified in the frame) may add a value to a slot of another frame. The second slot may have an **if-added** demon associated with it. Therefore, when the **if-needed** demon adds a value to the second slot, the associated **if-added** demon is activated. The **if-added** demon may perform operations which activate other demons, thus causing further demon activations throughout the system.

Demons are associated with slots. Some slots inherit information from frames higher in the sort hierarchy (the **IsA** or **AKO** hierarchy). When a demon is activated, demons in many other parts of the system can be activated: some demons will be concerned with performing operations as the result of inheritance, some will fill in values, some will delete values and some will perform arbitrary actions (e.g., sending a message to the user). When a demon is activated, it is not usually possible to determine with ease what other effects will be produced or where they will appear.

The way demons in frame collections are controlled is not particularly modular, even though they are distributed. The initiating demon (the one which caused all the other demon activations) has no direct influence over the actions of the other demons it has activated (and this activation may be indirect). In other words, although demons themselves are highly modular in the sense that they are typically constructed as fairly short segments of code which typically encode only one action or else encode a highly restricted set of actions, they are spread across the frame collection in such a way that any particular control thread may be very, if not impossibly, difficult to find. The modularity problem, in this sense, is that the effects of executing any particular demon may be felt in some part of the frame collection which was thought to be unconnected to the place where the demon resides.

This situation contrasts strongly with the CASSANDRA control model. Indeed, the comparison of the CASSANDRA model and frame systems is like comparing chalk and cheese. In the CASSANDRA model, control is distributed but the effects of a control decision are usually highly localised. When a local control decision impacts upon other Level Managers in the system, the control information is passed along specified channels which ensure that the control information (and, perhaps, some of the results of that decision) is passed on a need-to-know basis only to those Level Managers which actually need to be aware of it. In frame systems, control is so decentralised that many frames in widely separated parts of the system may be affected by the activation of a single demon.

A form of frame problem* occurs when demons are activated in frame systems: it is hard to know what has *not* been altered. In the CASSANDRA model, there is considerably greater locality. Because all communications are routed through defined channels, only a small portion of the system need be altered by any control decision. When global control decisions are made, it is known *a priori* that many, if not all, Level Managers will be interested in that decision.

4.8.3. Procedural Models

In this section, the CASSANDRA control model is compared with procedural control models. In particular, the CASSANDRA model is compared with local and remote procedure call mechanisms.

The discussion will begin with an examination of the semantics of local procedure calls. In the interests of brevity, local procedure call will be termed 'procedure call'.

Procedure call mechanisms depend upon a central store or state and upon the immediate passing of control from the point of invocation to the body of the procedure. When a procedure is called, the state current at the calling point is saved and a state composed of the original state at the time of call extended by the state defined by the procedure body is substituted.** When the procedure returns, the original state is restored, even though it may have been modified during the execution of the body of the procedure (global variables or other variables in scope during the execution of the procedure body may have been assigned new values or an end of file condition may have occurred, for example).

The CASSANDRA control model is based upon message passing and the separation of local and global control. When a message is sent from one Level Manager to another, it is not guaranteed that the message will be attended to immediately. If the message is intended to be of use to one or more Knowledge Sources in the destination Level Manager, it is not the case that the message is visible to them as soon as it arrives: the reasons for this have been given above. The first condition on procedure call is not met, therefore. The second condition, that the state of the caller be saved before the called procedure is executed, is not met either. When a message is sent from one Level Manager to another, the sending Level Manager

* This should not be confused with frames, the structuring principle. The *frame problem* is the problem of determining which parts of the world are not affected by a given action (cf. (McCarthy, 1969)).

** Note that this definition, which differs from the usual informal definition is, in fact, more accurate than the usual account. Readers wishing to check this point are advised to consult a work on denotational semantics, e.g., (Stoy, 1977).

does not suspend its actions and enter a waiting state: instead, it continues its operations as usual. The reason for this is that a Level Manager will contain other tasks which will need to be attended to and they comprise part of the local state of each Level Manager. It is conceivable that a Level Manager may send a message and then decide to halt all internal processing. However, the transit time for the message is finite (assuming that the message is delivered) and message-passing cannot be considered to be an instantaneous event. These arguments show that the CASSANDRA control model is not reducible to local procedure call.

The alternative form of procedure call is remote procedure call (RPC). There are different accounts of this mechanism and each depends upon the model employed.

One version is the simple send model remote procedure call. In this model, a message is sent from one procedure to another. The sender continues its actions while the receiver accepts the message and processes it. In this first model, there is no requirement that the receiver return a value to the sender. In a variation on this model, the sender transmits the message and then suspends until the receiving procedure has completed (this, of course, is a variation of the coroutine concept). Although the two procedures may be in different machines or in different address spaces, the sender is required to wait for the completion of the receiver.

The second model is the send-wait model. In this model, the sender transmits a message to the receiver and then suspends. The receiver processes the message and returns a value. This model is similar to a function call for it requires a result to be returned. The third model is similar to the **rendezvous** mechanism found in the ADA programming language. In this model, both sender and receiver must be in a state in which communication is possible. The sender reaches the point at which the message must be transmitted and then suspends. Similarly, the receiver continues processing until it requires the information from the sender: when it does so, it also suspends. When both processes are in the wait state, the communication goes ahead and both processes are resumed. When they are resumed, both processes continue in unsynchronised processing.

The send model in its first version is closest to the CASSANDRA model of control. When Level Managers communicate, they simply send messages and continue processing. If a two-way communication is required, it is performed using this basic, asynchronous, model. Level Managers may request information from other Level Managers, but they do not suspend and wait for the reply. Instead, they continue internal processing until the reply is received. In a saturated system (one in which there are many entries in each local database), there will be Knowledge Source scheduling and execution activities to perform. If Level Managers were permitted to suspend while waiting for messages from other Level Managers, this processing could not be done. There would also be a risk of deadlock, for, if all internal activities were suspended, Level Managers requiring the results of internal activities in other Level Managers would have to wait for those results. This could starve other parts of the system of needed information, possibly causing deadlock. The CASSANDRA control model does run the risk of problems when one party to a communication is removed from the system for some reason. If this happens, it is possible for essential information to fail to be available. The model, as currently viewed, though, has the advantage that if a Level Manager is removed, it is unlikely to cause deadlocks for some time because of the availability of information within Level Managers. This does, however, assume that some critical Level Manager is not removed and that the system is saturated. As with any distributed system, the risk cannot be totally avoided.

RPC is a mechanism which implements the lowest level of a control policy. The same is true of the CASSANDRA model. Inter-Level Manager communication is only a device which transfers information across the system. Message passing is used in the control model and dictates some aspects of that model. It does not, on its own, constitute the entire control model. The CASSANDRA model translates into a system of independent communicating sequential processes which are controlled internally and externally.

4.8.4. Summary

When comparing the CASSANDRA control model with other models, the first thing to be said is that it has two components, one decentralised, the other global (and possibly decentralised). Most other control models have just one component, which is, by definition, centralised. Demon systems are a partial exception to this, for they rely mostly on the control model of the language in which they are implemented (usually LISP): that is, demons are usually structured as sets of procedures which call each other either directly or indirectly (indirectly via mechanisms such as the **if-needed** and **if-added** demons in FRL-0) via the procedure call mechanisms supplied by the implementation langauge.

The second thing to note about the CASSANDRA control model is that it is *knowledge-based:* it deals with strategies dependent on knowledge of the solution space for particular problem instances. This is the opposite of general, weak methods such as Means-End Analysis, depth-first and A* search. The CASSANDRA control model also contrasts with the control strategies employed by many production systems. Control in production systems is based upon fairly superficial properties of production rules (the length of the situation-fluent, or the time, in terms of the number of interpreter cycles, that an element has been in working memory) and not upon the contents of productions or of working memory elements or the relationships between these contents (for example, the kind of information typically found in semantic networks). In terms of its knowledge content, it is very much closer to Hayes-Roth's Blackboard Control Model than to the other models discussed in this section.

When comparing the CASSANDRA control model with procedural control models, it does appear to be the case, I think, that it has closer links to the control models of operating systems than to individual programs: even here, there are differences. The scheduler in an operating system like VMS, VM/370 or UNIX* is not usually able to tell the processes it operates upon what they should be doing. The CASSANDRA model allows the global controller to tell Level Managers to concentrate on KS instances with certain attributes or to avoid communication with some other Level Managers; local schedulers can make similar decisions for themselves, based on purely local information. Operating system schedulers and dispatchers are usually left to decide on the order in which processes should be executed on the basis of parameters such as memory requirements, previous I/O requests, page faults and so on. The point, here, is that the CASSANDRA control model is based upon very much more knowledgeable control mechanisms and they are knowledgeable because they have access to higher level information than most, if not all, operating system schedulers.

From these comments, and the more detailed arguments of this section, it seems clear that the CASSANDRA control model is not simply reducible to one other model and that it has advantages over many other control models employed in current AI architectures.

* VMS is a registered trademark of Digital Equipment Corporation; UNIX is a registered trademark of AT&T.

4.9. DELETIONS

In this section, the deletion of entries from the local database in CASSANDRA systems is discussed. The model of entry deletion presented below is one which requires the explicit representation of information upon which decisions to delete entries can be made. It is general to both blackboard and CASSANDRA systems. This, in turn, makes it possible to reason about when to delete blackboard entries. Such explicit reasoning is performed by the deletion Knowledge Sources.

The deletion of entries from the blackboard is essential in real-time domains and in domains where there are many entries generated, only some of which will remain useful to the problem solving process. In continuous, real-time systems, the number of entries can grow indefinitely if no deletions are performed, and, at some stage, the store of the machine on which the system is running will become exhausted. For these reasons, it is important to remove entries from the blackboard when they are no longer required or when they represent information which is too old, or when there are logical reasons for removing them.

In the literature, there has been no discussion of entry deletion in a blackboard system to my knowledge. Penny Nii has informed me that the sonar analysis system HASP/SIAP did not perform deletions at all. Instead, it made a summary of the situation board and relied upon InterLISP to perform regular storage maintenance.

In CASSANDRA-II and WordSys, there are special Knowledge Sources which delete entries from the local databases. Deletions are performed by special-purpose Knowledge Sources for the following reasons. If deletions were performed by ordinary Knowledge Sources, the rules governing deletion would redundantly appear in many places. It would, though, be quite possible to replace the deletion Knowledge Sources by a centralised deletion procedure. The centralised approach is, though, forbidden in the CASSANDRA architecture. Next, entries may be deleted only under certain circumstances. In the airspace monitoring domain, entries may be deleted when they have passed their expiry time or when they have been matched by all relevant Knowledge Sources (this point will be explained in detail in chapter 6 below).

An arbitrary Knowledge Source cannot simply delete an entry when it has finished with it because there may be other Knowledge Source instantiations in the control database waiting to operate on the entry. If KSs simply deleted entries when they had finished with them, the pending tasks would never be run (they would be removed from the control database when the entry upon which they depend is removed from the blackboard). The individual problem solving KSs cannot decide to perform a deletion because they have access only to local knowledge about the usefulness of any entry.

Deletion Knowledge Sources were introduced to avoid this problem. They were also introduced because it was considered that knowledge about when to delete an entry from the blackboard is of a different type to knowledge used to solve problems. Deletion Knowledge Sources contain knowledge *about* entries and not knowledge *of* entries and not of what to do with the information held in entries.

Deletion Knowledge Sources in CASSANDRA-II contain information about links between entries; they access information about the length of time each entry has been in its database, and they access information about the number of successful matches for each entry. This information is, in a sense, meta-knowledge. Since deletion Knowledge Sources contain structural information which may be considered to be at a higher level than the information contained within problem solving Knowledge Sources, it was considered that there should be a complete split between deletion and problem solving Knowledge Sources.

There was another justification for introducing the distinction: scheduling difficulties. It has been argued above that an arbitrary Knowledge Source cannot reasonably be charged with deleting entries because it does not have access to the right kind of information. If one were to permit problem solving Knowledge Sources to perform deletions, one would have to make sure that they were scheduled at the right times -- that is, once to solve the problem and possibly a second time to perform the deletion. This imposes impossible demands upon the scheduler, for it must keep a record of the most appropriate time to re-schedule a KS in order to make a deletion. In the light of the argument above, it seems to make no sense at all to require ordinary problem solving Knowledge Sources to make deletions. Therefore, the CASSANDRA-II system contains independent deletion Knowledge Sources which are instantiated and scheduled like ordinary Knowledge Sources.

Deletion Knowledge Sources have the advantage of making the entry deletion process explicit. If deletions were performed by normal (problem solving) KSs, it would not be possible to distinguish deletion from other activities. The addition of deletion KSs also permits a system (blackboard or CASSANDRA) to reason about one of its resources: the entries on the blackboard. Deletions, according to this model, are caused when some entry attributes reach certain values (in CASSANDRA-II, these are length of residency in local databases, number of matches and the number of supporting links). When these attributes reach the assigned threshold values, they cause deletion Knowledge Sources to become interested. Once a deletion Knowledge Source has become interested (by triggering), an instantiation of the Knowledge Source is created which then becomes a schedulable task. In this model, entry deletions are explicit events and can be detected as such by an external observer.

Because entries are usually linked together in a network structure on the blackboard, deletion Knowledge Sources must be able to deal with links. When a deletion KS executes on an entry, it must ensure that all other entries which point to the one being deleted have their links updated. If links are not updated, the blackboard will become inconsistent because there will be dangling references: any attempt to follow these links (for example, to determine the strength of the hypotheses in some region of the blackboard) will fail. However, links in most blackboard systems are one-way pointers. It is clearly necessary for each link to be associated with an inverse.*

A link points from one entry to another. In order for deletion KSs to operate successfully, it should be possible for any entry to determine those entries which point to it: this requires an inverse to be stored in each entry for each of the links pointing to it. Given the presence of inverses, the deletion KS can find all the entries which point to the entry to be deleted and remove all references to it which exist elsewhere on the blackboard. If this information is available to deletion KSs, it is possible for them to ensure that there are no dangling pointers left behind by a deletion operation. In some cases, for example, HEARSAY-II, entry deletion will cause the re-evaluation of the strength of the entries which point to an entry which is to be deleted: this re-evaluation of entry strengths is part of the domain-specific component of deletion KSs.

The explicit representation of links with their inverses is another aspect of making the blackboard more explicit. It has been argued above that scheduling should be based on explicit knowledge of the problem, the current solution state and of the problem solving system. In some applications, of course, it is also

* It is probably not the case that one can say 'with its inverse' because there are almost certainly cases of links which have more than one inverse. If a link were a representation of a function, one would be able to stipulate that it have at most one inverse. However, many of the relationships defined by links are best considered as 2-ary relations: thus, a link between two entries which represents the *support-from-below* relation can have more than one inverse, depending upon what 'above' is taken to mean in *supports-above* since the link can relate entries on more than two abstraction levels and the entries on different abstraction levels can be thought of as being of different types.

based on the links which a particular entry possesses. Deletion Knowledge Sources require link inverses to be given an explicit representation so that the graph on the blackboard can be correctly modified when a deletion takes place. Links can contain useful information about the solution and its derivation (as they do in AGE, for example). By giving explicit representations to links, the information encoded in a link can become part of the general problem solving process.

Now, given the facts that deletions are caused by entry attributes reaching set values and that deletions are tasks in the system, it becomes clear that it is possible to reason about the existence of blackboard entries (one might call this a theory of 'lifetimes'). This directly parallels the use of explicit representations of control information in the Blackboard Control Model. In the Control Model, Knowledge Sources are able to reason about the system's activities because a vocabulary is present for that purpose. Similarly, in a system equipped with deletion KSs, there are attributes which permit reasoning about the lifetimes of entries. The deletion Knowledge Sources in CASSANDRA-II and WordSys already perform this kind of reasoning to a limited extent.

The deletion Knowledge Sources in CASSANDRA-II and WordSys exploit a few entry properties. There may well be many more which could be employed if a more detailed representation of entry attributes and the relationships between them were available (one might envision, for example, a theory which had some model of the importance, centrality or worth of an entry containing some particular kind of information). This kind of information is not present in CASSANDRA-II or WordSys and its provision was not possible because the background information was not provided.

The benefits of the deletion Knowledge Source approach is simply that it makes a difficult task explicit and, moreover, it is a workable solution. The deletion model employed in CASSANDRA-II and WordSys appears, *a priori*, to be generalisable. In some domains, it may turn out to be hard to find any attributes which give a complete guarantee of success (the air defence example given below is one such domain); in others, there may be fairly obvious attributes upon which deletion decisions can be based.

In order to see the problems with removals, let us consider an example. The example is based on a real system and a real application.*

---

* The example is simplified: there are cases which I do not consider. The radar tracking task is immensely complex and complicated, too complicated to be presented in detail here. All I have done is to give a flavour of the problem.

Consider the UK air defence task. It is necessary to monitor the UK airspace for invaders. The airspace covers not only the UK and Eire, but extends in the north to northern Norway and in the west to the middle of the Atlantic Ocean. If invading, hostile aircraft are detected by radar, they have to be tracked and intercepted. The size of the airspace means that there will be many tracks detected within any period time. A system performing the track monitoring task has to base its decisions on the tracks it has observed. It uses track information to decide whether an aircraft is hostile, whether friendly; it also uses track information to attempt to predict the behaviour of hostile aircraft so that interceptors can be accurately vectored to eliminate them.

The obvious times for deletion are: when an aircraft leaves UK airspace, when a track is too old to be useful and when a track is no longer visible. The first case is a genuine criterion for deletion. The problem is that the airspace is large and so one would expect the majority of tracks never to leave it. A fourth case arises when it is known that an aircraft is not hostile: commercial flights are a case in point. Commercial and light aircraft also tend to fly in recognisable patterns and they almost all fly below the speed of sound and tend not to take the kinds of risks a hostile aircraft would take. In these last few cases, deletions can be made immediately and by the techniques which are described below. The case in which a track is too old is problematic, for just how old must a track be to be *too* old? This and track visibility are discussed in the next paragraph.

The problem comes when tracks are considered over time. Sometimes, tracks disappear for a few seconds. This can be because there is some obstruction between the aircraft and the detector. Aircraft can fly through the radar shadow of other aircraft, in which case the tracks merge. Clouds can also distort radar signals. Finally, there is the case of anomalous propagation: this is an atmospheric effect which distorts radar signals so that one can see over the radar horizon. When all these properties of tracks are considered, the deletion task becomes very difficult. When are two tracks the same? Where does one track end and a new one begin? If a track has been detected, then suddenly disappears, then to return with the same heading, are the tracks a record of one or of two aircraft?

This example shows the importance and the problems of deletion in a real domain. If all the tracks from UK airspace were held in store all the time, it would eventually fill, leaving no room for further processing. However, *arbitrary* decisions about those tracks which can safely be deleted cannot be made because valuable information would be lost: the decisions have to be reasoned.

Apart from showing some of the potential complications in what seems to be a simple task, this example also shows that a certain amount of domain-specific knowledge must be employed when deleting entries from the database. In operating systems, conventional database management systems and programming languages, it is possible to perform deletions or garbage collection on the basis of comparatively little information. When a process terminates, all of the store it held can be returned to the operating system for future use. In reference count store allocation systems, such as that employed in the InterLISP environment (Teitelman, 1975; Xerox, 1983), store can be freed when the reference counter associated with each storage cell reaches zero (indicating that there are no other cells dependent upon it).

In complex problem solving systems such as blackboard or CASSANDRA systems, deletions can only be made with reference to the utility or potential utility of the information considered as a candidate for removal. Deletion in problem solving systems is not the deletion or de-allocation of raw storage but the removal of a solution state component. If some items in a solution state were removed, one might find that they were needed at some later stage of the process. This suggests quite strongly that the deletion problem requires domain-specific information before it can be performed, and this information may be complex and varied.

In the air defence example, deletion KSs would be useful in some of the cases. The properties of commercial traffic and prior knowledge of commercial flights provides information which can be applied directly. Pilots intending to fly inside controlled airspace must notify air traffic control of their intention to depart: this is done by filing a flight plan. Flight plans can be filed at any time up to thirty minutes before departure. Commercial traffic uses the airways system, so any tracks following the airways could be deleted. Light aircraft tend to be very slow: they can probably be deleted. Aircraft leaving the UK sector can also be deleted. These deletions could be performed by deletion Knowledge Sources in a fairly obvious fashion: each one of these cases can be determined on the basis of entry attribute values. The result of their use would be a working memory in which only the more dubious tracks were left. Deletion Knowledge Sources could also remove some dubious tracks, a risk which must be taken when it is acknowledged that only partial information is available.

The CASSANDRA-II and WordSys deletion Knowledge Sources, when executed, perform deletion by removing the entry and its components from the object list or current package (depending on LISP version). When the next LISP garbage collection occurs, the entry and all its components are returned to free store. These deletion Knowledge Sources make use of the interface to the object list (via the **remob** function). The deletion Knowledge Sources indirectly make use of the standard garbage collection mechanisms provided by the underlying LISP system and do not perform any low-level storage management tasks on their own.

The rationale for the CASSANDRA-II and WordSys deletion Knowledge Sources is that they should remove as completely as possible any entries which are known to be no longer required by the problem solving process. Since the CASSANDRA-II and WordSys deletion KSs do not have (nor do they require) a model of the structure of the store provided by LISP, they do not perform operations on marker bits or reference counters. Deletion KSs are charged with the removal of entries from the local database in each Level Manager. They do not need to collect garbage from other places in the system -- they rely upon the underlying LISP system's mechanisms for storage management.

4.10. SUMMARY

A number of critical points have been made in this long chapter. In this section, I will attempt briefly to summarise them.

- Level Managers. CASSANDRA systems are composed of one or more Level Managers. A Level Manager contains a private, local database in which the partial results of *purely local* problem-solving activities are stored. Each Level Manager contains one or more Knowledge Sources which operate on the contents of the local database. The Knowledge Sources in a Level Manager can only operate on the local database and can respond only to changes in it: Knowledge Sources may not directly access information not held in their owning Level Manager.
- Level Managers each have a local controller. The local controller controls the execution of Knowledge Sources only in its Level Manager. The local controller can make decisions only on a

local basis: that is, a controller can only schedule Knowledge Sources in the Level Manager in which it resides. It can only make decisions with local impact. A local controller implements control strategies which are most appropriate for the Level Manager in which it resides. All local controllers are independent of each other and are tailored to meet the specific needs of their Level Manager. This means that a change to a local controller (say, the replacement of one strategy by another) does not entail an extensive change to any other component in a CASSANDRA system.

- Communications are effected between Level Managers by means of ports and channels. Channels are uni-directional data paths between Level Managers. At each end of a channel, there is a port. Ports are declared to be either input or output: a port may never be input-output. Channels carry messages between Level Managers. Messages can be used to convey data, results of problem-solving activities or control information. Before a channel can be used, it must be set up: this involves creating ports on the Level Managers to be connected by it. A channel can only connect two Level Managers and conveys messages from the output to the input port. If one Level Manager requires two-way communication with another, two channels and four ports are required in total.
- Explicit inter-Level Manager relationships. By requiring all inter-Level Manager communications to be performed via pre-defined channels, the connections between Level Managers in a CASSANDRA system are made explicit. A problem with the blackboard architecture is that a Knowledge Source can make changes to any abstraction level on the blackboard: this makes the relationships between abstraction levels hard to check. In CASSANDRA systems, inter-Level Manager communication is only possible between Level Managers which have explicitly been connected via at least one channel: if there are no channels connecting a pair of Level Managers, there can be no communication between them. The explicit channels between Level Managers also provide a form of protection: since there are no global effects possible, the actions of the Knowledge Sources in one Level Manager cannot directly cause problems in Level Managers other than those with which they communicate via channels.
- Level Managers may be connected via channels into an arbitrary graph structure, the nodes of which are the Level Managers and the arcs the communications channels. This contrasts strongly with the

blackboard architecture in which a linear hierarchy is imposed on the central database. The ability to arrange Level Managers in arbitrary graphs gives CASSANDRA systems more flexibility than blackboard systems, but causes problems in concurrent implementations -- this is because arbitrary graphs may contain cycles and cyclic relationships in concurrent systems can lead to deadlock in certain circumstances. The benefits of having an arbitrary graph are considered to be of higher value than the demerit of permitting deadlock: it is left to the system-builder to inspect for deadlock in the chosen topology. The topology for any CASSANDRA system is determined by the problem or problems it is to solve.

- There are constraints imposed by the architecture upon communications. Specifically, the constraints are that no Knowledge Source which communicates with a Level Manager other than the one in which it resides may make direct communication. Instead, all inter-Level Manager communications are performed by the Level Manager itself. If a Knowledge Source wishes to obtain information from another Level Manager, it may do so only in its precondition. A request for information is sent to the Level Manager in which that information is thought to reside by the Level Manager in which the enquiring Knowledge Source resides. Similarly, when sending information to another Level Manager, the Level Manager in which the sending Knowledge Source resides actually sends the message. Only Knowledge Source actions can send information. In other words, *all* inter-Level Manager communications is performed by each Level Manager on behalf of its Knowledge Sources. Knowledge Source preconditions, in the CASSANDRA architecture, are interpreted in a three-valued logic: when a Knowledge Source is waiting for information from another Level Manager, its precondition evaluates to *undefined*. These properties of communications are intended to reduce the risk of deadlock in CASSANDRA systems.
- The local control model employed by the CASSANDRA architecture is different from most, if not all other AI architectures. Control is specified, in CASSANDRA systems, on a local basis: that is, each Level Manager has its own local control component. Local controllers have access to a variety of information about the Knowledge Sources in their Level Manager and about the local solution state. Local controllers are used to control the individual nodes which comprise a CASSANDRA sys-

tem. When one Level Manager has to influence the control of another, it must do so by sending messages. There is no global control component specified for the architecture: that is considered to be a problem- or system-specific matter. Unlike demon systems, the effects of a control decision are highly localised.

- CASSANDRA systems are extensible in the sense that the addition of a new Level Manager requires only that extra communications channels need be defined to connect the new Level Manager to those previously in the system. Since control is performed locally within each Level Manager, the addition of a new one does not impact upon the control in all other Level Managers in the system.
- Although not strictly part of the architecture, an entry deletion model has been defined. The deletion model is knowledge-based and is designed to remove unwanted entries from local databases. The model uses information about entry properties to select database items, or entries, for removal. The deletion model can be applied both to blackboard and CASSANDRA systems.

5. CASSANDRA-II: AN OVERVIEW

5.1. INTRODUCTION

This chapter is concerned with introducing the reader to the CASSANDRA-II system. The system implements some of the more novel features of the CASSANDRA architecture, in particular local control and deletion Knowledge Sources. The message passing component in CASSANDRA-II is simplified and might be considered to be an examination of the best-case performance. CASSANDRA-II is the first and larger of the two systems constructed to examine the properties of the CASSANDRA architecture.

CASSANDRA-II has as its task the monitoring of aircraft movements in controlled airspace. The purpose of the system is to warn air traffic controllers of the conflicts which currently exist in the airspace which they are monitoring. The warnings come in the form of stylised messages which are printed on the terminal screen (an edited trace of a CASSANDRA-II run can be found in Appendix 3). The system derives its input from a simulated airspace within which aircraft move about the sky. If the system were to go into service, it would take its input from radar.*

This chapter is organised as follows. In the next section, the task domain will be presented. In section three, an overview of the CASSANDRA-II implementation of the CASSANDRA architecture will be presented.

5.2. THE DOMAIN

This section is a very highly condensed account of the air traffic control problem-domain selected for the CASSANDRA-II system. The air traffic control rules which appear in CASSANDRA-II are given in Appendix 2. The reader is referred to Appendix 2 for details of the separation and allocation rules. A more general account of air traffic control can be found in Appendix 1.

---

* Tests of the system using real input from radar would not be practical or possible at present. It would not be practical because it would entail physically interfacing the system to a radar system and constructing interface software (a lengthy, but comparatively straightforward process -- it uses, basically, the information sent to the cathode-ray display consoles): for operational reasons, it is unlikely that the Civil Aviation Authority would give permission to do this interfacing. In addition, it would not be possible to interface CASSANDRA-II to radar because the information required by the system cannot be derived from the current Mode C radar: a field test would have to wait until Mode S radar becomes available sometime during the 1990s.

CASSANDRA-II monitors the movements of aircraft in controlled airspace. Whenever two aircraft fly too close to each other, there is a *conflict*. The definition of 'too close' is given by the air traffic control regulations. One of the goals of air traffic control is to reduce the number of conflicts because they can pose safety problems. Conflicts come in a variety of types: they basically deal with the horizontal and vertical separation between aircraft. The minimum separation standards are given as a set of rules in the Manual of Air Traffic Services (MATS -- CAA, 1). CASSANDRA-II implements these rules as Knowledge Sources.

Horizontal conflicts can be of one of two types: lateral or longitudinal. Lateral separation conflicts, for controlled airspace, are determined by reference to navigational beacons. Navigational beacons are radio transmitters placed at various points on the ground. Aircraft typically fly by following a sequence of beacons.

Longitudinal separation can be based upon time or distance, and can be based on horizontal distances when aircraft are climbing or descending. Longitudinal separation rules also involve the *t.a.s.* (true air speed) of aircraft, with the basic stipulation being that if one aircraft is following another, the first aircraft must be maintaining a t.a.s. of 20 knots or more greater than the following aircraft and the distance between the aircraft must be five nautical miles or more. There is no conflict if these conditions are met.

In both lateral and longitudinal separation, there are special cases which need to be taken into account. These cases constitute the rationale for the Knowledge Sources implementing these rules.

Vertical separation is concerned with the vertical distance between two aircraft. There are rules which govern the minimum vertical distance between aircraft. The rules depend upon the altitudes at which aircraft are flying.

CASSANDRA-II also contains information about the altitude at which aircraft should fly. This information is in the form of cruise level allocation rules. These rules are based on measuring altitudes in terms of *flight levels*. A flight level, in this instance, is a band of air one thousand feet thick: aircraft must fly on those flight levels specified either by the rules or by instructions from ground control. There are rules for relating altitude to the heading on which an aircraft is flying. There are two basic rules: they are based upon either a division of the 360 degrees of the compass into two or into four. The division of the compass into two is normally employed in airways (the type of controlled airspace monitored by CASSANDRA-II): this is called the *semi-circular* rule.

There is a specific rule which forbids aircraft to fly at an altitude of 24,500 feet (Flight Level 245 or FL245; flight levels are notated in hundreds of feet). This rule is included in the CASSANDRA-II system.

The knowledge in the CASSANDRA-II system is encoded in Knowledge Sources. The system's Knowledge Sources detect violations of the separation rules and report them to the user. Because the various types of separation rule do not interact, a cruise level allocation conflict is independent of a lateral separation conflict. This suggests that each kind of knowledge can be independently represented in the system within an autonomous unit or Level Manager.

5.2.1. Reasons for Domain Selection

This section gives some of the reasons why the controlled airspace monitoring problem was chosen for the first implementation of the architecture. Specifically, this section deals with the reasons most directly connected with the CASSANDRA architecture and constitutes an elaboration of the remark that the airspace monitoring problem seemed an appropriate one on which to test some aspects of the architecture.

The first reason for selecting this domain was that knowledge was clearly parititioned into separate units, each of which could be represented by a Level Manager. Each type of separation (longitudinal, lateral and vertical) was found to be relatively indendent of the others (vertical separation checks are performed only on aircraft within five nautical miles of each other -- this horizontal distance check is performed as an integral part of the vertical separation operations), as was cruise level allocation. This suggested that they could be treated in an independent manner and represented by Level Managers.

A reason for selecting the airspace monitoring task was that different scheduling parameters appear in different kinds of conflict detection task. The separation problems provide distance information upon which to base schedulers but the cruise level allocation problem does not. Given the comments above about independence, this appeared to be a suitable test of the ideas about providing different scheduling mechanisms for each Level Manager. In other words, this aspect of the problem tested the viability of the purely local control requirement of the architecture.

The third reason for the selection of the airspace monitoring task was that the communications between the different kinds of knowledge in the system appeared to be very simple. Since this book is not concerned with an evaluation of communications mechanisms, the structure of the domain suggested that inter-Level Manager communications could be simplified. Communications between Level Managers in the CASSANDRA-II system is always uni-directional (there are no feedback loops): this represents the simplest possible form of inter-Level Manager communication allowed by the architecture. Since the focus of the CASSANDRA-II investigations is on testing the viability of local control in CASSANDRA systems, this simplification in communications appeared beneficial because it served to focus attention on testing the basic architecture.

The final reason for selecting the domain was that there were clear rules for triggering Deletion Knowledge Sources. The entries on the blackboard represent information about one or two aircraft, accurate to one sweep of the surveillance radar. After each sweep, the information is updated. This suggested one criterion for deletion. A second criterion is that the Knowledge Sources charged with performing separation checks can apply only once to each entry in the local database of each Level Manager. Once a particular KS has triggered on a given entry, it makes no sense for it to trigger there again. Entries are not modified by KSs external to the Level Managers in whose local database they reside, so once a KS has triggered on an entry it should never need to trigger on that entry again. Although not a central issue in the architecture definition, the problem of entry deletion appeared to be important and the knowledge-based approach seemed worthy of testing.

Thus, the chosen domain appeared to be ideal for testing the viability of the Level Manager construct, local control and deletion Knowledge Sources. It also had the advantage of being self-contained and relatively small: in other words, the domain offered the advantage of providing a doable project.

The domain differs in some respects from domains chosen for most of the blackboard systems described in the literature, even though it does possess all the real-time properties often associated with blackboard systems. The most obvious difference is that entries at one level of abstraction do not engage in much interaction with entries at another. Otherwise put, KSs do not depend upon and use partial results to generate a complete picture of the airspace they are monitoring (the WordSys system, the second system implemented using the CASSANDRA architecture *does* require more interaction and its KSs *do* depend upon partial results generated elsewhere). The CASSANDRA-II system does not rely particularly upon a strict abstraction hierarchy: instead, it employes a 'natural' representation of the domain in which abstraction hierarchies are secondary. If abstraction were exploited to a greater degree, more conventional cross-level interactions would be in evidence, although they would still be less in number than the blackboard folklore would lead one to expect.*

5.3. CASSANDRA-II

This section is concerned with the structure of the CASSANDRA-II system, the program constructed to test the major issues in the CASSANDRA architecture.

5.3.1. System Structure

The structure of the CASSANDRA-II system is shown in figure 5.1. The system contains Level Managers for each separation class (lateral, longitudinal and vertical), and Level Managers for cruise level allocation. It also contains a Level Manager for handling and filtering input data from the airspace simulation. The data flow through CASSANDRA-II is shown in figure 5.2.

Each separation class and the cruise level allocation process is represented by a pair of Level Managers: the upper and lower Level Managers. The upper Level Manger is concerned with removing references to aircraft or to pairs of aircraft (depending upon separation class) from consideration when it is known that they can never engage in a conflict. This operation is referred to elsewhere as 'pruning'. The upper Level Manager in each pair is also concerned with the passing of messages to the lower Level Manager. The messages contain entries which refer to one or two aircraft and, optionally, a beacon, again depending upon the separation class. The messages are received by the lower Level Manager which is responsible for performing the actual separation tests.

The upper Level Manager in each pair removes references to aircraft which cannot enter into a conflict. This reduces the amount of work which must be done by the lower Level Manager in each pair.

* The PROTEAN (Hayes-Roth, 1984b) system is another example of a blackboard application which lacks enormous amounts of cross-level interaction: it tends to operate a top-down strategy, with deviations when data-gathering is needed.

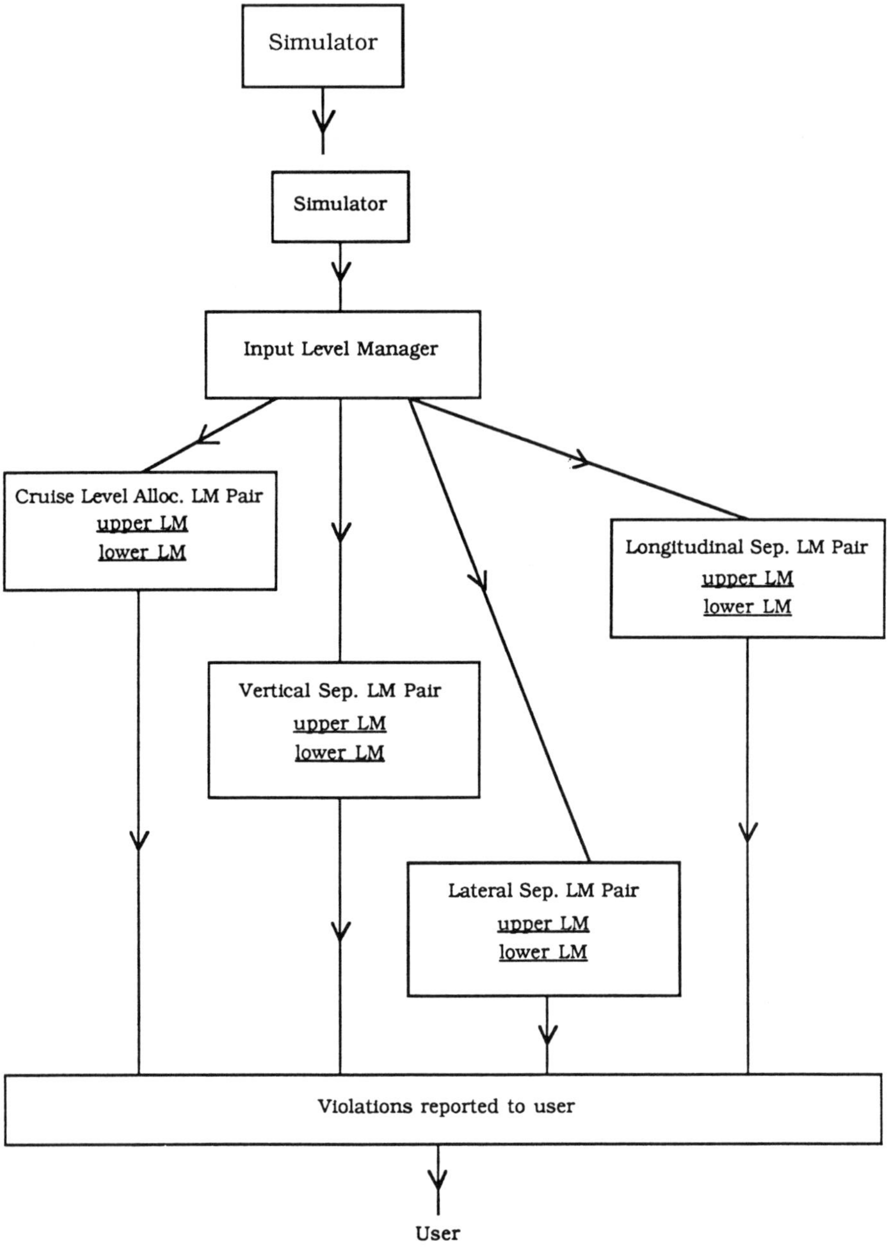

Fig 5.1

CASSANDRA-II global structure

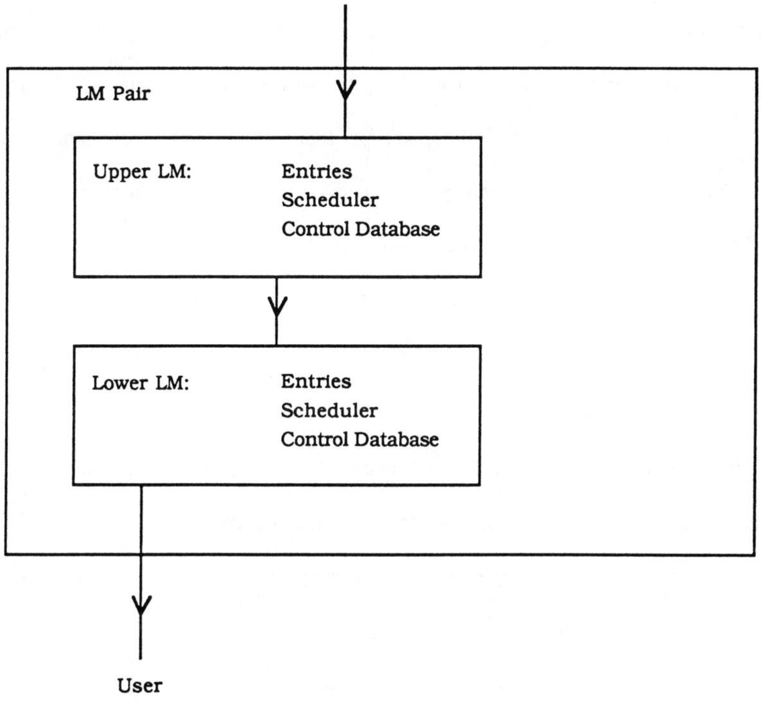

Fig 5.2

Information flow through a panel in CASSANDRA-II

When the aircraft references have been pruned, the upper Level Manager sends messages containing references to the remaining aircraft to the lower Level Manager via the message-passing system. The messages contain entries which refer to one or two aircraft, or to two aircraft and a beacon. In the case of the vertical and longitudinal separation Level Manager pairs, the entries contain references to pairs of aircraft. The upper Level Manager of the lateral separation pair sends messages containing an entry which refers to two aircraft and a beacon. The upper cruise level allocation Level Manager sends entries containing a reference only to one aircraft (cruise level allocation only concerns individual aircraft). The entries which are sent as messages are of the correct type for the lower Level Manager: that is, each lower Level Manager does not need to operate on the information contained in a message -- all it need do is add the entry to its local database. When an entry is received, it is placed in the database local to the receiving Level Manager.

The input Level Manager is concerned with interfacing to the input stream. The input stream consists of sequences of descriptors generated by the airspace simulator. The descriptors contain information about the altitude, heading, speed and position of each aircraft. The simulator sends a sequence of descriptors to the monitor on each cycle (a cycle is intended to represent one complete sweep of the radar antenna and represents a period of about six seconds).

The descriptors received by the input Level Manager contain references to many more aircraft than are in the sector or airspace region being observed by the monitor. The input Level Manager removes all references to aircraft which are outside the boundaries of the monitored sector, for they are of no interest to the system.

The next thing the input Level Manager has to do is to find all pairs of aircraft. The pairing algorithm finds *all* possible aircraft pairs so that none is omitted: in other words, every possible conflict can be detected because all pair-wise interactions between aircraft are taken into accout. The Level Manager performs this pair-finding operation because the separation rules are concerned with pairs (any combination of aircraft can be reduced to a set of combinations of pairs). Once the pairs have been created by the pairing Knowledge Source, the input Level Manager schedules a KS to see if any aircraft have crashed; if any have crashed, the user is informed immediately. The final tasks the input Level Manager has to perform are to send messages to the separation and cruise level allocation upper Level Managers. These messages contain references to sequences of aircraft: the upper Level Managers contain Knowledge Sources which operate on sequences of aircraft. Again, the messages contain entries of the correct type for the receiving Level Manager.

The Knowledge Sources in the input Level Manager are scheduled in a strict sequence. The rationale for this unusual scheduling regime is presented below (section 5.3.3).

Level Managers in CASSANDRA-II conform to the structure given above in the definition of the architecture. The implementation of the system was on a single-cpu machine and in a LISP dialect (FranzLISP) which possesses no facilities for concurrent programming. The implementation of CASSANDRA-II simplifies the architecture in only one respect: message-passing is performed by sets of functions which pass entries directly from one Level Manager to another. As far as the Level Managers are concerned, they communicate via a message-passing system.*

5.3.2. Local Control

Each Level Manager in CASSANDRA-II has its own local scheduler. The local scheduler makes control decisions which are wholly local to each individual Level Manager. Schedulers within each Level Manager are not able to make decisions based on direct inspection of the state of another Level Manager. The localisation of each scheduler to its containing Level Manager is enforced in the code which implements the system. Similarly, all Level Manager components are actually present in the data structures. The local schedulers in CASSANDRA-II employ different control regimes depending upon the nature of the task assigned to the Level Manager.

Local control decisions in CASSANDRA-II are limited by the matcher tagging mechanism. The KS matcher leaves tags on those entries each KS has successfully matched. A constraint in each CASSANDRA-II Level Manager states that entries can only be matched once by any particular Knowledge Source. This issue is described in greater detail in chapter 6.

There are three generic local scheduling regimes employed in the system: sequence (this has already

* When describing the second CASSANDRA system, WordSys, a more complex communications system will be discussed. The communications mechanism in WordSys is very much more interactive than the one in CASSANDRA-II: this is because WordSys Level Managers require two-way communications in many cases.

been seen informally in the input Level Manager), LIFO, and priority queue or agenda (this is the most common regime). Each Level Manager in the system has an instance of the appropriate generic scheduler.

(a) **Sequence** is used when there is a definite sequence of events. Sequences usually occur in the upper Level Managers and one also occurs in the input Level Manager. In upper Level Managers, there are usually two tasks to be performed: pruning references to remove any which cannot participate in conflicts, and sending messages to the corresponding lower Level Manager. Sequence scheduling is used to ensure that these operations occur in the correct order (so that, for instance, references to non-conflicting aircraft pairs can never reach the lower Level Manager). Sequences appear to be controversial and are justified below.

(b) **LIFO** is used when there are no criteria upon which to base a priority calculation. A case in point is the control of the cruise level allocation lower Level Manager. In this Level Manager, there is no information upon which a priority assignment could be made. If an aircraft is on the wrong flight level for its heading, there are two adjacent levels to which it could be moved: there is no scheduling criterion, therefore, which can be based on proximity to the correct flight level. Speed might be considered to be a basis for priority assignment until it is considered that an aircraft might be on the wrong flight level and flying supersonically, but in a region of the airspace in which there are no other aircraft. Since the order in which cruise level allocation checks is to be performed is immaterial, they are processed in last-in first-out fashion based on the order in which the relevant knowledge sources were triggered. It is the fact that the order is immaterial that determines that the LIFO regime be used: it would be perfectly possible to use a FIFO (First-In First-Out) regime instead, but LIFO was easier to implement in the first (and only) version of the CASSANDRA system.

(c) **Priority Queue** or **Agenda**. This regime is used whenever there is information which can partially order KS instantiations. In the case of the vertical, lateral and longitudinal separation lower Level Managers, the distance between aircraft (horizontal or vertical as appropriate) is used to generate the ordering. The orderings are always represented with the least distance coming first in the sequence and the greatest distance last. Clearly, if one is interested in determining the most important tasks, the shorter the distance the greater the importance or risk of conflict.

The local control regimes chosen for CASSANDRA-II reflect the requirements of the application domain. The sole exception to this is the use of sequences in the input Level Manager and the upper Level Managers. CASSANDRA-II's local control components reflect the properties of the tasks to be performed in each Level Manager and are intended to make the system work as quickly and as accurately as possible. There are some complications with the implementation of these regimes. In particular, there is an interaction with the deletion KSs: this interaction is discussed in chapter 6 below.

5.3.3. Knowledge Sources

CASSANDRA-II Knowledge Sources have a tri-partite structure consisting of precondition, condition and action. This structure was selected because it was found that not much of an advantage was to be derived from using event-based triggering (the system can be made to operate using it, but it fractionally reduces its runtime performance -- this is because event-based triggering systems retain event information for use by preconditions): for this reason, the term *precondition* is used and not trigger. Because KSs have a precondition, it was felt that what is normally referred to as the precondition would be better termed the *condition.*

The precondition of each Knowledge Source is concerned with checking that the blackboard entry against which the KS is being matched is of the correct type. In some CASSANDRA-II Level Managers, more than one entry type is present in the local database (the input Level Manager is a case in point: it contains entries of two types: **List** and **PairList**). It is essential, in such cases, that KSs are properly applied. Preconditions can also perform quick checks on the consistency of the information contained in an entry: they represent a computationally inexpensive test of the entry being matched.

Conditions represent the major test applied to any entry. Conditions can perform arbitrary computations. It is often the case (although it is not enforced) that the computational cost of conditions be greater than or equal to that of preconditions.

KS preconditions and conditions operate only on entries in the database local to the Level Manager in which they reside. Because of the way the system is structured and because of the lack of a need to gather information from outside a Level Manager, it is not possible in CASSANDRA-II for a KS precondition or condition to access information outside of the owning Level Manager.

Actions in CASSANDRA-II Knowledge Sources perform the functions normally associated with KS actions. In the case of the separation rule KSs, it is the action which tests for the negation of the condition specified in MATS (CAA, 1): the rules in the manual are concerned with maintaining minimum separation, and CASSANDRA-II is concerned with violations. Actions also interface to the message-passing system in the manner described above. Actions can send messages to other Level Managers by making a request to their owning Level Manager. Finally, actions can add, modify or delete entries in the local database.

CASSANDRA-II contains many Knowledge Sources, each of which is about the same size as a production rule.* In some cases (for example, in the input Level Manager), there are many small KSs where one would expect to find a considerably larger one. In these cases, the Knowledge Sources are explicitly scheduled in a sequence. It might seem that it would be very much easier to construct one large Knowledge Source in which the sequence was performed by serial composition in the implementation language (CASSANDRA-II is written in LISP) and with lower control overheads.

Indeed, this is the case. There is, however, a point to splitting the large KSs into smaller ones and having them scheduled as independent units. It is claimed that the CASSANDRA architecture can support different kinds of local scheduling regimes. Scheduling regimes can range from sequences at the low end to complex mixtures of opportunism and other strategies at the high end. The sequential scheduling employed in some parts of the system is designed to show that these different regimes may be implemented in the same system and that different regimes may exist in the same system with the benefits argued for them above. In order to test this hypothesis, some Knowledge Sources were broken up and turned into small KSs and given a sequential scheduling regime. That is to say, sequences were introduced to add extra cases to test the claim that independent, local scheduling is viable. Sequential scheduling tests the local control hypothesis by examining its applicability in boundary cases (sequential scheduling can be considered a boundary case): this seems to me to be good experimental method.

There are other advantages in having short Knowledge Sources which execute in sequences. One

* This comparison is only relative, it should be noted. In HEARSAY-II, Knowledge Sources were anything between a few tens and a few hundred of pages of SAIL. A typical production rule requires less than one page of A4 for its statement.

particularly good reason is that the KSs are easier to construct because they are all smaller than the KS which would have been constructed if they had been collected together. It also permits the triggering conditions of each sequenced KS to be evaluated on the blackboard: this contrasts with the usual KS action which employs a conditional statement or expression to perform internal decisions. The final reason is that the KSs which result from this breaking up of large Knowledge Sources are very much more modular than would otherwise have been the case: this implies that the actions performed by KSs in the sequence are available for other tasks, thereby avoiding, for example, repetitions of code sequences in KS actions. There is, in any case, a tendency to reduce KS size: this is very much in evidence in the BB1 implementation of the Blackboard Control Model (Hayes-Roth, 1985b) and in the PROTEAN system (e.g., Hayes-Roth, 1984a).

The reader should, in any case, note the fact that the BB1 implementation of the Blackboard Control Model (Hayes-Roth, 1985b; Hayes-Roth, 1984b) uses sequences. In the case of BB1, control KS sequences are generated by control decisions at various abstraction levels and sequences may be interrupted by the execution of tasks not in the sequence. However, given the existence of, say, a Focus decision, a sequence of KSs will be scheduled which execute sub-components of the Focus.

Even though sequences can be replaced by larger Knowledge Sources which contain the sequence in the body of the action, there may still be reasons for permitting sequence to appear as a distinct control regime, even though it is reminiscent of local procedure call. Sometimes, tasks have to be performed in a definite order. It can be argued that better modularity results from the fact that accepting that separate operators perform the steps in the sequence and checks might have to be made to ensure that each operator in the sequence is being properly applied. In the current system, however, sequence was introduced as an experimental technique to add more weight to the demonstration of the validity of local control.

Each Level Manager has a purely local Knowledge Source matcher and action interpreter. The matcher has been briefly mentioned above. The action interpreter executes the action of the Knowledge Source KS instance on the entry: the Knowledge Source and the entry are found in the task (in CASSANDRA-II, *task* is a technical term denoting a KSAR) or Knowledge Source instance being executed. The provision of purely local matching and action interpretation is dictated by the modularity arguments presented in chapter 4 (section 4.3); it also has the advantage that very different knowledge representations may be employed in different Level Managers. In CASSANDRA-II, however, the knowledge representation is relatively uniform across the system (it reduces to an attribute-value form which is almost universal in blackboard systems). The local matcher and action interpreter could, though, be structured to operate in different ways in different Level Managers.

5.3.4. Typed Entries

The blackboard in CASSANDRA-II is strongly typed. Each Level Manager contains entries of a limited number of types in its local database.

The types in the current version of CASSANDRA-II are:

blob **List.** Entries of this type refer to unordered lists of aircraft references.

blob **PairList.** Entries of this type refer to unordered lists of aircraft reference pairs. PairList entries are used when attempting to order aircraft references on the basis of separation distance and for collision detection.

blob **PrioList.** Entries of type PrioList contain an ordered sequence of aircraft reference pairs. The sequence is ordered with the pair representing the least separation distance as the first element and the greatest distance as the last element.

blob **SingleAircraft.** Entries of this type refer to one aircraft. SingleAircraft is the entry type used to represent aircraft in the cruise level allocation lower Level Manager.

blob **AircraftPair.** This type contains a pair of aircraft references. Entries of this type also have a distance attribute which represents the distance between the aircraft in the pair.

blob **Beacon.** This entry type contains a reference to a navigational beacon and an aircraft pair. This entry type also contains an attribute denoting the distance between the aircraft.

Knowledge Source preconditions are sensitive to the types of entries which they are attempting to match. If a Level Manager declares that it is interested in entries of only a few types, KS instantiations which refer to those types and those types only will appear in the control database, thus preventing accidental matches and instantiations.

In the input and the upper Level Managers, typed entries restrict the activities of Knowledge Sources and contribute to the proper sequencing of KS activations. Typed entries in these Level Managers also prevent knowledge sources from triggering on inappropriate entries.

In CASSANDRA-II, typed entries also serve as an error-checking device so that Knowledge Sources can only match on the correct entries. This is particularly important when entries are passed in messages. If there were no type restrictions in force, it would be possible for one Level Manager to send what it wanted to any other Level Manager, causing the receiver extra work. When typed entries are present, errors can be trapped before entries ever enter the local database.

Entries in CASSANDRA-II also have a slot which contains links. Links are used basically to record the derivation history of any given entry. Each link is provided with inverses as specified by the entry deletion model.

If an entry is in an upper level of a Level Manager pair, or in the input Level Manager, it has a *Dependents* slot. This slot contains the identifiers of the entries created as a result of the execution of tasks which have been scheduled for this entry. This slot is used by the deletion KSs, as is its inverse slot, *Parent.* An instance of a *Parent* slot points back to the entry which caused the entry with the *Parent* slot to be created. While *Dependents* slots can contain zero or more entries, the *Parent* slots are constrained to contain only one reference (that is, an entry can only have one parent). *Parent* and *Dependent* slots can refer to entries in the same Level Manager, but it is more usual for them to refer to entries in the other Level Manager of the same Level Manager pair: it is forbidden for a *Parent* or *Dependent* slot to refer to an entry in any other Level Manager pair.*

5.3.5. Message-Passing

CASSANDRA-II contains a message-passing system. Message-passing in CASSANDRA-II is always uni-directional. The input Level Manager contains output ports which connect to the separation and cruise level allocation upper Level Managers. The upper Level Managers have one input port each: the input ports are connected to the input Level Manager via a channel. Information flows from the input Level Manager

* This is because of the constraints imposed by a distributed environment. The message-passing mechanism sets the *Parent/Dependent* slot to **nil** when sending a message. This is a CASSANDRA-II-specific feature of message-passing.

to each upper Level Manager. Each upper Level Manager has one output port: this is connected to the single input port of each lower Level Manager. Information flows from upper to lower Level Managers. Finally, each lower Level Manager has one output port: these ports are connected to the user interface. Information flows from the lower Level Managers to the user interface. The connections for the system are given below using the channel connection notation of chapter 4 section 3.

```
typeof Chan1 iff List;
Chan1 : simulator.out arrow inputLM.in

typeof Chan2 iff List;
Chan2 : inputLM.out1 arrow CruiseLevelUpperLM.in
typeof Chan3 iff PrioList;
Chan3 : inputLM.out2 arrow VerticalSepUpperLM.in
typeof Chan4 iff PrioList;
Chan4 : inputLM.out3 arrow LongSepUpperLM.in
typeof Chan5 iff PrioList;
Chan5 : inputLM.out4 arrow LateralSepUpperLM.in

typeof Chan6 iff Aircraft;
Chan6 : CruiseLevelUpperLM.out arrow CruiseLevelLowerLM.in
typeof Chan7 iff CruiseLevelWarning;
Chan7 : CruiseLevelLowerLM.out arrow UserInterface.in1

typeof Chan8 iff AircraftPair;
Chan8 : VerticalSepUpperLM.out arrow VerticalSepLowerLM.in
typeof Chan9 iff VerticalWarning;
Chan9 : VerticalSepLowerLM.out arrow UserInterface.in2

typeof Chan10 iff AircraftPair;
Chan10 : LongSepUpperLM.out arrow LongSepLowerLM.in
typeof Chan11 iff LongSepWarning;
Chan11 : LongSepLowerLM.out arrow UserInterface.in3

typeof Chan12 iff Beacon;
Chan12 : LateralSepUpperLM.out arrow LateralSepLowerLM.in
typeof Chan13 iff LatSepWarning;
Chan13 : LateralSepLowerLM.out arrow UserInterface.in4
```

Since there is a restriction on the entry types which can legally be passed between Level Managers, each channel can be assigned a type. This has been done using the notation

typeof <channel-name> *iff* <type>;

where <channel-name> is the name of a channel and <type> a legal entry type. Types whose suffix is 'Warning' are warning message types. Warning message types contain information to be presented to the user: they have been added for completeness.

From the connections given above, it can be seen that CASSANDRA-II contains no loops and is, therefore, deadlock-free. This result follows immediately from the connections and is reassuring should CASSANDRA-II ever be required to operate in the field.

5.3.6. Deletion Knowledge Sources

Each Level Manager in CASSANDRA-II is equipped with deletion knowledge sources. These Knowledge Sources remove entries from the local database when they are no longer required.

The model of deletion has been presented in chapter 4; a detailed account of the functioning of deletion KSs will have to wait until chapter six. For the time being, suffice it to say that there are two attributes of an entry which cause it to become a candidate for deletion: the time it has been resident on the blackboard and the number of successful KS matches in which it has participated. In some cases, inter-Level Manager links are used to determine whether or not an entry can be actually deleted. Deletions in CASSANDRA-II can interact with the scheduler -- the arguments are complex and best left until chapter six where the implemented system is described in detail.

6. HOW CASSANDRA-II WORKS

6.1. INTRODUCTION

This chapter describes the CASSANDRA-II system in detail. CASSANDRA-II is the larger of the two experiments performed to test the viability of the CASSANDRA architecture (the other is discussed when considering the generality of the architecture in chapter 7). This chapter concerns itself with this *implemented* system: in some cases, the implemented system contains features which are not specified by the architecture or features which are present only to make implementation possible within a limited period of time -- examples in the latter category should *not* be taken as indicating that full implementation of the corresponding feature is not possible. In both cases, the features are the way they are, only because to do otherwise would require more time than was available for the construction of the system.

The CASSANDRA-II system contains two major components:

- an airspace simulator, and
- a monitoring system.

The second of the components is the program CASSANDRA-II, the first implementation of the CASSANDRA architecture. The simulator provides an environment within which the CASSANDRA-II program performs the airspace monitoring task. The reader is advised to consult Appendix One and the glossary for explanations of Air Traffic Control terms and concepts.

6.2. THE SIMULATOR

The simulator, although not logically part of the monitor system is there for three main reasons:

(i) real airspace was not available for the experiment;

(ii) the problem of interfacing SSR (Secondary Surveillance Radar) and primary radar output in digitized form was considered too complicated, though not intellectually very demanding, and would have absorbed many man-months of effort (and, in any case, not all the information required by CASSANDRA-II is provided by Mode C radar), and

(iii) the information required by CASSANDRA-II (e.g., *tas* (true air speed) and heading) is difficult to extract from radar data and would have required additional software to perform track analysis tasks. Real airspace could not be used for a variety of reasons. If CASSANDRA-II had been built using real data in real time, it would have required an interface to radar: this would have entailed installing equipment and interfacing to SSR (Secondary Surveillance Radar) channels, both of which were not possible. Use of real airspace would also have entailed that an ATCO (Air Traffic Control Officer) be trained to use the system: for an experiment, this seemed also to be impracticable. A simulation has the advantages that the contents of airspace can be varied at will and that aircraft parameters can be easily adjusted so that small variations in the system's response can be observed. A simulation also permits unusual mixes of traffic to be used, thus CASSANDRA-II can be made to work in simulated conditions that are somewhat unlikely.

Simulation frees experiments from being limited to traffic conditions at any one particular ATCU (Air Traffic Control Unit): traffic over the Rocky Mountains (using FAA (Federal Aviation Authority) rules) or over the Netherlands (using EuroKontrol rules) or over Central and Southern England (using the present rules) can be simulated with little difficulty. A further point is that, by using a simulation, tests of CASSANDRA-II tailored to other sets of rules can be made by changing the KSs in the monitor component. These points are important in the context of the desire of ICAO (International Civil Aviation Organisation). and the CAA (Civil Aviation Authority) to interface more effectively with EuroKontrol (the joint European Air Traffic Control organisation).

The simulator produces two kinds of output: one relating to the current state of the airspace being simulated (which will be termed *real* airspace); the other (generic) output is a projection into the future of the state of airspace. Projections are intended to help the ATCO decide whether a clearance is going to have the desired effects, or whether it will have adverse effects some time into the future.

The simulator produces its output for real airspace on a regular basis. The simulated time representing the rate of output (the clock-rate) is user-controlled. Output from projections can occur at any time from when the request was made for the projection to some time before the end of the period into which the projection is made. Projections should, of course, be handed over for analysis in sufficient time for the monitor to analyse the state of the projected airspace and for the ATCO to evaluate the results of the analysis. Currently, projections are handed over to the monitor as soon as they have been produced (all updates in the simulator are performed during the same cycle, so all outputs are ready at the same time - this is just an implementation convenience): it is the responsibility of the monitor to see that as many analyses are performed as possible in time.*

For the remainder of this section, the distinction between real and projected airspace will be ignored. The mechanisms are the same.

The simulation uses two kinds of model: airspace and aircraft. The airspace model contains a description of the boundaries of the airspace (currently a 4-tuple of Cartesian 2-space co-ordinates -- all airspaces are rectangular at the moment), and the locations, identifiers, types and ranges of beacons in the airspace. The airspace also contains information on the transition altitude and transition level (set to defaults of 3000 ft. and FL 30 respectively): the transition level is the default bottom of the airspace used by a KS in the input Level Manager to determine whether an aircraft is within controlled airspace -- if the aircraft is below the transition level, it is considered to be outside the jurisdiction of the monitor. The contents of the airspace model are static -- they are not updated during a monitoring session. The weather inside the simulated airspace is assumed to be standard temperature, pressure and humidity: meteorological data is exceptionally hard to integrate with airspace models and no aircraft documentation I possess shows the performance variations due to weather.

The airspace model provides a framework within which to monitor the aircraft which fly in it. It allows the monitor to know which aircraft are inside controlled airspace, which aircraft are flying too close to the airspace boundaries and which aircraft are flying too low (and are risking going out of controlled airspace). The airspace also notes what its type is (controlled airspace, airway, special rules, etc. -- the default is airway).

Within this framework, aircraft movements are simulated. Aircraft in the simulator are represented as descriptors. Descriptors are tuples of parameters which describe an aircraft at any point in time. The parameters in a descriptor are divided between static and dynamic parameters. Static parameters are set up

* At some later date, it might become desirable to perform simulations involving projections on a priority basis and present output in priority order - first would come real airspace output, then those projections relating to the next immediate time are performed, then the next one after that, and so on recursively. Thus a projection for five minutes into the future has a higher priority than one for ten minutes; neither, however, has as high a priority as output from real airspace.

at the start of a simulation and describe the flight kind, the type of aircraft, and so on. Dynamic parameters describe the state of an aircraft at any point in time and are updated on every simulation cycle.

The parameters in aircraft descriptors are as follows. First, the static parameters.

- aircraft identifier (e.g., BA544);
- flight category (i.e, A, B, C, D, Normal, etc.);
- flight type (IFR, VFR, etc.);
- aircraft type (e.g., Boeing 747-200).

The dynamic parameters are:

- altitude (actually measured in feet, but converted to level numbers where necessary);
- position (a cartesian 2-space co-ordinate);
- speed (in knots);
- heading (expressed in degrees magnetic).*

All dynamic parameters are updated on each cycle of the simulator. This ensures that the current altitude, position, etc., are always available.

Dynamic parameters are maintained as lists of values. This is done so that the behaviour of an aircraft throughout its flight can be available for explanation and justification. Some KSs also need access to historical information (most notably when determining separation when levels are crossed). In order to avoid recomputation of values, previously computed values are kept in the form of history lists.

Dynamic parameters are not simple values. They are record structures of one of two types: constant and variable. Constant records denote the fact the parameter is not changing for the present (positions are always recorded as constants -- the position is found on a sweep and varies between sweeps, but as a function of other parameters). Variable records indicate that the value of the parameter is changing over the course of a number of sweeps. Altitude, speed and heading can be variable**. Variable records contain the

* A track is also maintained by the simulator. Tracks are vectors and headings are scalars. Heading represents the compass bearing of the aircraft. A track is a sequence of <position, heading> tuples.

** Due to the difficulty of calculating the rate of turn (it requires knowledge of the banking angle), headings are assumed constant. When an aircraft changes heading, it simply adds a new constant heading to the front of its heading list (the system was implemented in LISP and this operation was performed using the LISP primitive *cons*). Heading changes are, in any case, rather difficult to work out -- some pilots cut the corner when turning, some go wide and some waggle about.

value of the parameter at the time the manoeuvre was started, the time it started, the value which is to be attained and the value which the parameter currently has. When the current value is identical to the target value, the variable record is replaced by a constant record: this avoids a one cycle lag between attaining the desired value and recording the fact that the value has, indeed, become stable.

Variable records have one extra property. They record the kind of manoeuver which the aircraft is making. This recording is symbolic and is used for checking and for value calculation. The permitted values are:

- Altitude - climb or descend;
- Speed - accelerate or decelerate;
- Track - turn.

The simulator examines the flight parameters in sequence. If the latest value is a constant, that value is used to create a new constant value for the next cycle. The new constant is time-stamped to indicate the cycle for which it is valid.

When the most recent value is a variable, it is updated according to its type, so deceleration or descent causes a decrease in the magnitude of the current value of the parameter, and acceleration or climb causes an increase. The new value is calculated according to the simulator clock rate and the rate of change of the parameter. When a new variable is created one of two things happens: if the current value is equal to the target, the record is replaced by a constant record; otherwise a new variable record is created. Both types of record are added to the front of the parameter's list.

It should be noted that the calculation of a variable parameter represents a series of linear approximations to the curve which would be described by a real aircraft. The approximation can be improved by having the simulation clock tick at a higher rate.

Position updates have a special status. If an aircraft is turning or increasing or decreasing speed, its position relative to the co-ordinate origin will change in a manner different from that it would be if the speed or heading parameters were constant. An increase in true airspeed entails that an aircraft cover more

---

Thus, it is best for the time being to employ the scheme adopted in CASSANDRA-II.

ground than if the parameter were held constant (and conversely for deceleration); if the aircraft is turning, the position of the aircraft will alter with respect to the co-ordinate origin (the track of an aircraft is a *vector* and not a scalar -- that is the easiest way to explain it). The position update calculation can be performed only *after* the speed and heading updates have been performed (for obvious reasons). Because altitude has been separated out, altitude changes have no effect on aircraft positions.*

The simulator contains facilities akin to demons to cause an aircraft to change one or more of its dynamic parameters. The facilities (called *sim-demons*) allow aircraft to change levels, heading and speed at specified times during the simulation or at specified points in the airspace. Sim-demons allow aircraft to do such things as turn at beacons, climb to the wrong level, refuse to leave controlled airspace, and so on.

Sim-demons are applied to real airspace at the time specified by the demon or when the aircraft to which the demon applies reaches a certain co-ordinate or level. In projections, a little more has to be done.

A projection starts immediately after it has been requested and the changes to aircraft parameters are carried on until the projection has reached the time it is intended to represent. Thus, if the current time is 60 and the projection is for 360 (i.e., is meant to represent the state of airspace in 5 minutes' time), the projection clock starts at 60 and runs (in a separate 4-space from real airspace) until it indicates a time of 360. During the 300 seconds which separate the start and the finish, sim-demons are run on aircraft in the projection, causing them to change direction, etc., just as if they were in real airspace. Projections are performed on data structures which are kept logically distinct from real airspace. Sim-demons are applied during projection to make the result as close as possible to what it ought to be. Sim-demons, in CASSANDRA-II, are a way of representing flight plans, although the flight plan cannot be inspected as a declarative structure by the system.

The user can request changes to the parameters of one or more aircraft. Such a request can start a projection: the user specifies the time which should be projected in order to see the possible effects of the parameter changes. The user might, for example, see what the effects of clearing an aircraft to climb from FL210 to FL230 will be in five minutes' time. The projection is performed to provide a representation of

* This entails that the following assumption is made by the simulator: during climb or descent at a fixed speed, the actual speed measured against the ground remains constant. This is a fiction: true airspeed decreases when climbing and increases when descending, but that matters little for present purposes.

the consequences of that clearance.

Internally, descriptors are held as records on a property of a LISP atom. This makes the interface between the simulator and CASSANDRA-II simple. Every time an aircraft enters real airspace, an atom is **newsym**ed for it and the descriptor is attached on the atom. When a projection is performed, new atoms are created for each aircraft in the airspace and the descriptors physically copied: this removes any difficulties with updating the descriptors. When the simulator has completed a cycle, it hands the real airspace list and any projection lists to CASSANDRA-II. When an aircraft leaves the co-ordinate system, the atom on which the descriptor hangs is returned to Lisp free space, as is the record. The reader should note that controlled airspace is a sub-space of the space known to the simulator -- airspace has its own boundaries within this larger space.

The interface between the simulator and CASSANDRA-II is just the set of lists handed over on any cycle. The input of lists to CASSANDRA-II is described more fully in the next section.

6.3. CASSANDRA-II: THE MONITOR

CASSANDRA-II is the monitoring component of the CASSANDRA system. The monitor is the component which gives the system its name. The system is composed of a collection of Level Managers, the structure of which is shown diagrammatically in figure 6.1.

The reader should consult Appendix 2 for full details of the KSs which are actually implemented in the current version of CASSANDRA-II.

6.3.1. A Cycle Through CASSANDRA-II

CASSANDRA-II operates on a cyclic basis. The cycle consists of the input of lists of aircraft descriptors from the simulator, conflict detection and message output. The descriptors arrive from the simulator at a regular rate which corresponds to one or more sweeps of the radar antennae. Given the comparative stability of airspace over short periods of time and the fact that individual radar sweep rates vary somewhat, the average time for a sweep is six seconds. This figure can be altered by the user, and for experimental purposes, a sweep time of one minute has been found useful.

<u>Level Manager</u>

- Entries
- Knowledge Sources (including garbage collection KSs- KSs belong to this LM only)
- Matcher (for this LM only)
- Scheduler (for this LM only)
- Control Database (for this LM only)
- KS Action Interpreter (for this LM only)
- Number of entries
- LM pair to which LM belongs } for checking only

Fig 6.1

The fine structure of a Level Manager in CASSANDRA-II

The input to CASSANDRA-II is in the form of one or more lists of references to aircraft descriptors. One of the lists *always* refers to real airspace: the others refer to various projections into the future. Projections are only generated on request from the user and are generated either to find out what airspace will look like at some future time, or to see what the likely effects of one or more clearances might be.

When an input list is generated by the simulator, a blackboard entry of type **List** is created for it* and the entry is placed in the input Level Manager's local database. Over the next few problem solving cycles, input Level Manager KSs are scheduled to remove all references to aircraft which are outside airspace and then to create an entry which contains all possible pairs of aircraft (with duplicates removed: a pair <ac1, ac2> is considered to be identical to a pair <ac2, ac1>). The next KS scheduled determines whether there are any collisions between aircraft.** If there are any collisions, the pair referring to the crashed aircraft is removed from the list of pairs and an emergency message is sent to the user. After collision detection, KSs are scheduled to create entries containing lists of aircraft ordered by vertical and horizontal distance. These lists have the least distance as the first element of the list and the greatest distance as the last element of the list. These ordered lists are used by the lateral, longitudinal and vertical separation Level Manager pairs and are sent to the upper Level Manager of each of these Level Manager pairs. Another KS is also scheduled: it takes the list of aircraft pruned by the first KS in the sequence and posts it to the cruise level allocation panel upper Level Manager (upper LM).

During this basic interpreter cycle, the deletion KSs may be triggered, causing entries to be deleted from the local database. There may also be outstanding tasks from other cycles. Outstanding tasks result from scheduling decisions and the relative priorities of tasks (i.e., KSs whose triggers have been satisfied, but whose actions have not been executed -- in CASSANDRA-II, the term *task* is preferred over KSAR). When there are outstanding tasks of sufficiently high priority, the basic cycle described above may be interrupted by other tasks. This is, really, a matter for the individual Level Manager scheduler. There might, due to the distribution of priorities at any time, be a continuous sequence of KSs which operate on the same

* CASSANDRA-II has a strongly typed blackboard. Each entry is of exactly one type. The type scheme is discussed in section 6.3.3.3, below.

** A collision is defined as vertical separation of less than 30 ft. and a horizontal separation of less than 100 ft. - these figures are derived from the average dimensions of the aircraft likely to be in airspace. Even if the aircraft are smaller, these distances mean that if they ever get that close, they are in trouble.

input data and follow exactly the sequence described above. The only invariant of the input Level Manager processing is that for each entry, the KSs bound to the input LM must always act upon it in that order. This point has been discussed in more detail above (chapter 5).

When an entry is passed by an input Level Manager KS to another Level Manager pair, it is sent to the upper Level Manager of the destination Level Manager pair.* What happens then depends upon the Level Manager to which the entry has been sent. This description continues with the cruise level allocation Level Manager pair, the simplest of the four Level Manager pairs.

The cruise level allocation upper Level Manager checks for two conditions:

- that each aircraft has not been allocated FL245 as a cruise level, and
- that the aircraft is allocated the correct level for its heading.

The 'correct' cruise level for the heading is derived from the semi-circular rule. This rule determines the level upon which an aircraft may fly by dividing the compass into two segments, each of 180 degrees. If an aircraft is on a heading less than 180 degrees ($0 \leq$ heading < 180 degrees), it must fly on an *odd* cruise level (e.g., 25,000 ft. or Flight Level 250). If an aircraft is on a heading in the range 180 degrees $\leq$ heading < 360 degrees, it must fly on an *even* cruise level (e.g., 26,000 ft. or Flight Level 260).

An entry placed in the local database of the upper Level Manager of the cruise level allocation LM pair contains a list of aircraft descriptor references. The upper LM contains one KS. This KS sends one entry to the lower LM for each aircraft reference in the list. Each entry in the lower Level Manager is tested by two KSs which perform the checks mentioned above and send messages to the user. The cruise level allocation upper Level Manager is somewhat unusual in that it has only one KS and that its scheduler does not use separation as a prioritization mechanism (the latter is a feature it shares with the input level): this is because the LM pair operates on single aircraft and not on pairs.

The three other LM sets operate on pairs of aircraft and use separation distance as part of the scheduling process. As an example, to give the reader a flavour of the rest of the system, the longitudinal separation panel is described before moving on to a brief summary of the cycle.

---

* The information flows through CASSANDRA-II are shown in figure 6.2.
* The reader is recommended to consult Appendix 1 for more details on Air Traffic Control regulations.

When an entry is placed in the local database of the longitudinal separation upper Level Manager, a number of KSs operate on it. Entries on this Level Manager contain lists of aircraft pairs. That is, they are of type **PairList**.

The longitudinal separation rules require that the aircraft in question are within 100 nm (nautical miles) of the DME (Distance Measuring Equipment - a device attached to a navigational beacon for measuring distances between aircraft and beacons) used by the aircraft to determine their distance from the associated VOR (all the longitudinal separation rules in CASSANDRA-II require aircraft to be navigating via a VOR, or VHF Omni-directional Range which is one kind of navigational beacon). There is a longitudinal separation upper Level Manager KS which checks that the aircraft in a pair are within 100 nm of a DME. The second KS in this upper Level Manager removes all aircraft pairs from the ordered list if the aircraft in question are separated by more than 50 nm.* The function of this KS is to remove from consideration all those aircraft pairs which cannot possibly represent a confliction: the maximum of the separation minima specified by the rules is 45 nm. This pruning KS serves a similar function to other KSs which are found in upper Level Managers: it serves to reduce the space which must be searched for conflictions and helps to increase the performance of the system. The analogous KSs for the other upper Level Managers are:

(i) Vertical Separation. The pruning KS removes all aircraft pairs which have a vertical separation greater than 5000 ft.. The minimum separation between supersonic aircraft flying above FL450 is 4000 ft..**

(ii) Lateral Separation. The pruning KS removes aircraft pairs according to horizontal distance and absence of a common beacon. (This KS is quite complex).

---

* 50 nm was chosen so that there would be something else to do after the pruning operation: thus, the possibility of error on the part of some KSs is deliberately permitted. In a live version of the program, 45 nm would be the value chosen for efficiency reasons.

** An improvement to this KS would be to examine the altitudes of the aircraft in a pair and prune by an amount relevant to the altitude. This needs a little explanation. Consider the simplest case of two aircraft in supersonic flight at or above FL450: the minimum separation is 4000 ft. Therefore, any pairs of aircraft which are separated in the vertical by more than 4000 ft. should not be considered. The other cases follow immediately: for aircraft not in supersonic flight and flying above FL245, the pruning is performed on a 2000 ft. basis; for aircraft below FL245, 1000 ft. is the pruning parameter. Thus, in each case, where an aircraft pair is in one of the altitude bands, the minimum separation figure is used to determine whether or not the pair is to included or excluded from consideration.

Once the pruning operations have been performed, entries are sent to the lower longitudinal separation Level Manager for detailed tests to be performed. One entry is created for each aircraft pair in the pruned list. The scheduler ensures that the pruning operation is performed *before* the posting operation (a similar process is used by the schedulers in the vertical and lateral separation upper Level Managers): this is to ensure that there are no unwanted checks performed by the lower Level Manager. When the entries are received by the longitudinal separation lower Level Manager, they can be checked by eight KSs. The KSs generate user messages if a confliction is detected.

In the present context, a check is represented by executing a task which has been created by the satisfaction of the precondition and condition of a given KS (e.g., *LongitudinalSepKS1* which checks that two aircraft are separated by at least 20nm longitudinally - the check is that one aircraft is following the other, that the first aircraft is maintaining a true airspeed of 20 kts or more than the following aircraft and that the aircraft are separated by 20nm longitudinally -- i.e., the check is a conjunction of conditions in this case).

A dataflow diagram for the Longitudinal Separation upper and lower Level Managers is given as fig. 6.2.

6.3.1.1. Summary

In any configuration of CASSANDRA-II, the simulator (or radar processing equipment in a live version) produces a set of descriptors, one for each aircraft. The descriptors are sent to the input Level Manager. The input Level Manager prunes away all aircraft not in airspace and creates ordered lists of descriptor references. It also sends a list of references to the vertical separation upper LM and tests to see which aircraft have crashed. The other LM pairs in the system then activate and produce messages when conflictions are detected. In a parallel or distributed configuration, each Level Manager operates totally independently of the others save for the fact that it must wait on some other LM for input. In a parallel version, messages are merged non-deterministically before being presented to the user. In a serial configuration, similar to the current one, the Level Managers in the system are run in some pre-defined order or are selected according to some scheduling rule to run for a certain time, then to be suspended and another Level Manager chosen for execution.

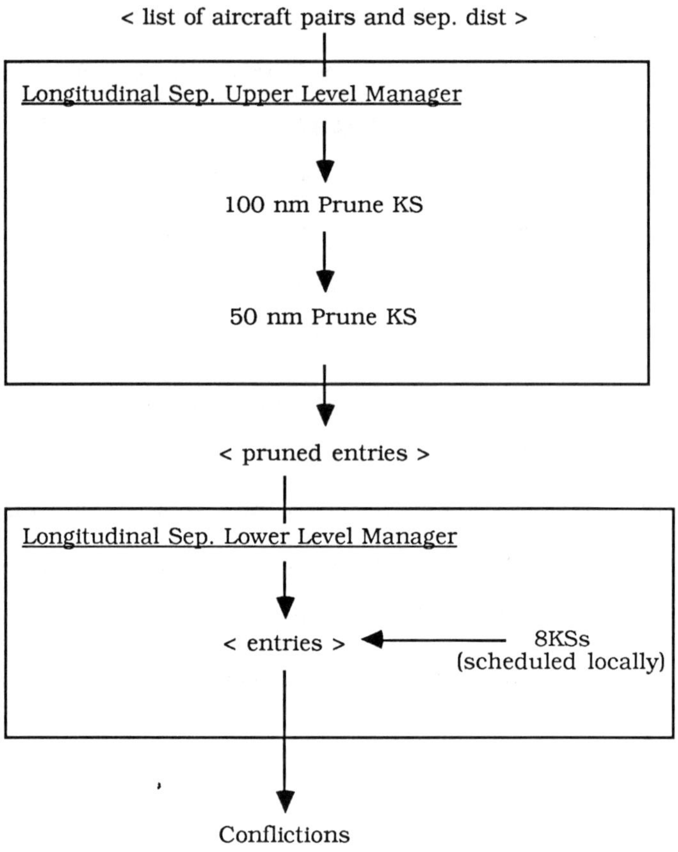

Fig 6.2

Notional flowchart for Longitudinal Separation LM Pair

6.3.2. Detailed Structure and Rationale

Having described the operation of CASSANDRA-II and having introduced some implementation details, it is time to go into the detailed structure of the system. This detailed description is aimed at showing the reader how CASSANDRA-II works.

6.3.2.1. Local Control and Schedulers

Everything in CASSANDRA-II Level Managers is geared to making all KS components operate in a purely local environment. This is particularly true of the schedulers bound to each Level Manager. The fact that there is a scheduler bound to a Level Manager entails that it can make its own decisions independent of all other Level Managers. Each local scheduler does not need to know of decisions made elsewhere in the system or of their rationale. It is a feature of the CASSANDRA-II task domain that once an entry has been placed in the local database of some Level Manager (and this applies particularly to lower Level Managers), any decisions which are made can be made in total isolation: the other Level Managers in the system may either be wholly irrelevant to the task performed by the Level Manager in question or may be the consumer of the entries created as a result of executing KSs in that Level Manager. The relationship between the upper and lower Level Managers of a pair and the relationship between the input Level Manager and the other pairs in the system is one of producer and consumer* and implies that the producer and consumer (upper and lower LMs and input LM and all other LM pairs) may proceed at their own rate, with the proviso that the consumer must occasionally wait for entries generated by the producer. There is no concept of a global solution state in CASSANDRA-II and an individual level may not inspect the state of another level. The producer-consumer relation between Level Managers is depicted in fig. 6.3.

A lower LM depends for its entries upon the actions performed by KSs bound to the corresponding upper Level Manager of the same pair. While the upper LM continues to supply the lower Level Manager with entries, all goes well. If, however, the lower LM has exhausted its supply of entries, it has to wait for the corresponding upper Level Manager of the pair to produce some more before processing can continue.

The scheduler in each Level Manager manipulates two local data structures used for control pur-

* The concept here is exactly the same as the one used in concurrent progamming and Operating Systems.

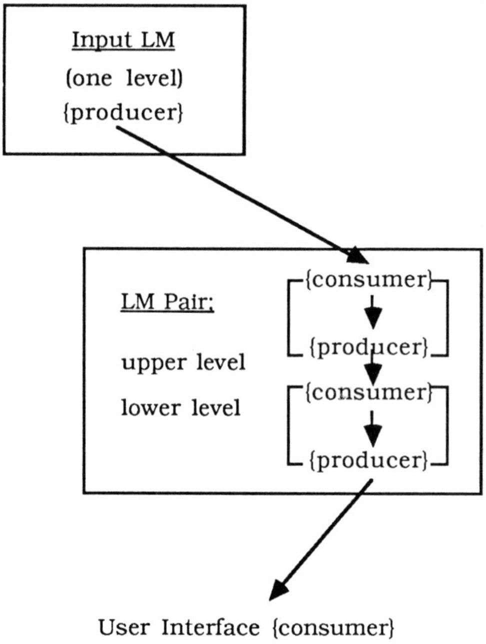

Fig 6.3

Producer-consumer relationships in CASSANDRA-II

poses. In many cases, these structures are agendas, but in some, they are just control lists. There are two structures bound to each LM: one deals with tasks pertaining to real airspace, the other with tasks for projections. Agendas are used when distance information is available, and are used by the lower LMs of the vertical, longitudinal and lateral separation LM pairs. Control lists are used in all other cases. Control lists are randomly ordered in the case of real airspace lists, and are ordered by time in the case of projections. Projection control lists are ordered so that the soonest time by which the projection should be completed is at the head of the list and the latest at the rear. Tasks are added to projection control lists according to the time which they represent. Figure 6.4 shows the details of the scheduler in diagrammatic form.

The fact that local schedulers operate on two data structures differentiates CASSANDRA-II from many other blackboard systems (for example, BB-1 and OPM). If CASSANDRA-II were to be used only for *en route* operations, a multiplication by one of the scheduling factors of a task (usually distance in real airspace) and by expiry time in the case of projections would be an adequate heuristic for generating a single agenda. CASSANDRA-II, though, is designed to have the flexibility to be applied to aerodrome operations* which entails that this simple scheme will not work. It will not work because aircraft are closer together than in an en route sector and projections must be shorter than the projections in en route working. Projections in en route operations can have periods of five, ten or fifteen minutes: in aerodrome or TMA operations, projections will be of the order of one or two minutes around an aerodrome and less than five elsewhere. These differences suggest that a non-deterministic control regime might result if simple numerical combinations were permitted. Therefore, the schedulers operate by (basically) selecting real airspace tasks first and then interleaving projections as and when time is available.

Non-determinism is not acceptable for at least two reasons. The first concerns the non-deterministic mixing of real airspace and projection tasks. If these tasks are executed non-deterministically, it would be conceivable that more projection tasks than real airspace tasks could be executed per cycle (if the algorithm were truly non-deterministic, this would be quite possible given the possibility that there would be many more projections to choose from, and thus the probability that the random selection yield a projection

* In particular, London Heathrow. Heathrow has an enormous number of ground movements each day and its Terminal Management Area is the busiest in the world. Before long, Heathrow will become a major bottleneck in the UK civilian air network.

— Scheduler (code)

— Real airspace task database

— Simulated (projected) airspace task database

Fig 6.4

The scheduler and its databases

would be increased). This would cause real airspace tasks to be overlooked. Real airspace is the true subject of CASSANDRA-II: if real airspace tasks are being overlooked, CASSANDRA-II is not performing correctly: if real airspace tasks are being overlooked in a 'live' version of CASSANDRA-II, real lives would be at risk. Non-determinism also entails, in this context, that there is no way to *guarantee* that real airspace tasks are being properly attended to. This, in turn, suggests that there is no adequate verification procedure which will give an assurance that real airspace has priority over projections.

The second major reason for banning non-determinism is that many tasks have a priority associated with them. If the control regime were non-deterministic, priorities would not determine the order in which tasks were executed. Non-deterministic control would not allow one to state which were the most important tasks and it would not guarantee that these tasks be executed before tasks of a lower importance. Thus, it would be possible, in a non-deterministic control regime, for conflictions to be ignored, even though, in the long run, all tasks would be attended to (assuming that the control regime were fair). However, the local possibility that important tasks could be ignored for some period of time suggests very strongly that non-determinism be avoided, at least within Level Managers, in this system.

The scheduler also makes use of a feature which will be described more fully in the next section of this chapter. When an entry is matched by a KS, it is tagged with the KS identifier. It is an implicit rule of the system that an entry may be matched by any particular KS only once. Using this information, the scheduler can select a KS to execute. This feature is particularly valuable when the scheduler has a sequence of KSs to execute (as is the case with the input Level Manager and some of the upper Level Managers). The scheduler knows the order in which KSs should be executed and it can determine whether the next KS in the sequence can be executed on the basis of the presence of an appropriate task in the agenda and the matching information on the entry. It is a property of the system that when a sequence is started it always elaborates to the correct sequence of entries and tasks with no gaps caused by missing entries or non-triggered KSs: this property is fairly difficult to analyse completely, but is also shared by the Blackboard Control Model (Hayes-Roth, 1985) amongst other systems. This pleasant property is rooted in the correctness of the triggering algorithm and the finite delay between triggering and execution. The tagging mechanism also has the advantage that it helps the system avoid loops. Loops could easily occur in

KS

— Precondition	(quick relevance test)
— Condition	(slower condition test - tests some condition in airspace)
— Action	(can: update entries, delete entries, create entries, post entries to another level)

Fig 6.5

Knowledge source structure in CASSANDRA-II

CASSANDRA-II if an entry remains on the blackboard long enough for the next match cycle to be performed. Loops generate extra entries and waste memory and processor time (both by repeating a task and by causing other tasks to be repeated).

6.3.2.2. Scheduling, Matching, Action Interpretation and Real Time Issues

Of the remaining slots in a Level Manager, the two which are most unusual are the KS matcher and the action interpreter slots.

Level Managers are designed to operate as independent processes, perhaps within a distributed processing environment, and are designed to be as autonomous as possible. As with the scheduler, the matcher and action interpreter operate on a purely local basis.

Knowledge Sources in CASSANDRA-II are held in a database associated with each Level Manager. Each Level Manager has a slot which contains the KSs triggering on entries in its local database. When a KS is needed, the system fetches the appropriate KS component. The structure of CASSANDRA-II Knowledge Sources is shown in fig. 6.5.

Each Level Manager also has a matcher which is specific to it and to the task in hand. The control flow through the matcher is shown in fig. 6.6. The reader should note that each Level Manager has its own, independent copy of the matcher; although the match algorithm should be fairly obvious, it has been included for the sake of completeness.

There is a complication in the story of the matcher, the scheduler and the action interpreter. Some Level Managers have entries which explicitly contain distance information, but others (the majority) do not. This is reflected in the types of task used in the two general cases: one contains distance information of some kind (vertical or horizontal) as a scheduling parameter, the other does not. It would be perfectly possible to have one global function for each of the matcher, scheduler and action interpreter, but these global functions would have to discriminate between the types of task they either create or handle, and this would cost time; if the global functions mapped tasks onto a single data structure, a space overhead would be incurred (and there would still have to be some type discrimination). It seems better, therefore, to provide an appropriate function for each possible use.

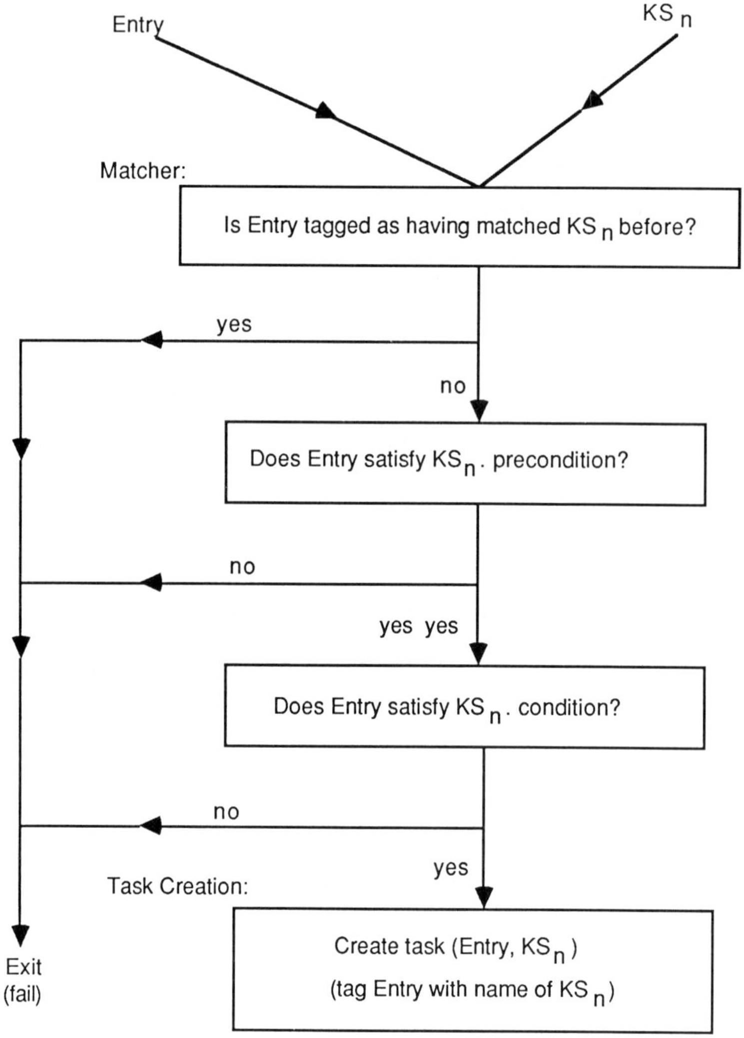

Fig 6.6

The KS matching algorithm

The action interpreters in CASSANDRA-II perform one basic task, they **apply** the KS action to the entry mentioned by the task obtained from the control structure. Given that there are two task types (one containing distance information, the other not containing distance information), there are two generic interpreters which are instantiated appropriately when bound to a Level Manager. The interpreters extract the KS identifier and the entry identifier from the task and fetch and apply the KS action to the entry.

Interpreters also tag the entry with the KS identifier (the reason for this is explained below).

There is, however, one unusual feature of the generic CASSANDRA-II matcher which needs some explanation.

KSs in CASSANDRA-II do not usually update local database entries and, when they do, it is a fact known to the scheduler. Entry updating is frequently associated with sequences of KSs: this is a feature of the CASSANDRA-II system and was dictated by the needs of the domain.

The matcher in each Level Manager, therefore, tags each entry with the identifier of the KS which has just successfully matched against the entry. When performing the basic match cycle, the matcher looks at the tags on each entry and, if the KS currently being considered has already successfully matched the entry, the next entry in the LM is tried (thus skipping over the KS which previously matched the entry). The tagging mechanism prevents duplicate tasks.

This scheme could be extended to the case where a KS updates an entry. The obvious modification requires knowing when an entry was last updated by a KS. If the matcher notices that an entry has been updated since the current KS was last matched with the item, the matcher can try to match the KS again because the update may have significantly altered the entry's contents. If there has been no such update, then the matcher skips to the next entry.

The tagging mechanism is also of use to the scheduler. Some Level Managers require sequences of KSs to be applied to an entry. At any time during the sequence, there is no guarantee that all of the KSs still to come in the sequence have matched against the entry (and, hence, have no tasks in the control database which can be scheduled), or, contrariwise, the relevant entries have not been generated by earlier KSs in the sequence. The scheduler can examine the tags on the entries which are associated with sequences and, should there be only a subset of the KSs in the sequences mentioned as tags, the scheduler can opt to schedule some other tasks. This process can continue until all the KSs in the sequence have been matched or the entry has become outdated.*

The scheduler also uses the tags on entries to determine the KSs which it can schedule. Apart from suspending some sequences because of the absence of tags, it can look at the tags to see how far a given sequence can go. When there is a sequence of KSs to be scheduled on an entry, the scheduler looks at the entry tags to find out if the first KS has matched, and if it has, the corresponding task is executed. The scheduler then looks for the second KS in the sequence, and so on. The scheduler could look directly at the tasks in the control database, but there is no guarantee that a deletion has not occurred, so the task may be out of date -- this risk is still there in the current scheme. The current scheme also allows the scheduler to check that the next KS has been matched and saves the memory required to take a copy of the control database for a full check. Once the check has been performed, the scheduler knows that it has the task to execute and can select the appropriate task from the agenda.

The reader should note that there is another use for tags. Discussion of this second use is postponed until the deletion KSs are considered.

6.3.2.3. Control and Entry Deletion

Although CASSANDRA-II exhibits many features in common with other blackboard systems (OPM, BB-1 and the author's own Ariadne-1, in particular), it differs most markedly in its control, although, even here, there are similarities. In CASSANDRA-II, control is divided into two components: local and global control. The reader is referred to figures 5.2, 6.1 and 6.4 for an overview of the local control component in CASSANDRA-II.

Just as effective control is important in any AI system, entry deletion is important in a real time system or in a system with limited memory. Having redundant entries around in the database means that the amount of memory required to operate the system will grow with time and, unless outdated entries are

* An entry might not be matched because it is new and has just entered the database, or an updating task has not yet been scheduled on the entry which prevents subsequent KSs from matching the entry. An interesting idea, which has yet to be followed up is to put more intelligence into the matcher, for example, making it a full KS in its own right. In such a scheme, the scheduler could direct the matcher to look at only *some* of the entries and KSs in the database, thus improving the focus of attention at any one time. This is not implemented in CASSANDRA-II because it costs both in time and in space. As was noted above, the current implementation is guaranteed to produce the correct entry sequence -- during this last paragraph, it should be observed, I am considering a more general case, so there is no contradiction.

flagged, they cause an overhead during matching and scheduling. Redundant entries on the blackboard can cause loops to form which further degrade system performance. CASSANDRA-II contains entry deletion KSs, therefore. Deletion KSs are attached to each Level Manager in the system. There are two deletion KSs per Level Manager: each deletion KS is a complete, independent Knowledge Source although they all use a common set of procedures in their implementation. The deletion KSs fall into two classes: time- and match-triggered. Each individual deletion KS examines the local state of its Level Manager's local database and removes entries when executed.

This section describes the control and deletion mechanisms in CASSANDRA-II. Control is discussed first.

The facts that Level Managers are wholly independent and require only the input of data from elsewhere and that the links between entries on the blackboard are used only for entry deletion imply that any serial global control strategy must be at best wholly arbitrary. The facts also imply that a concurrent or distributed implementation is natural. In what follows, a detailed account of local control is given: this is followed by a description of a global control regimes.

6.3.2.3.1. Local control

For this discussion, the longitudinal separation panel is chosen for all examples.

It can safely be assumed that in upper Level Managers there will be exactly one entry referring to real airspace during any one cycle. This is because real airspace entries exist only for one cycle and are then deleted. The Knowledge Sources in upper Level Managers operate on one entry per cycle. This is because the pruning KS removes aircraft references directly from the entry which was received as input for the current cycle: a copy operation was considered too expensive both in terms of time and in terms of memory cells to be implemented in CASSANDRA-II.

Real airspace entries represent the situation in real airspace at the time of their appearance in the system (actually, a short time before they appear, due to processing delays). There is only ever one real airspace being monitored. Thus, there is only ever one upper Level Manager entry at any time which relates to real airspace: that entry contains all aircraft references which are relevant to a given LM pair. It should be noted that some real airspace entries may remain in local databases because they have not yet been deleted: these will never be considered for task creation because they will have been matched by all relevant KSs during the cycle on which they appeared in the local database -- they are, therefore, wholly irrelevant and may be ignored for the purposes of local control.

There may be, however, an arbitrary number of entries referring to projections, but, again, for any projection time, there may be at most two entries (one for a general projection and one for a clearance -- this is enforced by the way in which the simulator allows the user to create projections).

Upper Level Managers have a control database divided into two components -- one for real airspace (which contains only one reference by the above assumption) and one for projections. These components are control lists (not agendas) and contain the tasks which are scheduled for execution. Upper Level Manager tasks do not contain distance information.

Upper Level Manager control lists are derived from the previous contents of the list and from the output of the KS matcher (the reader will remember that KS matchers add entries to control lists directly). When a KS precondition and condition have both evaluated to true, a task is created and added to the control list.

Upper Level Manager schedulers concentrate on real airspace tasks first until none remain. The longitudinal separation Level Manager contains two KSs, and there may be one or two real airspace tasks in the control list at any time. When the real airspace tasks have been exhausted, the scheduler can turn its attention to projections. The obvious reason for this is that real airspace tasks may only remain in the system until the next input from the simulator (or the radar) and so must be attended to first; also, the purpose of CASSANDRA-II is to provide the user with as accurate a picture of real airspace and real conflictions as possible, so real airspace tasks should always be preferred.

If there is insufficient time for the system to attend to a real airspace task, it is deleted when it expires. It can be deleted because a new entry will shortly be generated by the simulator (radar). Similarly, when the system has insufficient time for a projection task, it expires and is removed from the Level Manager (projections can always be restarted). CASSANDRA-II will increase priorities (by dividing the numeric value by two) when a task has not been executed and has expired. It will also update the triggering entry expiry time to the next clock tick so that it cannot be deleted by time-triggered deletion KSs: the entry is also annotated to indicate this fact. The priority reassignment mechanism is closely related to the time-triggered deletion KSs, so a detailed examination will be made when the deletion KSs have been discussed.

The reader should note that in a live version of the system, deletions such as those discussed in the last paragraph may not be wise because it is sometimes possible for a radar to 'lose' an aircraft on one sweep and recover it on another. In addition to this property of radar systems, it is also possible that aircraft become lost because of a variety of physical effects such as shadowing (in this case, the radar 'shadow' produced by one aircraft will obscure the trace of another and render the second invisible). Under such circumstances, it might be better to project all aircraft positions forward in time on each radar sweep so that effects such as those just mentioned are mitigated: this approach was not adopted in the implementation under discussion because they increased its complexity to a considerable degree.

The longitudinal separation upper Level Manager has two KSs, *PruneLongitudinalSepItems* and *PutLongitudinalSepTestEntries*. The KSs are scheduled in that order. Both KSs will, however, match the **PrioList** posted by the input Level Manager, so *PutLongitudinalSepTestEntries* cannot be executed until *PruneLongitudinalSepItems* has been executed, thus removing all aircraft references which should not be considered by the lower LM KSs. When *PruneLongitudinalSepItems* is to be executed, its task is removed from the control list and the action applied to the entry mentioned by the task.

On the next match cycle, *PruneLongitudinalSepItems* cannot be matched again because it side-effects the entry on which it was triggered, and that same entry still resides in the upper LM database. The tagging scheme in the matcher will ignore the entry and so fail to match the entry a second time. There is no task in the control list which refers to the pruning KS, and so the second KS, *PutLongitudinalSep-TestEntries* is selected. *PutLongitudinalSepTestEntries* sends an entry to the lower Level Manager for every aircraft pair in the pruned **PrioList.**

So far, discussion has centred on real airspace tasks. There is also a need to account for projection tasks. The simplest is to select tasks on the basis of expiry time: the time which is closest to the current system clock value is selected. Projection tasks in control lists are ordered by time and this scheme merely amounts to selecting the first task in the list each time through the cycle.

In cases where KS sequences are longer than two, for example in the input Level Manager, the scheduler cannot rely on the matcher to ensure that tasks are executed in the proper order. Instead, it has to use a table of entries and KSs. All the KSs which are in a sequence are placed in the table when an entry is matched by the first KS in the sequence. The knowledge of the sequence is compiled into the scheduler. That is, the scheduler contains a table which contains the identifiers of the KSs in the sequence in the order in which they are to be executed. When a task has been executed, the entry in the scheduling table which contains its KS identifier is marked and the next task is chosen on the basis of the next KS identifier in the table. When the sequence is completed, the table entries are un-marked and the process begins again from the top of the table. If a sequence has to be interrupted, its table is saved and marked as suspended: a copy of the table is used to start the next sequence. Each table contains references to the entries upon which the sequence is to operate: this reference is used to ensure that each sequence is being applied to the correct input data. Where a sequence spans more than one entry (as it does in the input Level Manager), the Dependents and or Parent links of entries are inspected to find the next entry and sub-sequence (in this case, the links represent a temporal ordering over the entries). The matter of sequences has already been discussed in detail above (chapter 5).

On the lower level of the Longitudinal Separation LM pair, there are few of the conveniently simplifying assumptions which can be made for the upper LM. The lower LM contains eight domain KSs, and an aircraft pair can be matched by one or more lower level KSs (although this is rather unlikely).* The fact that an entry can be matched by more than one KS does not really induce loops in the execution of the system: there are no side-effects on lower LM entries and the matcher removes the possibility of direct looping. If an entry is matched by more than one KS, it simply means that the aircraft in the entry are potentially involved in more than one longitudinal separation conflict, and this matter should be reported to the user. The lower LM scheduler operates an agenda scheme and selects the first task in the agenda. Agenda entries are ordered by distance in the, by now, familiar way. Once again, the scheduler selects tasks from

* A comparatively simple modification to the current scheduler would detect multiple matches in the agenda - i.e., matches by the different KSs with one and the same entry. The multiple matches could be scheduled first, thus improving the focus of attention. As one of these tasks is selected, it is removed from the agenda in the normal way. The modification consists of a few lines of code and a table. It was not considered worth building this feature because the likelihood of such a case is remote.

real airspace and then selects projection tasks. Projection agenda entries are ordered both by time and by distance, so the top task on the agenda has the earliest expiry time and the shortest distance, the next one has the same expiry time and a greater distance or a greater expiry time and the shortest distance for that expiry period.

An interesting point about lower Level Managers is that once a match cycle has been executed on a given set of entries, there is no need for a further match cycle until there are new entries input to the level. The matcher is called after each schedule in the normal way, however: this is because projection entries may have been placed in the Level Manager between task execution and the next match cycle.

The control regime described above is wholly typical of the four domain Level Manager pairs in CASSANDRA-II. The exception is the cruise level allocation LM pair which cannot employ distance as a scheduling parameter: control lists are the only control mechanism which can apply. The cruise level allocation LM pair, therefore, represents two instances of the generic upper Level Manager control regime.

6.3.2.3.2. Global control

It has been remarked above that serialised control in CASSANDRA-II is a somewhat arbitrary process. The natural way to schedule Level Managers in CASSANDRA-II is to run them all in parallel. Just so that the reader forms a picture of the control regime used to derive the annotated trace of Appendix 3, a serial control mechanism is described here.

The major decision, when designing a control structure for a serialised CASSANDRA-II, is to determine the amount of non-determinism to be permitted in the system. If the control structure is highly non-deterministic, it will better model a concurrent implementation, though at the cost of the extra processor time required to make a non-deterministic selection. The global control regime described here is totally deterministic.

The global control regime (called 'Simple') was used during system testing.

The Simple regime basically activates each Level Manager in the system according to some predetermined order. The order actually used was based upon the complexity of the operations performed by each Level Manager with the proviso that the input level is always the first to be activated (it provides

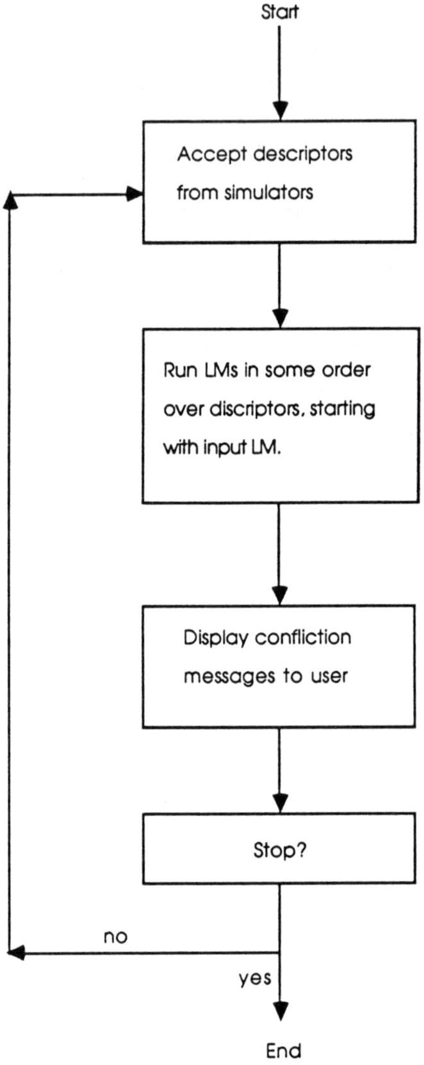

Fig 6.7

Global control in CASSANDRA-II (Simple algorithm)

input to all the other Levels Managers in the system). The easiest way to explain Simple is to present it as an algorithm. It is shown as a flowchart in fig. 6.7.

Simple

1. Accept lists of aircraft descriptors from the simulator and send them to the input Level Manager;
2. Activate the input Level Manager and let it run to completion (i.e., let it run until all tasks have been executed), sending entries to the upper Level Manager of each of the other LM pairs;
3. Activate the other Level Managers in the system and let them run to completion in the following order: Cruise Level Allocation upper Level Manager, Cruise Level Allocation lower Level Manager, Vertical Separation upper Level Manager, Vertical Separation lower Level Manager, Longitudinal Separation upper Level Manager, Longitudinal Separation lower Level Manager, Lateral Separation upper Level Manager, Lateral Separation lower Level Manager. (Note that the upper Level Manager is *always* run before the lower Level Manager - this is so that the lower Level Manager has input to work on);
4. Display messages. This is actually done after each Level Manager has run to completion.
5. Go back to 1.

6.3.2.3.3. Entry deletion

CASSANDRA-II is a real time system. The Level Managers which comprise the system contain entries which are used by the system's KSs to generate user messages or other entries. Entries last for only a certain time, after which either they represent a picture of the airspace which is either out of date or else they represent projections which are no longer required because the time by which the projection was needed has past and the user could see what was happening in real airspace rather than in a projected airspace.

When entries are sent to a Level Manager, they are matched by the KSs in that Level Manager. Any given KS may match a particular entry exactly once. This entails that, once all the KSs which may match an entry have matched it and after they have executed, there is no point in retaining the entry in the local database for it simply represents useless information.

Entries in a Level Manager are held in lists. Unwanted or out-dated entries serve no useful purpose and occupy storage which could be released for other purposes (like holding new entries).

In a real time system like CASSANDRA-II, the amount of memory allocated partially determines the performance of the system. In a flat addressed system, if there are too many unwanted entries in store, the space which they occupy will not be available for allocation to new entries and, eventually, the system will stop for lack of space. In a virtual storage system, if there is a large quantity of storage allocated, there is an overhead in the number of page faults which have to be executed in order to bring pages into real memory. If the storage required by CASSANDRA-II can be reduced to a minimum, there will be a performance benefit. CASSANDRA-II is also designed to be a continuous system, and so the amount of memory it uses must be controlled.

CASSANDRA-II contains a set of deletion KSs. Deletion is performed on every cycle of each Level Manager of the system and deletion KSs are matched in the ordinary way with local database entries: that is, deletion KSs are basically ordinary Knowledge Sources. The difference comes at schedule time when at least one deletion KS is always executed if there is a deletion task. Deletion KSs do not simply remove the identifier of an entry from a level: they completely destroy the entry and return it to Lisp free-space (this is done via calls on functions provided by the FranzLisp system). Thus, once a deletion KS executes on an entry, all of the memory used by the entry is given to the LISP storage manager for re-use.

Deletion KSs, however, trigger on conditions different than other KSs. In particular, they have a precondition which *always* evaluates to true, and they are not sensitive to entry contents. For each Level Manager, the deletion KSs do check that the entry being matched is of an appropriate type (the deletion KSs in the input Level Manager check that an entry is of one of the three types normally found there): this is more a matter of system convention than absolute necessity. The conditions of deletion KSs fall into two types: time-triggered and match-triggered conditions.

Time-triggered deletion KSs look at the expiry time of an entry. If the expiry time is greater than or equal to the current system time, the condition evaluates to true and a task is created. When this occurs, it means that the entry is out of date and can be removed from the Level Manager's local database.

Match-triggered deletion involves the examination of the tags left behind on an entry by the matcher and the action interpreter. Match-triggered KSs do not examine the system clock to determine the current time. A match-triggered KS retrieves the tags left by the matcher and those left by the action interpreter. If the two sets of tags are identical, the entry can be deleted and the condition evaluates to *true* so that a task can be created. The theory behind match-triggering is that when all the tasks which have been created for the entry have been executed, the entry is no longer required and can be deleted. If the tags left by the matcher and the interpreter are not the same, then there are outstanding tasks, and the entry must not be deleted.

Match-triggering deletes entries at times earlier than expiry and is designed to spread the time spent in deletion over a number of cycles. Time-triggered deletion may only cause deletions when an entry has expired, so, if there are many entries which expire at the same time, there will be an overhead in removing them, assuming that the scheduler runs all pending deletion tasks on each cycle (which it may choose not to do). By introducing match-triggered deletion, an entry can be removed as soon as all the tasks requiring that entry have executed.

The actions of deletion KSs do not simply remove the entry which matched the condition. In time-triggered deletion KSs, the action performs operations based upon whether it is bound to the upper or lower level of a panel and upon whether the KS is bound to the input Level Manager. In the case of upper and lower level time-triggered deletion KSs, there are links in the entry to be deleted which are followed.

If a time-triggered deletion KS is bound to an upper level, the action examines the Dependents slot of the entry: if the slot is empty (i.e., there are no dependents), the entry can be deleted immediately. If, on the other hand, the slot is not empty, the action deletes each entry from the lower level mentioned by the slot: only when all these entries have been deleted does it expunge the upper level entry. The reasoning behind this is as follows. All dependents of an upper level entry have the same expiry time, and so can be deleted when their parent is deleted. The order in which the upper and lower level entries are deleted is somewhat arbitrary, but it is, in fact, symmetrical to the order in which lower level collection KS actions operate.

Lower level time-triggered deletion KSs examine the Parent slot of the entry to be deleted. If the slot is empty, the entry can be deleted immediately. If, however, the slot contains a reference to an upper level entry, the KS action goes to that entry and deletes the reference to the lower level entry from the Dependents slot if that is not empty (this should actually performed by sending a control message to the upper Level Manager: in the current implementation, the removal is direct because all Level Managers occupy the same virtual address space). If the Dependents slot is empty or becomes empty, the parent entry is deleted and the lower LM entry is handed to the LISP garbage collector. If the Dependents slot in the parent entry is not empty and does not become empty, the lower LM deletion KS will just delete the lower level entry and exit. The reason for not deleting an upper level entry when the Dependents slot is not empty is purely arbitrary -- all lower level time-triggered deletion KSs are immune to the non-existence of the parent entry.

Match-triggered deletion KSs only ever delete the entries on which they are triggered. Thus, match-triggered KSs only ever operate on the Level Manager to which they are bound.

There are two kinds of deletion KSs because match-triggered KSs may fail to trigger on a given entry because the scheduler has not executed all the tasks pending on that entry. When this happens, there has to be a catch-all: the catch-all is provided by time-triggered deletion KSs which delete only on the basis of time.

Time-triggered deletion KSs can interact with the scheduler. Match-triggered deletion KSs examine the tags left behind by the matcher and only delete entries when no more KSs can match on them. When no more KSs can match and all the tasks generated by the entry have been executed, the entry can be deleted for it is no longer required. In the CASSANDRA-II system, match-triggered KSs are guaranteed to produce the right results; time-triggered KSs, on the other hand, are not. Time-triggered deletion KSs can delete entries when their expiry time has been reached or exceeded. This allows the possibility that the tasks associated with a particular entry may never be executed. Given the fact that there is new information input to the system on every radar sweep, this may not seem too much of a problem. In theory, it is possible for an aircraft to move through a sector without being attended to by any KSs: this is because the load on the CASSANDRA-II system would be so high that the tasks associated with entries referring to the aircraft are never executed. In such a case, time-triggered deletion KSs would remove the entries from the local databases and the associated tasks from the control databases.

Consequently, it is necessary to prevent time-triggered KSs from doing what they are supposed to do when a task has not yet been executed. This is done by dividing the priority of the task by two, thus potentially making it higher than any other priority in the Level Manager -- a priority of zero is the highest possible priority. Next, the entry referred to by all over-due tasks is flagged so that time-triggered deletion KSs will ignore it. The expiry time is also increased: it is increased by an equivalent of one radar sweep period. The latter (together with the marking process mentioned above) is necessary for the correct implementation of deletion in Level Managers which do not prioritise their tasks.

The above scheme, although workable, has a disadvantage: it will prefer old entries to new ones. This entails that the system becomes increasingly out of synchronisation with the real airspace. In mitigation, it must be said that this scheme does not permit aircraft to pass through the monitored sector unnoticed; it would only be required when the load on the system was so great that all real airspace aircraft cannot be attended to within the cycle time of each Level Manager.* If very fast hardware were available, CASSANDRA-II might never enter this state: CASSANDRA-II has to wait until the 1990s for field trials even to become conceivable, so fast enough hardware might be available.

In the input Level Manager, there are both match- and time-triggered collection KSs. Here, though, only an entry which matches a deletion KS condition is deleted. This is because there are no temporally-ordered links between entries (there are, actually, only Dependent slots in the entries on the input level, so inverses are not available).

Deletion KSs are selected by the normal scheduler bound to a Level Manager. It is a purely local scheduling decision to execute one or more deletion tasks. In the normal run of things, it would be beneficial to run all the match-triggered tasks and at least one time-triggered task just to keep the Level Manager's local database to a reasonable size. If a resource-sensitive scheduler were available,** the pay-off between deletion and leaving outdated entries on the blackboard could be calculated and a scheduling decision made on that basis. The basic scheduling regime used when deletion KSs are present is shown in

* An open question is how to get systems to reason about their resources and their limitations. Alternative schemes might be employed as the load increases: such schemes could be invoked as a result of explicit reasoning about resources.

** This is difficult to build in FranzLisp because the amount of information about memory occupancy and object size given by Franz is insufficient to make sensible decisions.

fig. 6.8 (note that more than one KS can be scheduled per cycle).

The deletion KSs in CASSANDRA-II know about the links between entries in the local database and, so, can modify the entry which is at the other end of the link from the entry which is being deleted. Because of the uniformity of the link structure in CASSANDRA-II and because of the fact that there are so few link types, deletion Knowledge Sources determine the action to be performed for each link type by executing a case statement: the knowledge of links in CASSANDRA-II is compiled into Knowledge Sources in the sense that it is represented as executable code.

Knowledge of link type and link inverses is an issue which was discussed when introducing the model for deletion KSs: the links between entries should have explicit inverses so that a deletion KS can traverse the link to find the entry or entries which caused the one which is being removed to exist. Without knowledge of inverses, the deletion KSs will leave dangling pointers which will reduce the performance of any KSs which follow links.

6.4. CONCLUSIONS

Having examined the implementation of CASSANDRA-II, it is necessary to consider those ways in which the system better implements the airspace monitoring task than would a blackboard system and just which parts of the architecture CASSANDRA-II has tested.

A straight blackboard implementation was first considered for CASSANDRA-II. There were problems with this, particularly in finding a suitable abstraction hierarchy. CASSANDRA-II monitors aircraft within a single sector. Within sectors, there are beacons and there is a division between upper and lower airspace. One abstraction hierarchy could be derived by grouping together beacons by geographical proximity: if that is done, there is the immediate problem that aircraft will, in general, be assigned arbitrarily to geographical areas and, hence, to abstraction levels. A slightly more natural way to arrange the blackboard would be to have three abstraction levels: one for the entire airspace, the next for the sectors and the last for individual aircraft. The problem with this is that CASSANDRA-II is designed for sector operation, so there is no airspace abstraction required. The final approach is to assign an abstraction level to each kind of conflict (vertical, longitudinal and lateral separation) and to cruise level allocation. Under this third

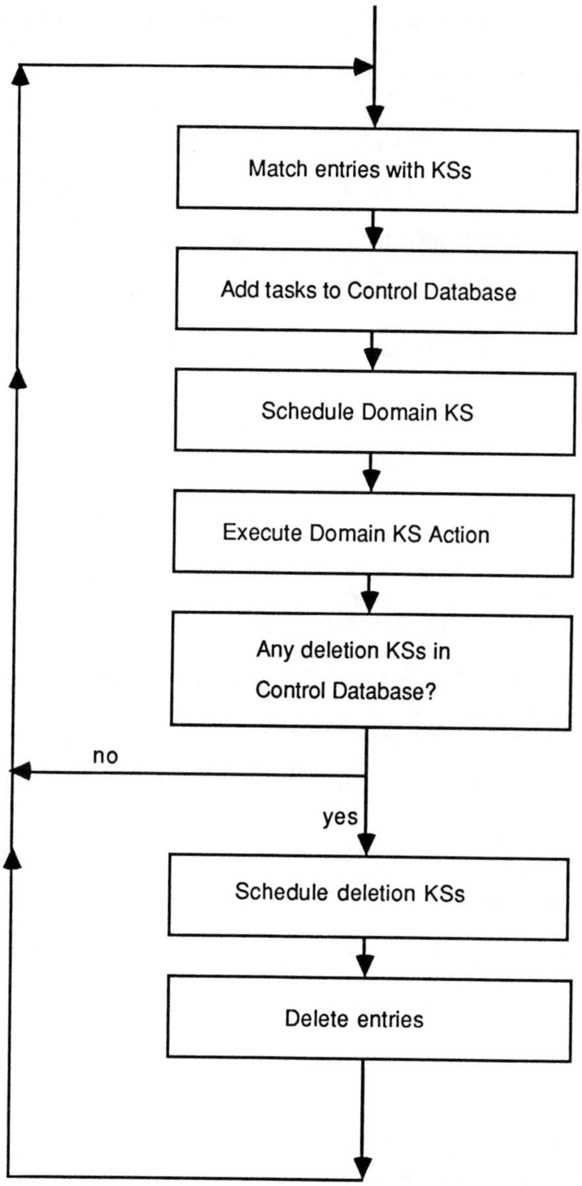

Fig 6.8

Scheduling with entry deletion KSs in a Level Manager in CASSANDRA-II scheme, there is no hierarchy, just a collection of levels each dealing with separate things. The blackboard architecture, therefore, imposed requirements which could not be met in this domain.

It has been pointed out that the airspace monitoring task was selected because the relevant knowledge appeared to be clearly separable into non-interacting categories and this, indeed, proved to be the case. The implementation of CASSANDRA-II tested the viability of the Level Manager construct by assigning a pair of Level Managers to each distinct area of knowledge possessed by the system: that is, there are Level Manager for Vertical, Lateral and Longitudinal separation, as well as for Cruise Level Allocation. Each Level Manager was equipped with a collection of Knowledge Sources which could trigger only on the contents of the owning Level Manager's local database.

Each Level Manager also had a purely local action interpreter and control component. The control components in CASSANDRA-II all operated on an independent basis and controlled the execution only of those Knowledge Sources held in the same Level Manager as the controller. The controllers implemented instantiations of generic control strategies (such as LIFO and Agenda) according to the individual needs of each Level Manager. Since the system functioned appropriately with local control, it can fairly be stated that the local control component of the architecture has been tested and shown to work satisfactorily.

A global control component was supplied to the system to co-ordinate the operations of the individual Level Managers. The global controller was extremely simple and activated Level Managers in a fixed sequence to ensure that information was propagated through the system in the correct manner. The inclusion of a global controller indicates that it is possible to control CASSANDRA systems at a level above that of the individual Level Manager if the problem requires it (the architecture specification is neutral as to the provision of global control, it should be noted).

Deletion Knowledge Sources were provided in CASSANDRA-II to test the knowledge-based deletion model. These Knowledge Sources functioned according to specification. This result indicates that the deletion model has some utility.

The main results of the CASSANDRA-II experiment is that the Level Manager construct, local control and the entry deletion model are all viable.

The major area which needed testing was inter-Level Manager communications. The task assigned to CASSANDRA-II was not interactive: information flows in only one direction through the system and hypotheses are not formed using any kind of feedback or feed-forward mechanisms. Clearly, this is an area which must be tested further: the WordSys experiment described in the next chapter was designed to test communications using a problem which is very much more interactive than is CASSANDRA-II's.

7. WordSys: A SECOND EXPERIMENT

7.1. INTRODUCTION

In order to assess the generality of the CASSANDRA architecture, a second experiment was planned. For the test to be genuine, it was necessary to find a problem which had none of the convenient properties of the airspace monitoring task. In particular, the problem had to be more 'interactive' than the previous experiment in the sense that Knowledge Sources in Level Managers should communicate in ways more varied than by simply sending messages without requiring information to be returned. In the airspace monitioring system, CASSANDRA-II, KSs in upper Level Managers just send entries to the corresponding lower Level Managers: they do not depend upon inter-Level Manager communication for anything other than to provide information upon which other KSs can directly operate.

In a more 'interactive' problem, KSs would have to send information to other Level Managers which would cause the incremental construction of solutions. That is, messages have to be sent back and forth during the construction of a solution.

To perform the second experiment, it was decided actually to construct a new system rather than to engage in a mere design experiment. This approach entails that more actual experience with the architecture is gained and new problems encountered (the hope was that severely limiting factors would be encountered).

During the period in which the second experiment was being considered, the NBB system (Craig, 1987) was being developed. It seemed reasonable to use one of the problems selected to test NBB as the second CASSANDRA experiment. Furthermore, it was decided to use a problem which had been specifically chosen for the blackboard system and to adopt it as a CASSANDRA test case *before* it had been implemented as a blackboard system. The reader should note that although the problem was *chosen* as a CASSANDRA test case before implementation of the CASSANDRA system was attempted, the NBB version, for a number of reasons, was the first implemented.

7.1.1. Aims

The specific aims of the second experiment were

(i) to test the applicability of the CASSANDRA architecture to a second domain, and

(ii) to test the validity of the message-passing component of the architecture.

The problem chosen for the second experiment was based on the word recognition problem examined by Rumelhart and McClelland (Rumelhart, 1982; McClelland, 1981). The problem seemed to be interesting and comparatively small; it also seemed to be a problem which required significant amounts of control. The chosen problem has the benefit that it is small enough to permit a comparatively full and complete description in a few pages.

7.1.2. Chapter Structure

This chapter is structured as follows. In the next section, the word recognition problem is described. The precise formulation differs from that of Rumelhart and McClelland insofar as no attempt was made to make the implementation faithful to human processing (so, for example, letter context is not considered), nor was the input as fine-structured as was the case in Rumelhart and McClelland's experiements. In section three, the CASSANDRA implementation of the system to 'solve' the recognition problem is described in some detail.* Section four considers the two experiments together. Section five of this chapter is a review of the CASSANDRA architecture: it considers the CASSANDRA architecture in the light of the theoretical problems raised about blackboard systems in chapter 3. The chapter concludes with a short, general review.

7.2. THE PROBLEM

This section presents the problem chosen for the second experiment. The problem is due to Rumelhart and McClelland (Rumelhart, 1982; McClelland, 1981). The problem can be stated as follows: From a sequence of stimuli which encode (in some fashion) a sequence of letters, try to discover the English word represented by the letter encodings. In other words, the problem is to try to find English

* The word *solve* is in quotes because the solution sought is to the question "how do humans recognise words?". The system described in this chapter answers another question: what does a CASSANDRA system which performs the word recognition task look like?

words whose constituent letters can plausibly be derived from an input which represents a sequence of letter encodings. The input to the system is intended to be complete in the sense that it will always contain four letters or a sequence of letters and non-letters whose length is always four; it is not intended that there be missing letters in the input sequence.

The input letters are encoded in a form which could be said to be similar in some respects to what is thought to be produced by the visual system when viewing sequences of letters on a page. In other words, there is noise present in the input which prevents the system from immediately reaching a correct solution to the problem.

One representation for letters which would approximate the sensory representation is a field of dots, each cluster of which represents a letter feature. This representation has the advantage that additional noise can be introduced into the 'visual' signal so that the hypothesised recognition mechanisms can be purturbed at will by the experimenter. From this input, letter features are extracted so that individual letters can be hypothesised. Once letters have been hypothesised, it is possible to determine English words which contain those letters in the order provided by the input representation. Notice here that there is an important constraint: the word hypotheses must be English words and not random collections of letters. This suggests that if a sequence of letters does not correspond to an English word, one or more letters must be rehypothesised. In addition, it is possible to use rules about word-formation in English to determine plausible letter hypotheses -- for example, the letters 'q' and 'k' rarely, if ever, appear next to each other in English words, but the letters 'c' and 'k' appear quite commonly in the order 'ck'.

A dot-based representation also permits non-letters to appear in the input. This entails that the quality of hypotheses may be subject to considerable variation, thus generating a large space within which to search for plausible letter hypotheses. Similarly, the effects of letters in sequence generates a large space within which to search for word hypotheses, given the possibility that letters within a sequence may be under-specified or that they may be 'non-letters' (combinations of dots, in the original representation, which do not form a letter in the Roman alphabet). These factors suggest that a considerable amount of control must be exercised in order that a system which solves this problem converges on a solution in an acceptable time.

The Rumelhart and McClelland experiments used a specially-designed font to represent characters.

For the purposes of the NBB test and the CASSANDRA experiment, a letter representation was chosen. The representation was designed so that it could still cater for variation in the input, but the size of the letter hypothesis space was somewhat smaller than would be one based on a dot representation. The reasons for this were that the amount of time which could be spent on experiment and on test preparation was limited, and that the existence of a program to help in the preparation of input data was considered to be beneficial if it would reduce the time required to set up a test. Rather than adopt a dot-field representation, the second experiment (and the NBB test) used a representation based on bit strings: a 32-bit word was used to represent each letter, with bits being set where there was a feature present in the input sequence.

The letter features encoded in this representation were lines: each of the 26 letters of the Roman alphabet was given a description as a set of line segments and each line segment was mapped on to a number. A total of 17 line segments was required to encode all letters, leaving 15 bits free for the introduction of random noise. This letter encoding, although it reduces the hypothesis space, still permits a large number of additional states. This is because extra line segments may be introduced into each letter, segments which do not appear in the encoding of standard English letters may be introduced, or the two effects may be combined. In addition, segments may be removed from an encoding or they may be displaced (e.g., a segment may be moved from position 10 to position 21).

The second simplification of this experiment was dictated by time: the time I could reasonably spend on this CASSANDRA experiment was highly limited. It was decided that the experimental system should not attempt to be faithful to the putative human processes which would account for data gathered from human subjects performing the word recognition test. The word recognition system was intended to be a fairly short test of an interpreter and of the CASSANDRA architecture, not an attempt to reproduce the results reported in (Rumelhart, 1982) and in (McClelland, 1981). This allowed the system to employ whatever means were at its disposal to hypothesise words. In turn, this permitted the NBB implementation to exercise features which would be expected to be used in other systems; in the case of the CASSANDRA implementation, similar reasons prevailed in addition to testing the architecture. In particular, this simplification allowed the coding of search methods as procedures in Knowledge Sources. It also allowed intermediate representations of letter and word hypotheses which are almost certainly not used by humans (the bit string representation, for example).

Although the implemented systems embody these simplifying assumptions, they still have fairly difficult tasks to perform simply because of the sizes of the search spaces involved. In addition, a dictionary of about 2100 English four-letter words was provided. The size of the dictionary (which could be expanded at will, for there was nothing in the system which dictated a word length of four -- four seemed to be the smallest number which would provide an interesting set of words) and the constraint that all hypothesised words be genuine English words added to the search task.

7.3. INTERACTION

It was stated above that a second experiment was decided upon because a more interactive problem was required. Interactive problems require message traffic between Level Managers. CASSANDRA-II employed only uni-directional communications and did not test the viability of the channel construct. The new problem had to involve two-way inter-Level Manager communication so that the behaviour of the architecture when interfaced to a message-passing system could be examined.

The word recognition problem, I believe, requires this kind of communication. It does so for the following reasons.

The recognition problem requires that words be constructed from letters which have been hypothesised from some representation of a perceptual input. The latter can be thought of as a feature-extraction process which still retains some noise in the input signal: features are not extracted in a pure form, but still retain some of the noise inherent in the environment. Letters are hypothesised from collections of features. Since the identification of a coherent set of features is not certain -- this is, initially, due to noise -- each letter hypothesised from the features must be open to revision. The input to the system consists of words of exactly four letters, so groups of four letter hypotheses, one letter hypothesis per letter position, are taken to form words. Since an individual letter may be incorrectly hypothesised from the input features, it is possible that the word formed by including an incorrect letter hypothesis in a given letter position will not appear in the English language. When a word does not appear in the English language, it is necessary to re-hypothesise one or more letters, thus making a correction to the word hypothesis. To re-hypothesise a letter, the input features must be consulted and an hypothesis which is better according to some set of criteria must be created.

The interactions between letter and word hypotheses are shown pictorially in figure 7.1.

When a word is not found, then, to be in the English language (or in the dictionary in the case of WordSys), one or more letters have to be identified as faulty and corrected.

Translating this into CASSANDRA terms, if we assume that there are three Level Managers, one for input, one for letter hypotheses and one for word hypotheses, there is two-way traffic between at least the letter and word hypothesis Level Managers. A rough outline of how the system operates is then as follows. Initially, the input is accepted by the input Level Manager and letters are hypothesised. The letter hypotheses are sent to the letter hypothesis Level Manager which groups them and sends them as words to the word hypothesis Level Manager. The word hypothesis Level Manager checks to see if the word hypothesis it has just received is in the dictionary. If it is, the word is a good hypothesis. If a word hypothesis is acceptable, this uni-directional transfer is perfectly acceptable and there is no interaction between the Level Managers in the system.

It is when a word hypothesis is unacceptable that interaction becomes an important factor in the system. When a word is rejected, one or more letters have to be re-hypothesised. Letter hypotheses are represented in the letter hypothesis Level Manager where they are retained in case of the need to re-form an hypothesis. When the word hypothesis Level Manager rejects a letter, therefore, it has to send a message to the letter hypothesis Level Manger informing it of the letter to re-hypothesise. Note that the word hypothesis Level Manager does not make any suggestions as to which replacement letters would be suitable candidates: the word hypothesis Level Manager is restricted to knowledge about words as complete entities: this is a highly restrictive assumption and, in a more interactive version (similar to Rumelhart and McClelland's original), such information could be made available to the letter re-hypothesisation process. When the letter hypothesis Level Manager has re-formulated an hypothesis for the letter, that hypothesis has to be sent back to the word hypothesis Level Manager. Since it is not guaranteed that the letter

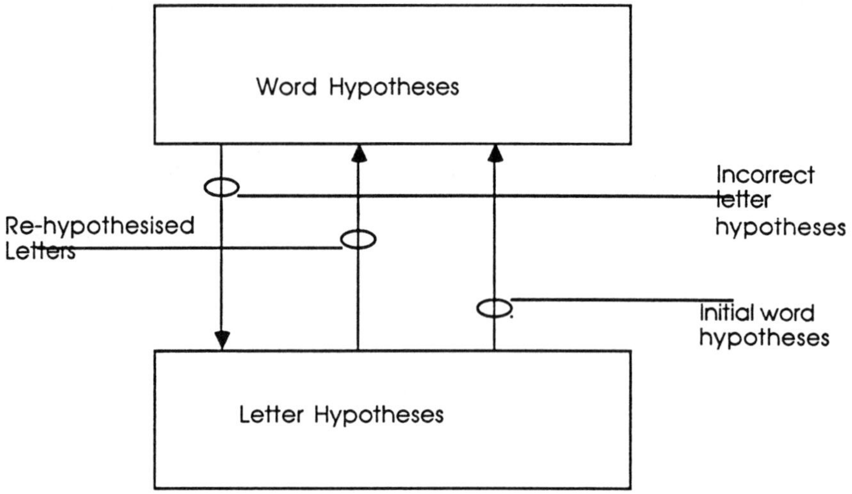

Fig. 7.1

Interactions Between Letter and Word Hypotheses

hypothesis Level Manager will find the correct letter hypothesis first time (and the presence of more than one incorrect letter in a word makes this unlikely due to the combinatorial effect of multiple, incorrect letters), there can be a sustained, two-way exchange of messages between the letter and word hypothesis Level Managers.

Depending upon how one sets up a CASSANDRA system to perform word recognition, there is a variety of ways in which one can arrange inter-Level Manager interaction. The scheme outlined above is the simplest and is the one actually adopted in WordSys, the reasons being that it is the simplest to arrange and that the simplest case may give some insights into more complex ones.

One alternative is to allow two-way interactions between all the Level Managers in a CASSANDRA implementation. When a letter hypothesis is rejected, for example, the letter hypothesis Level Manager sends a request to the input Level Manager for a new hypothesis to be formed from the input data for the letter position. When the input Level Manager has analysed the input data and formed a new hypothesis, the letter is sent to the letter hypothesis Level Manager to be forwarded to the word hypothesis Level Manager. This scheme was, in fact, rejected because all possible letter hypotheses were formed in the input Level Manager and stored in an independent database: this made the implementation easier and made processing a little faster.

Another alternative is to let the word hypothesis Level Manager communicate directly with the input Level Manager when it finds one or more incorrect letters. This would replace the bi-directional message-passing between the word and letter hypothesis Level Managers with communications between the word and input Level Managers, thus bypassing the letter hypothesis Level Manager. Since the word recognition problem can be formulated in terms of an abstraction hierarchy, this arrangement seemed inappropriate for it violated the hierarchy constraints; it could also make the letter hypothesis Level Manager redundant after the first processing of the input.

The main feature of this problem is that it requires bi-directional exchange of information between two Level Managers. Which Level Managers engage in information exchange depends upon how the implementation is arranged. It is possible also to increase the amount of interaction between Level Managers by changing the knowledge they possess and by changing the effects which determine hypothesis rejection. The implementation described below makes no use of contextual effects: it is a simplification, in this respect. WordSys could be extended to take context into account and such an extension would require the addition of knowledge of which letters may be adjacent in valid English words and knowledge of syllable structure, amongst other things. Such an extension of the basic system was not undertaken because of time constraints.

7.4. THE CASSANDRA IMPLEMENTATION

The CASSANDRA implementation of the word recognition system (called WordSys) contained three Level Managers, one each for the perceptual input, letter hypotheses and word hypotheses. WordSys was constructed on a single cpu machine so the effects of parallelism could not be judged. The WordSys Level Managers will be called **Perceptual-Input, Letter-Hypothesis** and **Word-Hypothesis** below.* In addition to the Level Managers and their KSs, the system contained two separate databases: the letter database and the dictionary. These databases were wholly separate from the Level Managers, but the letter database could be consulted by KSs belonging to the Perceptual-Input and Letter-Hypothesis Level Managers; the dictionary could be consulted by KSs belonging to the Word-Hypothesis Level Manager. In both cases, the external databases were read-only.

Each Level Manager contains hypotheses about a particular kind of entity in the word recognition problem. The Word-Hypothesis LM contains entries representing hypotheses about English words which can be derived from the input sequence. The Letter-Hypothesis LM contains entries representing hypotheses about individual letters. The Perceptual-Input Level Manager contained entries which represent the input sequence from which word hypotheses were to be derived. The entries in the Perceptual-Input Level Manager's local database are placed there by an external function. Once an entry has been received by the Perceptual-Input LM, the recogntion process can begin.

The Level Manager configuration is shown in figure 7.2. The arrows connecting Level Managers denote communication channels. In the case of the channels which carry information between Level Managers (and not between Level Managers and the outside world), the type of information which can

* The convention in this chapter is that Level Manager names are hyphenated and KS names are not. Word-Hypothesis is a Level Manager name; HypothesiseWord is a KS name.

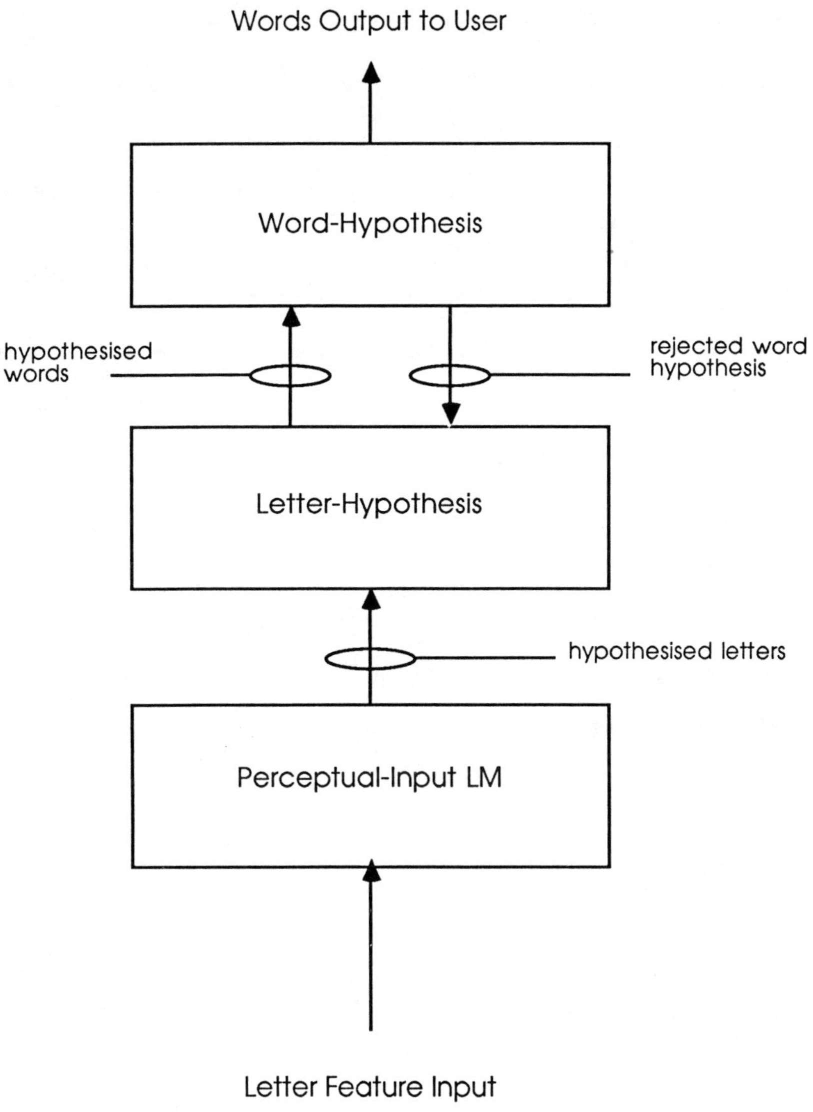

Fig 7.2

WordSys Level Manager Configuration

legally be passed is indicated in the figure.

The CASSANDRA implementation of WordSys contains nine Knowledge Sources: the NBB conventional blackboard implementation contains six. Two of the additional KS were due to the division of a task into two components -- the divisions were caused by the requirement in the CASSANDRA architecture that there should be no action-at-a-distance (i.e., the actions of a KS should cause only local state changes unless the action contains a *send* operation); the third was required to halt the system when acceptable word hypotheses have been generated. The KSs contain knowledge of various kinds which enable the system to hypothesise words from the input representation. They differ in internal structure from the KSs in CASSANDRA-II. KSs in WordSys have an event-based trigger condition, a state-based precondition and an action composed of a set of production rules. In addition, the KSs in WordSys had *obviation-conditions*, that is, extra conditions which, if they evaluate to *true*, cause the KS instantiation to be removed from the control database. Obviation-conditions are evaluated immediately after preconditions have been tested. The role of obviation-conditions is to provide an extra check in KSs, but one which is aimed at determining why the KS should *not* be considered for execution. One obviation-condition was found necessary during the construction of WordSys.

WordSys KS actions are composed of production rules. The actions associated with the rules are of two basic kinds: local and non-local. Local rule actions add or modify entries in the database local to the Level Manager in which each KS reside. Non-local actions send information to other Level Managers. Both kinds of action are represented by a generic **PROPOSE** action, the arguments of which determine the kind of action to be performed. The use of a single **PROPOSE** action also allows checks to be made that the action is being used correctly: the version of **PROPOSE** used in WordSys has access to system configuration information. **PROPOSE** is, in fact, a generalisation of the corresponding NBB function.

The basic strategy for assembling word hypotheses is to proceed bottom-up from Perceptual-Input, through Letter-Hypothesis to Word-Hypothesis. The three Level Managers in the system can be thought of as building an abstraction hierarchy with Perceptual-Input the lowest level and Word-Hypothesis the highest. When an entry has been sent to Perceptual-Input, letter hypotheses can be formed and sent to the Letter-Hypothesis Level Manager. The letter hypothesis entries in Letter-Hypothesis' local database form the basis for generating word hypotheses to be sent to the Word-Hypothesis Level Manager. Output from the system is taken from Word-Hypothesis.

The basic bottom-up strategy works well when the input sequence posted to Perceptual-Input is such that an English word in the dictionary can be directly matched (i.e., matched completely with no gaps indicating faulty letter hypotheses) as is the case when a perfect representation of the word 'DICK' is input to the system.* By 'perfect representation' it is intended that each representation of a letter in the input sequence contains exactly the same features as the entry for the letter in the letter database -- there are no additional features, nor any missing features, nor any altered features. Since 'DICK' appears in the dictionary and because each of the letters 'D', 'I', 'C' and 'K' precisely matches the templates in the letter database, the system is able immediately to output the word as the best word hypothesis. The derivation of the hypothesis 'DICK' from the input was a simple bottom-up process because the information in the input was perfect.

In the case of another input which represented the non-word 'OICK' (derived by exchanging the first letter of 'DICK' for the feature sequence for letter 'O'), the bottom-up process is clearly not adequate. The reason for this is that the dictionary contains no word composed of the letters 'O', 'I', 'C' and 'K' (there may be such a word in English, but the fact remains that it was not in the dictionary). In this case, the initial hypothesis 'OICK' cannot be correct because of the initial letter, so another letter has to be hypothesised for position one in the string. Rehypothesising a letter involves requesting the Letter-Hypothesis Level Manager to create a new letter hypothesis which could plausibly occur as the first letter of this sequence. In the implemented version of WordSys, the re-hypothesis task is performed not by trying to find a letter which can plausibly start a word ending in 'ICK', but by trying to find a letter which best matches the input letter's features (in this case, the features which determine the letter 'O').

Although this is not actually the best way to do the re-hypothesis task, it has the advantage of generating a number of spurious hypotheses which exercises the message-passing system. Since hypotheses and requests to re-hypothesise a letter are sent between the word and letter hypothesis Level Managers, the generation of spurious hypotheses causes extra messages to be sent. It is also worth noting, at this point,

* The dictionary was generated from the spelling dictionary provided with UNIX. It contains a number of proper nouns.

that Knowledge Sources in WordSys never wait for information: that is, Knowledge Source preconditions do not send requests to other Level Managers. The reason for this is that there is no need to use this feature of the architecture: since the system could be built without it, it appeared to be better engineering not to force waiting preconditions upon the system.

After three attempts to find letters which are close to 'O' in terms of features and generating word hypotheses, WordSys determined that the best word hypothesis to be 'LICK' (the letter 'D' in the letter feature database is encoded in a form which closely resembles the lower case form -- 'd', that is -- so 'LICK' is none too bad an hypothesis).

Similar experiments were performed by altering letters in the string 'DICK' and by changing features within individual letters -- in each case, the output hypotheses were considered to be fairly reasonable. In an experiment in which the letter 'I' in the input sequence 'DICK' was modified to contain one erroneous line segment, WordSys correctly identified the input word as 'DICK' in exactly the same number of interpreter cycles as it had when the input was perfect for 'DICK'.

7.4.1. Representations

This section is concerned with the representations of letters and words in the WordSys program. A number of different representations are employed by the system, the simplest of which is the word representation: it consists simply of a string of ASCII upper case alphabetic characters. Letters are also sometimes represented as ASCII upper case alphabetic characters and sometimes as bit strings of length 32. The easiest way to see where the different representations are used is to examine the formation of input and its consequent processing.

For each run of the system, the user has to create new input. WordSys will only process one input letter sequence at a time (this is to make experiments simpler). A separate program is used to create the input which is placed in a file. The input-creation program asks the user to input four upper case letters. It then asks if any of the letters is to be altered. When each letter is input by the program, it is converted into a list of features -- each feature is a line segment. Line segments, which are denoted by numbers in the range 0 ... 16, represent the lines which together form a letter. If the user states that s/he wishes to alter a feature, it is the feature list representation which is operated upon. When a feature is altered, its numerical value can be changed (the value has to be in the range 0 ... 31), or one or more new features can be added to the feature list. When features are added, or features are changed, noise of a fairly obvious sort is introduced into the letter representation. A feature can be removed from the feature list by setting it to a value already present in the list. The input program writes the features off to file for use by the WordSys recogniser.

When a letter features file has been created, it can be supplied to WordSys. WordSys reads in the feature lists and converts each letter's feature list into a bit string of length 32. Each number in the feature list corresponds to a bit position in the string.* Within each bit string, the feature is marked as *present* when the bit in the position indicated by the feature list element is *on*. A complete input word is represented by a vector of four bit strings (four is a convenience -- there are no manifest constants nor any length declarations in the actual code: four is the length of all inputs because the dictionary contains only four letter words). The vector of bit string representations is held in entries in the Perceptual-Input Level Manager's local database.

When a letter is to be hypothesised, the word vector is accessed and the corresponding bit string is fetched. Each bit string represents a letter with varying amounts of noise. The letter hypothesis-forming KSs look the bit string up in the letter database and determine the closest match. The match process is accomplished by considering the bit string as an unsigned 32-bit number (this is one of the two reasons for selecting the bit string representation: the other was its compactness). An arithmetic comparison determines the goodness of match and a difference measure is also computed from the letter database entry and the input letter representation. When the best letter candidate has been retrieved, the representation changes to ASCII upper case letters. The letter database contains bit strings as keys and ASCII upper case letters as data, so the matching process yields an ASCII letter as well as a similarity measure. When a letter hypothesis is created from the letter database lookup, the entry in the Letter-Hypothesis Level Manager contains the original bit representation, the similarity measure and the best hypothesis expressed as an

* An alternative to the representation chosen here is one in which the feature numbers do not map onto contiguous bits. At present, feature 0 maps to bit 0, feature 1 maps to bit 1, and so on. An alternative, which introduces the possibility of clustering noise around features, is to map features to alternate bits, clustering some features into sequences, but others into distinct regions of the bit string.

ASCII upper case letter. In addition, the entry contains the index into the input letter feature vector so that the letter hypothesis' position in the word to be hypothesised can be determined.

Word hypotheses are generated from letter hypotheses. Word hypotheses are represented as strings of upper case ASCII letters. They are assembled from the constituent letter hypotheses in a direct fashion: the ASCII letters are taken from the letter hypotheses currently active in the Letter-Hypothesis Level Manager and are assembled in order to form a word hypothesis.

The multiple representations in WordSys are motivated by the following considerations. Firstly, the input to the system should permit variations in letter input, and, in particular, should allow arbitrary amounts of noise to be included. Second, by encoding letter features as bit strings, a compact representation is to be had; it was also the case that fairly simple and obvious numerical and bit operations could be employed to derive information from the features (for example determining the goodness of match) -- the operations required by the letter manipulation processes correspond very closely to what could easily be achieved by employing a basically numeric representation (this appeared to be good software engineering practice). The ASCII character representation was motivated by the need to present the WordSys user with word hypothesis output in an easily recognisable form: that requirement clearly suggested that the character rather than internal code representation be used.

7.4.2. Knowledge Sources

WordSys contains nine Knowledge Sources, most of which engage in communication between the Letter-Hypothesis and Word-Hypothesis Level Managers. An additional *Stop* KS was added to the CASSANDRA implementation: this KS belongs to the Word-Hypothesis Level Manager and causes the system to halt when an acceptable word hypothesis is present in the local entry database.* The Stop KS works by sending a **STOP** message to all other Level Managers in WordSys. The remaining KSs implement word recognition knowledge fairly directly. The problem solving KSs in WordSys are: *HypthesiseLetter, HypothesiseWord, MakeCompleted, FindWordCandidate, ReHypothesiseLetters1, ReHypothesiseLetters2, AddNewWordCandidate* and *NewWordHypothesis*. The majority of these KSs were adapted from the NBB

* This KS was altered in some runs to permit multiple solutions. Since the KS is a very small module, the modification task was relatively simple.

implementation of WordSys fairly directly: their texts needed only minor edits to cope with the changed environment. The edits were of two basic types:

(i) a change of the trigger condition to reflect the fact that triggering may only occur locally (all preconditions in the NBB version evaluated locally to the triggering level), and

(ii) a change to each **PROPOSE** action so that entries would be posted to the local database or would be sent to the appropriate external Level Manager.

The major changes involved the KS called *ReHypothesiseLetters*: in the CASSANDRA implementation, this KS had to be split into two new KSs to avoid action-at-a-distance. The new KSs are called *RehypothesiseLetters1* and *ReHypothesiseLetters2*. The KS *AddNewWordCandidate* is completely new to the CASSANDRA implementation. The WordSys Knowledge Sources will now be described briefly: the descriptions roughly follow the order in which the KSs are executed.

The relationships between the various Knowledge Sources and Level Managers in the system are dipicted in figure 7.3. In the figure, each Level Manager is represented as a horizontal line. The Level Manager within which each KS triggers is shown as a ring on the corresponding line, and the Level Manager to which information is sent is represented by the line at the end of the arrow representing the KS's action.

HypothesiseLetter triggers on the contents of the Perceptual-Input Level Manager entry database. When a new letter feature sequence is input to the system, this KS triggers. The KS examines all the letter features and attempts to hypothesise a letter for each list of features. It does this by consulting the letter database. When the letter database is consulted by this KS, what amounts to a best-first search is initiated. HypothesiseLetter finds the best matches for the features on which it has triggered and, by doing this, it creates a table containing successively worse matches (the table is ordered by the goodness of match). This table is used for all subsequent letter feature matches to optimise search times. Upon finding the best matches for the input sequence, one entry is created by HypothesiseLetter for each letter in the input sequence and inserted into a message: the messages are sent to the Letter-Hypothesis Level Manager via the message-passing system. The message contains the letter hypothesis together with similarity and location information. The table used for subsequent best-first searches in the space of letter hypotheses is also

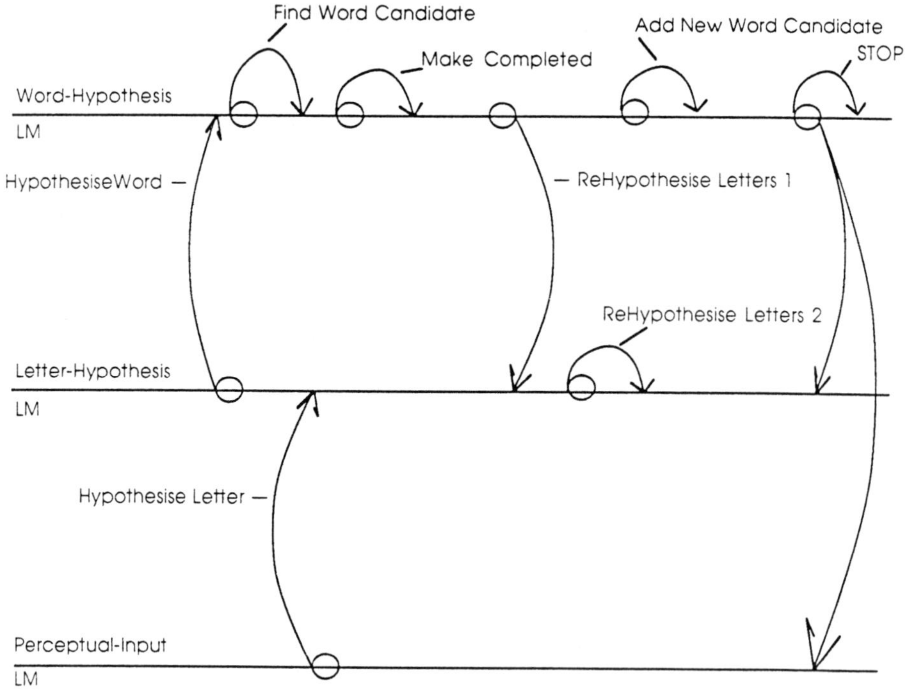

Fig 7.3

The Relationship between KSs and LMs in WordSys

conceptually sent to the Letter-Hypothesis LM, for once HypothesiseLetter has executed, no more use is required of the information held in the latest entry in the entry database local to Perceptual-Input (in the implementation described here, because the program ran in one address space and was sequential, the best-first table was shared).

Use is not required of information in entries in Perceptual-Input once HypothesiseLetter has executed because the relevant data (the location of the hypothesised letter in the input word, the bit string representation and the closeness of match) is sent together with the letter hypothesis to the Letter-Hypothesis Level Manager: this reduces the amount of communication required between Level Managers. In a conventional blackboard implementation, the search required to locate this information is also reduced -- this reduces the computational overhead in running the system.

Letter hypotheses are sent to the Letter-Hypothesis Level Manager in a **NEW** message. Messages in WordSys have information associated with them which tells the receiving Level Manager what to do with them. A **NEW** message tells the receiver that the entry should be added to its local database to cause a triggering event. A **MODIFY** message tells the receiver that the specified entry should have the attribute named by the message modified to hold the value provided by the message (**MODIFY** messages also cause triggering events, as do **ADD** messages). More will be said about messages below. When the Letter-Hypothesis LM receives the letter hypotheses generated by HypothesiseLetter, it adds them to its local database, thus causing HypothesiseWord to be triggered. (Note that messages and entries will be described henceforth as if they were identical).

HypothesiseWord triggers on entries in Letter-Hypothesis' local database. Unlike the majority of the KSs in WordSys, this KS has a fairly complex precondition. Specifically, the precondition checks to see that there are as many active letter hypothesis entries as there are letters in the input sequence (the length of the input sequence is held as an attribute of every letter hypothesis, so there is no need to provide HypothesiseWord with a constant word length nor is there the need for an enquiry message to be sent to the Perceptual-Input Level Manager so that length information can be provided).

An active hypothesis is one whose *Status* attribute holds the value *Active*. The values of the *Status* attribute are used extensively in WordSys, as will become clear. Only active hypotheses may be considered for inclusion in word hypotheses: an inactive hypothesis is one which has been rejected by another KS because it did not lead to an acceptable word hypothesis.

If there are fewer active letter hypotheses than letters in the input sequence, HypothesiseWord cannot execute. If there are as many active hypotheses as letter positions, the KS collects the hypotheses, orders them, extracts the ASCII letters and creates a string. The string, together with other information, is placed in an entry and is sent to the Word-Hypothesis Level Manager in a **NEW** message. The other information includes the identifiers of the Letter-Hypothesis entries which formed the word hypothesis: the identifiers are held in sequence order so that letter hypothesis entries can readily be identified if they represent incorrect or inappropriate letters. The *Status* of the entry sent to Word-Hypothesis is *Candidate* indicating that is should be considered for matching against the dictionary.

When Word-Hypothesis receives a **NEW** message containing a new word hypothesis it puts the entry held in the message in its entry database, and the FindWordCandidate Knowledge Source is triggered. This KS looks up the hypothesised word in the dictionary. The lookup procedure returns information about the closeness of match between the hypothesised word and the best matching entry in the dictionary. More importantly, the lookup procedure flags with an asterisk any letters which do not match the best fitting dictionary entry. FindWordCandidate puts a new entry in the local database of its LM (the Word-Hypothesis Level Manager). At the same time FindWordCandidate triggers (as a result of adding a new word hypothesis to the local database in the Word-Hypothesis Level Manager), the KS MakeCompleted also triggers. MakeCompleted checks the word hypothesis to see if it is in the dictionary in complete form (i.e., if there is a dictionary entry identical to the hypothesis): if it is, the word hypothesis entry's *Status* attribute is set to *Completed* and an acceptable word hypothesis has been found.

A constraint on word hypotheses is that they *must* be English words in the dictionary. MakeCompleted has a precondition which performs the dictionary check. The precondition requires the representation of the letter sequence in the word hypothesis to be in a form suitable for direct lookup in the dictionary: this representation is created by FindWordCandidate. Part of FindWordCandidate's action converts the word representation into a dictionary match record so that the match information returned by the dictionary interface can be handled in a clean fashion (the interface returns a number of items of information to the

KS, not just a letter string). In order that MakeCompleted's precondition be satisfied, the word hypothesis representation change must have been completed: this is an example of the *implicit* sequencing which is quite common in blackboard systems -- the same implicit sequencing was present in the conventional NBB implementation of WordSys (other examples can be found in PROTEAN and the Blackboard Control Model). In other words, because there is some attribute that is not filled or does not have the correct value, some Knowledge Sources are unable to trigger, but when the information becomes available, they trigger and can be executed. The point is that this mechanism can be exploited to create explicit sequences of Knowledge Source executions.

The KS ReHypothesiseLetters1 also makes use of an implicit sequence. It is triggered when a new word hypothesis appears in Word-Hypothesis' local database. This KS has a simple precondition: it checks for the presence of asterisks in the word hypothesis which caused it to trigger. Asterisks cannot be present unless the word hypothesis has been checked against the dictionary, so ReHypothesiseLetters1 depends upon the fact that FindWordCandidate has been executed by the time its precondition is tested. ReHypothesiseLetters1 does not examine the *Status* attribute of its triggering entry because, by definition, a completed word hypothesis contains no asterisks. ReHypothesiseLetters1's action changes the value of the *Status* attribute of its triggering entry to *Flawed* and then identifies the positions of the asterisks in the letter string. Once it has located the asterisks, it can determine the identifiers of the letter hypotheses which have been identified as faulty (this is done locally by correlating the letter positions with the contents of the attribute which represents the derivation of the hypothesis from entries in Letter-Hypothesis). ReHypothesiseLetters1 sends a **MODIFY** message to the Letter-Hypothesis Level Manager. The message tells Letter-Hypothesis to modify the *Status* attribute of each entry it mentions to *Rejected*.

When a *Status* value of a Letter-Hypothesis entry is modified to *Rejected*, ReHypothesiseLetters2 is triggered. The precondition of this KS checks to see if there are any more entries with a *Rejected* status. Since preconditions are checked some time after triggering, and since preconditions are checked on every cycle, the KS will always find the correct number of rejected letter hypotheses. In this implementation of the CASSANDRA architecture, entries in a Level Manager's input queue are processed during the triggering portion of the basic Level Manager cycle (the trigger-precondition-schedule-execute cycle typical of blackboard systems) at a time immediately after all locally generated triggering events have been processed. That is, a Level Manager only examines its input queue just *before* it is about to process preconditions. When the action of ReHypothesiseLetters2 is executed, it collects all letter hypotheses with *Status* equal to *Rejected* and changes the value of *Status* to *Cancelled*, thus preventing other instantiations of itself from having their preconditions satisfied. When all the *Status* attributes have been changed, the KS rehypothesises letters for each cancelled letter hypothesis -- it does this using the best-first search table created earlier. Each new letter hypothesis is added to the Letter-Hypothesis local database via a purely local **PROPOSE** action.

The entries created by ReHypothesiseLetters2 have an attribute called *WordHypothesis* which contains the name of the word hypothesis which was marked as flawed and which caused the re-hypothesise KSs to come into action. The *WordHypothesis* attribute is used to cause NewWordHypothesis to send a new word hypothesis to the Word-Hypothesis Level Manager. NewWordHypothesis works by finding all letter hypotheses which have a *WordHypothesis* attribute (letter hypotheses created by HypothesiseLetter do not have this attribute, so the condition is satisfied -- the interpreter considers an empty attribute to be the same as a non-existent attribute -- this is basically similar to the Closed World Assumption). It sends a **NEW** message to Word-Hypothesis which contains the letter hypotheses thus discovered: the message contains the individual letter hypotheses together with the indentifier of the originating word hypothesis. The arrival of the message causes the KS AddNewWordCandidate to trigger. This KS finds the originating word hypothesis -- the one which caused the re-hypothesis task to begin -- and merges its correct letters with the newly hypothesised corrections: each newly hypothesised letter is put in the correct place in the letter string contained in the word hypothesis. Note, though, that the letter string is copied: a new word hypothesis entry is created by AddNewWordCandidate and is linked to the originating word hypothesis via the *ExpandsWord* attribute -- this is so that the output routines can print the sequence of hypotheses which originated from an original incorrect word hypothesis. The entry added to the Word-Hypothesis Level Manager's local entry database causes FindWordCandidate to trigger, thus potentially repeating the rehypothesis events.

The activities of WordSys terminate when the Stop KS is executed. Stop, as was mentioned above, checks to see if there is an acceptable word hypothesis in the Word-Hypothesis Level Manager's local database. The KS was changed so that it would cause termination when there was more than one such word hypothesis and when a maximum number of word hypothesis entries had been added to Word-Hypothesis' entry database (the limit was typically set to 20 so as to avoid long runs). The unique action of Stop is to send the **STOP** message to all other Level Managers in the system. When a Level Manager receives this message it immediately terminates.

7.4.3. Deletion KSs

Deletion KSs were added to WordSys for some runs after it had been exercised on a few test cases. Deletion Knowledge Sources were comparatively easy to construct because the *Status* attribute changed its value to reflect entry utility. The conditions under which an entry could be deleted were quite easily discovered and so deletion KSs could be constructed with relative ease. For entries representing letter hypotheses, when the *Status* attribute changed its value to *Cancelled*, the entry could be deleted from the entry database. When entries in the Word-Hypothesis entry database had their status changed to *Superseded*, they could be deleted. The *Superseded* value for Word-Hypothesis entries was set by FindWordCandidate when it triggered on a word hypothesis which was created as a result of a re-hypothesise process.

The obvious condition for deleting the entry in the database of the Perceptual-Input Level Manager is that HypothesiseLetter has been executed. In fact, no deletion KS is provided for this Level Manager because none was considered really necessary.

Since deletion KSs depend upon the value of the *Status* attribute, and since changes to the attribute's value are important only after the KS which changes the value has terminated, deletion KSs are always guaranteed to execute in the correct order. It should be noted, in conclusion, that all deletion KSs operate locally: they do not cause any entry deletions to be made other than in the Level Manager within which they reside -- there is no actual use, therefore, made of the **DELETE** message type. It should also be noted that, due to the way in which the *Status* attribute changes value, there was no risk of deleting information in one Level Manager which could later be of use (an example of this is the deletion of word hypotheses which would furnish correct letters to complete an hypothesis created as a result of the presence of asterisks in the letter sequence).

7.4.4. Messages

Level Managers in the CASSANDRA architecture communicate by sending messages. The WordSys interpreter provides for four message types: **ADD, MODIFY, NEW** and **DELETE**. Of these, only **NEW** and **MODIFY** are used by WordSys.

A **NEW** message contains a complete entry. When a Level Manager receives a **NEW** message, it adds the entry to its entry database. When a Level Manager receives a **MODIFY** message, it extracts the entry specification, the attribute and value information from the message and changes the entry's attribute to contain the value specified by the message. In WordSys, the entry specification is always the identifier of the entry on which the attribute to be modified is held. This is possible because information was (somewhat) redundantly stored in entries. Specifying entries in **MODIFY**, **ADD** and **DELETE** messages by name avoids the description problem discussed when the architecture was presented. The receipt of a message of any of these types causes Knowledge Source triggering in the receiving Level Manager.

The **ADD** message type is very similar to the **MODIFY** type. It contains an entry specification, an attribute name and a value. The interpretation of **ADD** messages is that the attribute should be added to the specified entry and should have the specified value. A precondition of the add operation is that the attribute is not already present in the entry (if it is, a **MODIFY** operation should have been performed). The final message type, **DELETE**, has the interpretation that the specified entry should be deleted from the receiving Level Manager's entry database.

When a WordSys Level Manager receives a message, it interprets it according to its type. For example, when Word-Hypothesis receives a **NEW** message, it extracts the entry and adds it to its entry database. When the operation specified by the message being processed is performed, triggering events are caused: this is because the local database operations involved in interpreting a message are precisely those involved in KS triggering. Where Level Manager status enquiries are incorporated in the set of message types, triggering need not be an issue, but this depends upon how control information is represented -- in WordSys, all message types map directly to local database operations. No Knowledge Sources in WordSys need send enquiry messages, it should be noted: this is, in part due to the redundant storage of information and in part due to the task. The handling of inter-Level Manager messages in WordSys conformed to the constraints imposed by the CASSANDRA architecture.

7.4.5. Control

Since the CASSANDRA architecture is different because of its decentralised control, it is necessary to consider the treatment of control in WordSys. Control provided the biggest surprise in the experiments. Because of the apparent structure of the problem, a great deal of control was expected: this opinion was reinforced by the fact that the initial bottom-up strategy had to be followed by a period in which the locus of control passed repeatedly between Word-Hypothesis and Letter-Hypothesis Level Managers in the CASSANDRA implementation and abstraction levels in the NBB implementation. The NBB version was implemented without a scheduler during the initial construction phase: this was because the interpreter was under test and a scheduler could have provided spurious information upon which to base bug diagnoses.

It was intended that a scheduler be added to the NBB implementation once a significant number of the KSs had been tested (basically, after one KS from each abstraction level had been tested). The initial tests indicated that the *Status* attribute value changes were sufficient, together with the precondition tests, to cause the behaviour desired of the system. This remained true even after the full complement of KSs had been introduced into the system. In short, the change of value of the *Status* attribute was sufficient, when combined with the preconditions used in the various KSs to control the system. It is a fact that the NBB version of the system does not uselessly execute a KSAR during a run (KSARs are selected for execution when they are at the front of the agenda -- there is no scheduling criterion and the precondition matcher merely adds new KSARs to the front of the agenda when a KS's precondition has been satisfied).

There was also nothing unusual in the way in which the KSs had been constructed: they were programmed directly from a specification of the task they had to perform. If there was anything special about the way in which the NBB KSs were designed it was that they were designed without any thought of control -- control was to have been provided by a control blackboard and control KSs using the Blackboard Control Model. The *Status* attribute was introduced only to assist the control KSs when they were introduced. As KS development progressed, it became clear that the *Status* attribute was needed by some problem solving KSs, particularly during the re-hypothesis phase of the control strategy. Even when this attribute became important to the problem solving KSs, its use was restricted to cases in which it was considered genuinely useful. Similar remarks apply to the *ExpandsWord* attribute. The surprise was, in short, that so much control could be achieved using these attributes in conjunction with the preconditions so obviously suggested by the problem decomposition.** The decision to re-hypothesise was taken by Knowledge Sources. It would be possible to make the local controller in the word hypothesis Level Manager take it. Making the decision part of the control structure is equally valid, but costs an extra entry: it was decided that Knowledge Sources have the most immediate knowledge about hypotheses and this motivated giving them the decision-making power.

In the CASSANDRA implementation of WordSys a two-level agenda was maintained in each Level Manager. The agenda was divided into a sub-agenda for KSARs whose triggers had been satisfied and one for KSARs which had satisfied triggers *and* preconditions: only those KSARs with satisfied triggers and preconditions were eligible for execution. The local control structure in each WordSys Level Manager was: just execute the first eligible task in the local agenda's list of KSARs, just as it had been for the NBB implementation. This scheme worked very well for the NBB version and no reason was seen to alter matters for the CASSANDRA implementation. Each Level Manager had a local agenda as prescribed by the CASSANDRA architecture, although in this case the agenda was divided into two.

The local controller in each Level Manager in WordSys simply took the first KSAR from the agenda and executed it. The agenda was un-ordered, so the first KSAR executed was always the one most recently added. This control regime was used in every Level Manager in the system. It was expected that some genuine control strategy would have to be specified, but this scheme worked and worked quite well, so it was never altered. In a sense, the order in which tasks were executed was not constrained. For a number of KSs in WordSys, once its precondition had failed, it was never possible for the KSAR to become eligible for execution again because the precondition would never again become *true*. This indicates an implicit control structure in the system *over and above* the explicit scheduler.

At a more global level, there was also very minimal control. The passing of entries via the message-passing system and the value of the *Status* attribute were the basic control devices. In addition, Level

** The reader should, of course, not take these remarks as suggesting that this is the *only* way to structure a blackboard problem solver for this problem, but it is, nevertheless, a perfectly legal blackboard system insofar as none of the architectural constraints is ever violated.

Managers were selected for execution within a simple loop: each Level Manager in turn was activated (in the order Perceptual-Input, Letter-Hypothesis, Word-Hypothesis) and was suspended when all of the eligible KSARs in its agenda had been executed. Since there was only ever one KSAR in Perceptual-Input's agenda, it effectively ran only once per session. The message-passing system made entries available to Level Managers and, on receipt of a message, each Level Manager would take appropriate action, thus causing local triggering events. Local triggering events caused KSARs to be added to the local agenda. When executed, KSARs either changed the local state of the Level Manager or sent messages to other Level Managers.

In summary, local control relied upon triggering events and the KSAR status changes caused by precondition satisfaction. Global control was effected by changes in the value of the *Status* attribute in entries in the databases of the Word-Hypothesis and Letter-Hypothesis Level Managers and by the message-passing system. The latter fact indicates that global behaviour in CASSANDRA systems might be partially controlled by attribute manipulation. Further experiments are required to test this hypothesis, but it does not seem too surprising, for the Blackboard Control Model relies, to a great extent, upon attribute value change. The fact that the lack of global control manifested by the NBB implementation carried over to the CASSANDRA implementation indicates that the functionalities of the two architectures are very similar. It also indicates that there may be ways to implement control in CASSANDRA systems other than by procedurally specified schedulers.

7.5. WordSys REVIEW

This section is concerned with a review of the two WordSys implementations. Throughout the foregoing discussion, the reader will have noticed that some comparisons have been already made. This section is concerned with a rather more direct comparison of the two systems. The aim of this comparison is to determine the relative merits of the two architectures. Before progressing, it should be noted that the deletion Knowledge Sources were not introduced into the NBB blackboard implementation of WordSys: there was no particular reason for this omission -- the KSs are applicable to both the blackboard and CASSANDRA systems and perhaps at some stage in the near future they will be included in an NBB version. It should also be noted that the fact that the NBB version of WordSys was constructed first did have a marginal impact on the CASSANDRA version: the general decomposition of the problem was already known and so was carried over to the CASSANDRA implementation. In fact, it is fair to say that the decomposition was known before *either* implementation was attempted because there is adequate information available in the literature (Rumelhart, 1982; McClelland, 1981). Those changes that were made were mostly due to the distributed nature of CASSANDRA systems, as has been noted.

In terms of performance, the NBB version ran slightly faster than the CASSANDRA version. There was no attempt to construct the CASSANDRA interpreter as a distributed system (in fact, this would have been extremely difficult because the machine on which the tests were run is not connected to the Departmental Ethernet). As a consequence, the naturally distributed or parallel nature of CASSANDRA systems could not be examined. The delays inherent in the interpreter loop's running one Level Manager to completion before activating the next caused delays in processing, the biggest delay being caused by initialisation code for each Level Manager and the function (closure) call required to activate each Level Manager. Furthermore, the NBB and CASSANDRA interpreters contain different amounts of compiled code, a fact which made meaningful qualitative runtime comparisons impossible. In addition, the CASSANDRA implementation operates more slowly because it contains more KSs than the NBB version. The CASSANDRA version also had extra checking code in the **PROPOSE** action which requires time to execute.

Extra KSs had to be introduced into the CASSANDRA version of WordSys. The reason for this has been mentioned above: the architecture forbids action-at-a-distance. The addition of KSs to the system slowed its rate of generation slightly, simply because there were more preconditions to evaluate on each cycle for each of the Letter-Hypothesis and Word-Hypothesis Level Managers. This fact is mirrored in conventional blackboard systems: as the number of Knowledge Sources increases, the time required per cycle also increases. Since KS preconditions are arbitrary pieces of LISP code, there appears to be no avoiding this fact. Comparison of the two systems on the basis of cycle length is, I suggest, unfair. In a parallel implementation of WordSys, distributed across a number of processors with one Level Manager per processor, it is to be expected that the time required to generate word hypotheses would decrease (assuming that the inter-cpu communications medium does not approach saturation): this is because there would be fewer KSs active in each processor and, so, less time would be needed to check KS preconditions. *This* comparison is, I believe, fair, not because it shows the CASSANDRA implementation in a better light, but because it removes a problem with single-cpu blackboard systems. In a single-cpu blackboard system, there is nothing to do but accept the fact that the cycle time will increase in proportion to the number of KSs in the system. In a CASSANDRA system, it is possible to move Level Managers to distinct processors, thus reducing the load on each individual cpu: that is, if two or more Level Managers initially share a processor, the number can be reduced by assigning them to other processors, leaving the original processor with fewer Level Managers to compete for cpu cycles. This option is not available to users of the conventional blackboard architecture.

WordSys solves a problem that is more interactive than does CASSANDRA-II. In WordSys, hypotheses are passed between Level Managers and are sometimes rejected. There is a two-way flow of hypotheses between the letter and word hypothesis Level Managers. This contrasts strongly with CASSANDRA-II in which there was only uni-directional information flow.

When considering interaction, it can readily be seen that WordSys involves greater inter-Level Manager communication than did CASSANDRA-II. The main interactions were between the letter and word hypothesis Level Managers. Interaction became important when an hypothesised word was not found in the dictionary. It was a deliberate design decision to use a re-hypothesis process which could generate spurrious hypotheses: this was to test message-passing and its effects on the system. It has been seen that when a word hypothesis was found to be faulty, the offending letters were identified and a message was sent to the letter hypothesis Level Manager requesting that they be corrected.

Because of the semantics of the messages used in WordSys, such a request immediately caused some KS triggering. In the current implementation, when a word hypothesis was found to be faulty, no new word hypothesis Level Manager Knowledge Sources could be executed because their precondition was false, and the Level Manager temporarily halted, waiting for input. This was due to the fact that the system processed only one word at a time. The word hypothesis Level Manager began its activity again when a corrected hypothesis was sent from the letter hypothesis Level Manager. Activity in the system 'bounced' between the letter and word Level Managers when a faulty hypothesis was discovered in the sense that the word hypothesis Level Manager could go no further until the letter hypothesis Level Manager had corrected at least one incorrect letter hypothesies, after which the letter hypothesis Level Manager would suspend (in the sense that it could schedule no more Knowledge Sources) until called upon to correct more hypotheses. This may be reminiscent of CASSANDRA-II.

In the first system, each Level Manager executed all of its pending Knowledge Sources and then waited for input from another Level Manager. Level Managers in CASSANDRA-II did not, though, have to wait for corrections to be made and then re-start, as is the case with WordSys. In other words, once a CASSANDRA-II Level Manager had executed all of its pending Knowledge Sources, the information upon which they operated was sent elsewhere and was never re-used; in WordSys, however, Knowledge Sources operate on the same or on updated or corrected versions of entries until they are correct and this continued use of entries involves activities in other Level Managers.

7.6. CONCLUSIONS

This section is concerned with a general review of the CASSANDRA architecture in the light of the experience of implementing CASSANDRA-II and WordSys. The section will compare the CASSANDRA architecture with the blackboard architecture and consider the ways in which it improves upon the latter. The section begins with a fairly detailed overview of the architecture and then homes in on the lessons learned from the implementation of WordSys. The last paragraph of this section specifically addresses the issue raised when deciding to implement WordSys: is the CASSANDRA architecture general?

The first claim made about the CASSANDRA architecture is that it is more modular than the blackboard architecture. Systems constructed using the CASSANDRA architecture are built from independent Level Managers which tightly encapsulate a set of entries, Knowledge Sources and a purely local control component. The entries held in each Level Manager in a system represent solution elements generated by local or non-local Knowledge Sources. The CASSANDRA architecture requires a message-passing interface between Level Managers. The interface regulates the flow of information between Level Managers. That is, it is only possible to send messages from one Level Manager to a *pre-defined* subset of the other Level Managers in a system. If an attempt is made to send a message to a Level Manager which is not a member of the pre-defined set, an error condition results and the message is not passed on. The message-passing interface restricts the possible communications between Level Managers in a system so that only information which has been determined to be necessary to the receiving Level Manager may actually be directed there.

This contrasts strongly with the blackboard architecture in which inter-abstraction level communications are not regulated. In a blackboard system, it is only possible to determine the ways in which information flows across the blackboard database by examining the actions of the Knowledge Sources present in the system. It is possible, in a blackboard system, for a KS to send information to *any* other abstraction level in the system: thus, it is possible for a KS to send information to an abstraction level in error (and this can prove to be a difficult error to trap). The CASSANDRA architecture, on the other hand, requires inter-Level Manager communications to be pre-defined. Communication paths are associated with Level Managers in the form of ports, so the possible communications between Level Managers can be directly determined by examining the Level Manager and *not* the individual Knowledge Sources in the system: there will, in general, be far fewer Level Managers than KSs, so the amount of effort required to determine legal communication paths is reduced.

The blackboard architecture enforces a linear hierarchy between blackboard abstraction levels. In the CASSANDRA architecture, on the other hand, there is no such limitation. It is possible in CASSANDRA systems for Level Managers to be related in an arbitrary graph. Where linear hierarchies are required (as is the case with WordSys), the hierarchy can be created by connecting the component Level Managers in the appropriate way. Where no hierarchy is required, a CASSANDRA system can be configured to reflect this fact. As far as the relationship between Level Managers is concerned, the CASSANDRA architecture offers considerably more flexibility than does the older blackboard architecture.

By associating communications with entire Level Managers, it is possible also to control the development of CASSANDRA systems to a far greater extent than it is with systems using the blackboard architecture. The standard method for developing blackboard systems is to select an abstraction level, define its entry structure and then define the Knowledge Sources which trigger on it. The actions of KSs in a blackboard system may cause entries to be added to any other abstraction level in the system, and there is no check that entries are being posted to the correct level. In CASSANDRA systems, however, such checks *are* possible. The standard methodology for constructing CASSANDRA systems (if one may call it that with so few systems implemented) is to begin with the development of one Level Manager. The development of a Level Manager entails the definition of communication paths which may legally be used to send messages to other Level Managers. As has been stated, a message cannot be sent to a Level Manager if a port has not been defined for it. As a Level Manager needs to send messages to additional Level Managers in the system, the set of ports owned by the Level Manager can be extended. The point is that, at all times, the developer knows the destinations of messages sent by the Level Manager under development, *and*, what is more, the relationships between Level Managers are always explicitly represented in the developing system.

In addition to the modularity enforced by communications, there is the modularity caused by local control. The CASSANDRA architecture specifies that each Level Manager should have its own local control component (or scheduler in more conventional terminology). In the conventional blackboard architecture, there is only one controller or scheduler. The scheduler is concerned with controlling the execution of Knowledge Source instantiations in such a way that a solution is derived in a coherent fashion (although opportunism may cause deviations from any given strategy). The scheduler, in conventional blackboard systems, is responsible for co-ordinating problem-solving activity at both global and local levels. That is, the scheduler has to select the region of the blackboard which is most promising (or most in need of development) *as well as* determining the most appropriate Knowledge Source instantiation operating upon that region. This fact entails that local and global considerations must be considered at the same time when specifying the scheduler for a blackboard system (which probably accounts for the difficulty of that activity). In CASSANDRA systems, on the other hand, local and global control are separated by insisting that local control be performed by individual Level Managers. Control at any level in CASSANDRA systems is *always* knowledge-based, just as it is in the Blackboard Control Model, even though it may not be implemented as control KSs.

The separation of local and global control entails that control decisions which are restricted to any particular Level Manager are performed by its local controller. This, in turn, entails that local controllers be tailored to the specific needs of each Level Manager. By separating local and global control (as was done in the CASSANDRA-II system), the process of specification of the control component of a system constructed using the CASSANDRA architecture is simplified: it is possible to determine local control needs first, independently of global needs, and then specify a global behaviour (this may or may not lead to modifications of local control components, depending upon the particular problem to be solved). Alternatively, it is possible to define a desired global behaviour and design the local control component of each Level Manager so that the global behaviour is promoted.

Such a separation makes the construction of systems easier because it simplifies the specification of the control task. The separation of local and global control also simplifies the construction of systems: one does not need to have some form of scheduler in operation from the start of the development phase, as is necessary with the blackboard architecture. Indeed, the requirement that KS instantiations be scheduled at a global level at all times may tend to bias blackboard system implementations -- control has to be specified, in some form, from the start and this may tend to bias later efforts. In a CASSANDRA system, such biasing effects are less in evidence because of the separation of control. By separating the two levels of control, it is also possible to introduce or remove Level Managers from an implemented CASSANDRA system: all that need be done is to alter the global control structure to reflect the needs and behaviours of Level Managers. In conventional blackboard systems, the introduction of new abstraction levels can lead to severe problems with the scheduler.

The localisation of control imposed by the CASSANDRA architecture also permits the gradual development of global control as knowledge is added to the system -- since each Level Manager contains a controller specific to its needs, the global control component can be modified more easily since the range of operations it performs is more restricted than is the case with the more conventional architecture. The development method cited above was precisely that employed in the construction of the CASSANDRA-II airspace monitoring program: that program also showed the viability of introducing varieties of local control into the system. A similar, incremental, approach was adopted during the construction of WordSys, although in that system there was the surprise described above (section 7.4.5).

The conclusion one can draw about modularity of CASSANDRA systems is that they definitely improve upon the blackboard architecture in this respect. They also improve upon the blackboard in the ease with which an application can be constructed. An additional factor in the greater ease with which

CASSANDRA systems can be built is that the architecture does not force the requirement that there be an abstraction hierarchy present in any particular system. The CASSANDRA-II system has only an approximate hierarchy and that is very shallow; WordSys, on the other hand, has a fairly well-defined hierarchy. The difference is due to the different natures of the chosen problems.

This is an important point about the CASSANDRA architecture: it can be applied to problems very much more naturally than the blackboard architecture because it permits natural subsets -- where one does not need the power of abstration hierarchies, for example, they need not be constructed (abstraction hierarchies are formed, in the CASSANDRA architecture, by the structure of the message-passing network). With the blackboard architecture, on the other hand, it is always necessary to invoke abstraction hierarchies and to employ fairly complex control regimes (although the NBB implementation of WordSys suggests that control can be achieved in other ways, but it should not be forgotten that the NBB implementation relied upon the *implicit* control provided by the interpreter).

In other words, when one uses the blackboard architecture, one is committed to using it all. The CASSANDRA architecture is, on the other hand, very much more flexible -- architecturally acceptable CASSANDRA systems can be built which contain only one Level Manager: this is because the CASSANDRA architecture specifies the details of Level Managers and states that they communicate via message-passing. The architecture does not say how many Level Managers must be present in a system for it to qualify as a CASSANDRA system.

Because of this natural subset property, it should be possible to build well-structured and modular problem solving systems with many of the claimed benefits of the blackboard architecture *without* incurring the latter architecture's overheads (which, in some cases, are excessive). This is an empirical claim and will have to wait for confirmation or refutation until more CASSANDRA systems have been built.

The CASSANDRA architecture has been described in terms of parallel computations. Both of the systems implemented so far have been serial. Does this affect the status of the architecture in any way? I claim that it does not. One reason that it does not is that there are very clear mappings of the CASSANDRA architecture onto serial machines (one such mapping has been shown by the implemented systems). Even when *implemented* as a serial program, the architecture has modularity advantages over the blackboard architecture. The second reason is that the *vocabulary* of parallel computation has been used to describe the CASSANDRA architecture: by employing that vocabulary, advantages have been gained. Because one uses the particular vocabulary of parallelism does not necessarily commit one to parallel implementations. The use of concepts from parallel computation has, I suggest, been shown to provide a context in which a different perspective on problem solving architectures can be presented: the concepts have required greater justification of architectural features than has been evidenced before and it has forced discussion of possibly harmful interactions (such as deadlock). At the theoretical level, concepts from parallel computation have enriched the theory of the blackboard architecture and have suggested a more modular architecture.

Returning to the distinctions between horizontal and vertical organisations made by Fodor (Fodor, 1983), another argument runs as follows. Abstraction levels are specialised regions of working memory whose function is to enable vertical processing elements (KSs in the case of blackboard systems) to operate. Because the information held in abstraction levels is highly specialised, it does not seem appropriate, other than as an implementation convenience, to open up the possibility that anything can operate on the information contained there. In other words, because the blackboard architecture does not constrain abstraction levels other than by requiring their placement in a hierarchy and by requiring that there be Knowledge Sources which are able to trigger on the information held in each abstraction level, the architecture effectively contains a contradiction. Since abstraction levels contain specialised information and are operated upon by specialist processes, they should be considered to be highly separate within the abstraction hierarchy: that this is *precisely* what is not the case has been argued elsewhere. The CASSANDRA architecture, on the other hand, provides encapsulations for problem solving knowledge (in the form of Knowledge Sources and local controllers) and for their working memories (Level Manager entry databases). The CASSANDRA architecture takes the view that each abstraction level is something special and turns this into an architectural principle.

In conclusion, the following remarks are offered. To answer the question with which this chapter started, it would appear that the CASSANDRA architecture is not tied to any particular domain -- the evidence in support of this claim is in the form of the WordSys system. The CASSANDRA architecture improves upon the blackboard architecture by insisting on a greater degree of modularity. The additional modularity provided by CASSANDRA systems assists application-builders in the construction of CASSANDRA systems: the evidence for this comes from the construction of CASSANDRA-II and WordSys. Finally, the new architecture also seems to have a theoretical basis far stronger than the blackboard architecture: this must be seen as an advance over the older architecture.

8. CONCLUSIONS AND SUGGESTIONS FOR FURTHER WORK

8.1. INTRODUCTION

This last chapter contains suggestions for further work on the CASSANDRA architecture and on the CASSANDRA-II system itself. In the next section, the suggestions for future work are made and discussed. In the final section, a short conclusion is offered.

8.2. SUGGESTIONS FOR FURTHER WORK

There are a number of areas for further work. They can be divided into:

- work on the architecture, and
- work on the CASSANDRA-II system.

The major suggestion is that other systems be developed using the CASSANDRA architecture. To date, only two CASSANDRA systems have been developed. Unless further systems are constructed, the true range of applicability of the architecture and its limitations can be demonstrated only by argument. In particular, I would like to see a parallel, distributed implementation of the architecture: this would afford a better understanding of the problems inherent in using the CASSANDRA architecture in distributed AI environments.

8.2.1. Work on the Architecture

Throughout this book, a number of possible future developments and areas for further research have been mentioned. Some of these areas have been of a general nature, but some have been specific to the CASSANDRA architecture. I will mention the more general topics first because I believe that they are important for AI in general and are not just limited to the architecture presented in this book.

The first major topic is the explicit representation of problem solving and task knowledge. The CASSANDRA architecture requires control to be expressed in a basically knowledge-based form: this is achieved by separating the control component of a system into local and global components, with the local components being highly specialised and tailored to operate in highly constrained environments (i.e., they are constructed specifically to support their Level Managers). The current trend in blackboard systems (and other problem solving systems, for that matter) is to make far more information available to the system so that it can be explicitly used in the solution of problems. By explicitly representing more knowledge and information than is currently the practice, the system can reason about its own problem solving and other activities and thereby, one hopes, display more reasoned behaviour. The usual reason for making more knowledge explicit in a problem solving system is that it assists in the control of inference. In addition, though, the provision of greater amounts of explicit knowledge entails that a system can better explain itself to users and can possibly be employed in a teaching role.*

Because the CASSANDRA architecture is higly modular, it promotes the construction of systems composed of relatively small components. One may think of a Level Manager as being a small expert who collaborates or competes with other, small, experts in the solution of problems. The high level of modularity of CASSANDRA systems suggests that each component be more amenable to relatively complete description and explicit representation than other systems -- that is, the architecture seems actively to promote explicit description. Each Level Manager defines a very small space, and this reduction in size and relative isolation further suggests that explicit representation is possible, at least in theory.

Explicit representation of a system's knowledge assists problem solving and explanation. It can be of use when a system is unable to find a solution: this is similar to the behaviour of the Soar system (Laird, 1985). In an architecture like CASSANDRA, explicit representation could also be useful in enabling Level Managers to construct models of the progress of the system towards a solution from only partial information. When describing the CASSANDRA architecture, the speech act theory of natural language semantics was discussed and it was suggested that Level Managers may be able to infer something about the state of other Level Managers from the communication acts in which they engage. This is possible because there are rules governing the performance of speech acts and the application of one of these rules is determined by the knowledge state of the agent engaged in a communication act. This implies that knowledge of *when* and *why* a particular communication act took place can assist in the development of a model of the state of other agents. In order to reason thus, it is necessary for each Level Manager or agent to have knowledge

* The reader may remember the discussion of the implicit control imposed by interpreters when the WordSys word recognition system was discussed. An explicit representation should probably include a description or model of the architecture and its implementation. Work of this nature is planned as part of the BB-SR project (Craig, 1987).

about when and why and with whom to engage in each communication act. In order to reason about other agents or Level Managers, each agent or Level Manager must explicitly represent the communication act rules *and* its own knowledge state so that it can engage in this reasoning.

The ability to construct models of the state of a problem solving episode clearly becomes an issue in the context of distributed problem solving systems (and these are frequently considered to be the target of the CASSANDRA architecture). This is because distributed AI systems lack the concept of central, global state. If components of a distributed system had to build their own copy of the global state, the communication medium connecting them would probably saturate (thus preventing any real problem solving from taking place) and the agents would spend a good proportion of their time constructing their own version the model and the model would probably not be accurate. It seems more reasonable to expect agents or Level Managers to infer state information from other sources such as communication actions and intentional enquiries.

The explicit representations considered so far have been basically suggested for control purposes. Another need for explicitness has been shown in this research: entry deletions. It has been argued that an entry may only be deleted when it is *known* no longer to be of any use to the problem solver. In the CASSANDRA-II and WordSys prototype systems presented above entries can be deleted when certain attributes achieve specified values (complete match tagging and time expiry in CASSANDRA-II and special *Status* values in WordSys). It seems possible, to me, to develop a theory of lifetimes which would allow systems to infer that some of their information was no longer necessary or valid. Since both CASSANDRA-II and WordSys perform deletion by executing Knowledge Sources, it can be fairly claimed to be a knowledge-based activity. In neither CASSANDRA-II nor WordSys was the information on when to delete entries recorded in other than a procedural form: it was always encoded in the form of Knowledge Sources. This procedural encoding is a point of opacity in the systems and should, I suggest, be improved by including an explicit and declarative representation in addition to the procedural representation. The benefits of declarative representation are explainability (or accountability in cases where things seem to go wrong) and the introduction of the possibility that general mechanisms can be employed to operate on the declarative representation so that the Knowledge Sources which implement the deletion mechanisms can be created automatically, thus ensuring greater reliabilty in the resulting system.

In both of the implemented systems, the criteria upon which a decision to delete an entry could be made were very clear and were not subject to noise or ambiguity. It is expected that these properties will not be shared by other domains (the air defence example which motivated the discussion of entry deletion in chapter 4 is a case in point). Quite obviously, more work is required on this: one way to proceed would be to examine a number of problems and domains and try to discover deletion criteria and to try to quantify the level of uncertainty in the applicability of the deletion criteria.

Finally, a formal specification of the CASSANDRA architecture would be of great benefit. Such a specification could be produced using Hoare's CSP (Hoare, 1985) for example. The point of a formal specification is that it would provide a standard against which to judge implementations and upon which to base future developments. One problem with the blackboard architecture is that there is no single, agreed definition: as a consequence, there is often redundant discussion on whether or not a particular system is, indeed, a blackboard. If there were a formal definition and specification, such debate would be obviated. A second reason for producing a formal specification is that it permits formal theoretical analyses of the architecture with formal results. A problem with many current architectures is that it is very hard to determine their properties: a formal specification would provide this valuable information -- such information is valuable because it avoids reference to implementations constructed for particular tasks (and, thus, removes the need to "look behind" the task) and because it defines the properties of the architecture in a domain-independent manner (and this could, for example, be useful in determining whether or not to use the architecture for a particular application). Finally, a formal definition could point out the limits of the architecture far more succinctly and completely than could informal or semi-formal methods.

8.2.2. Work on CASSANDRA-II

CASSANDRA-II is the larger of the two example systems constructed using the CASSANDRA architecture. CASSANDRA-II is a system intended for real world application. If CASSANDRA-II were ever to be employed in the field, lives would depend upon its performance and accuracy. WordSys, on the other hand, solved a 'toy' problem, and is, therefore, far less important. WordSys is, in any case, relatively complete, but further work can be done -- the extra work can be devined by comparing the description of

WordSys with the papers by Rumelhart and McClelland (Rumelhart, 1982; McClelland, 1981). Given these remarks, the suggestions presented in this section are specific to CASSANDRA-II.

There are four suggested areas for further work on CASSANDRA-II. They are:

- performance improvements,
- user interface,
- focus of attention, and
- distribution.

CASSANDRA-II is currently implemented in LISP. It was implemented in a very safe way which used comparatively expensive operations: one clear way to improve performance would be to change many instances of safe list-manipulation operations into those which modify list structure directly.

The preferred way to increase the runtime speed of CASSANDRA-II is to re-code it in a conventional imperative programming language such as C or ADA. The majority of the data structures in CASSANDRA-II are of fixed length, so there would be few problems created by the need for extensive use of a heap (for example, allocation and deallocation of heap space -- these can be expensive operations and would tend to reduce the speed of the system unless managed very carefully). A second reason why CASSANDRA-II could easily be re-coded is that it was built using a (self-imposed) type structure: in a few places, there are union types, but they should not pose too great a problem in a re-coding.

The user interface provided by the current implementation of CASSANDRA-II is rudimentary to say the least. In addition to simply printing out warning messages, a graphical display of the current airspace state with highlighted conflictions would be an obvious improvement.* No graphics facilities were available on the system used to implement CASSANDRA-II, so this feature could not be provided. However, it should be noted that there are problems inherent in providing such an interface, the most important of which is information overload. ATCOs are already heavily loaded by voice communications, meteorological data, flight strips and the position display. The addition of an interface which presents warning messages and gives the user the ability to generate displays representing projections of airspace state would

* Projected airspace state would be treated in exactly the same way.

increase this load, particularly when it is considered that the interface has to be manipulated (say, to generate projections). Although the availability of high-quality graphics interfaces inclines one to suggest "hi-res graphics with everything", the CAA does not see this as a particularly good area for their deployment. As a temporary measure and for demonstration purposes, the addition of a graphics interface would improve the system, but other solutions must be sought for the longer term. Such work is currently underway within the CAA and elsewhere, but it is too early to make any definite suggestions in this respect.

Currently, CASSANDRA-II does not possess any global focus of attention mechanisms, for none were thought necessary. It tends to be the case that, if an aircraft is involved in one kind of conflict, it will also be involved in one of another kind. In the current implementation, one warning message is generated per conflict and the conflict detection mechanisms for each conflict type do not interact. This is a conservative strategy which ensures that the user always knows about *every* conflict in the airspace. Given the fact stated above that conflicts often come in multiples, a focussing mechanism could be added to the system. The focussing mechanism could be implemented as follows: when one conflict is detected, all other lower Level Managers are warned of its existence. Once they know that a particular aircraft is involved in a conflict, they could check their control databases to see if there are references to the aircraft in tasks waiting to be executed. If there are such references, the tasks involved could receive an increment to their priority so that they will execute before other tasks. This would ensure that potential conflicts involving a given aircraft were dealt with as soon as possible. In such a scheme, information overload could be reduced by ensuring that only one message which summarised the conflicts in which an aircraft participates be sent to the user. This problem was not examined during the experiments based on the current implementation of CASSANDRA-II because it was considered to be a large topic, and it was considered that the possible interactions between this mechanism and message-passing in a distributed processing environment would require far more time to examine than was available. Distributed focus of attention mechanisms and their interaction with the effects of parallelism are best left for future work.

Finally, physical distribution. The CASSANDRA architecture is naturally distributable over a communication network such as Ethernet. This is a result of the modularity of the architecture and the augmentation of the vocabulary in which the architecture is described to include concepts from parallel computation. Many real time systems are implemented as distributed systems: the argument for this is that distributed systems are much more fault-tolerant than centralised systems. Since CASSANDRA-II is designed for a domain in which reliability is essential, physical distribution should naturally be considered. A distributed implementation has not been attempted due to the limitations of FranzLISP and due to the fact that it was not possible to have access to a suitable network. The former problem has been eased with the improvement of the foreign function interface in FranzLISP, but the latter is still the major stumbling block. As was stated at the beginning of this section, a distributed version of the CASSANDRA architecture would be very welcome and would allow further experiments to be conducted. In the context of the CASSANDRA-II system, a distributed version would enable performance and accuracy tests to be performed in an environment more akin to actual use. This remains an area for further investigation.

8.3. CONCLUSIONS

This research has led to the definition and description of a problem solving architecture which improves upon the blackboard architecture in a number of respects, principally in its modularity and flexibility.

The new architecture, called the CASSANDRA architecture, improves upon the modularity of the blackboard architecture by the introduction of the Level Manager concept. Level Managers are encapsulations of abstraction levels and have their own local control component as well as Knowledge Sources and an entry database. The CASSANDRA architecture requires Level Managers to communicate via predefined communication channels so that modularity is enforced. The local controller in each Level Manager implements control regimes which are appropriate to the needs of the Level Manager and which are de-coupled from any global control regimes. The new architecture is more flexible than the blackboard architecture because it permits systems to be constructed from one or more Level Managers: this strongly contrasts with the older architecture which must always be used intact.

The CASSANDRA architecture has been used to implement two experimental systems. The systems operate in different task domains and solve very different problems. Both systems worked according to specification and were easier to construct than the blackboard equivalents. The fact that the architecture could be applied effectively to different tasks in different domains argues for the fact that it has some claim to generality. The claim is reinforced by the argument that the CASSANDRA architecture provides modular knowledge-based building blocks from which to construct complex systems. Furthermore, the facts that the two example systems could be constructed in either the blackboard or in the CASSANDRA architecture implies that they are functionally similar: an argument was presented when describing the CASSANDRA architecture to support this claim.

Complex systems can be built in a variety of ways, but the principle of defining clusters of Level Managers which solve classes of sub-problems, the solutions to which are passed to higher-level or simply to different clusters of Level Managers appears to be one approach for very big systems.

The additivity of the architecture just alluded to is a result of attempting to introduce parallel processing concepts into the blackboard architecture. This does not, though, necessarily force one to implement the architecture as a system of concurrent or distributed processes: indeed, both implementations of the architecture so far have been sequential programs. What is the case is that one can *describe* the CASSANDRA architecture as a parallel system of components while implementing it as one sees fit. The CASSANDRA *architecture* is just that -- a recommendation on structuring knowledge-based problem solving programs.

1. APPENDIX 1: AIR TRAFFIC CONTROL

1.1. INTRODUCTION

The purpose of this appendix is to outline the basics of air traffic control in general and then examine the particular aspects of the domain with which CASSANDRA-II is concerned. The role of air traffic control (henceforth, ATC) is basically to ensure that airspace is utilised to the maximum and to ensure that there is a minimum of risk to the pilots, passengers and crew of aircraft, at the lowest realistic cost to the tax-payer and the aircraft operators. Part of the role of ATC, which is, perhaps, sometimes forgotten, is the reduction to a minimum of inconvenience and risk to those on the ground (for example, the regulations concerning low flying and noise levels.)

ATC in the United Kingdom is provided by the Ministry of Defence (MoD) and the Civil Aviation Authority (CAA). Both organisations co-operate in the control of air traffic: MoD is concerned with military flights* ; CAA with civilian. This co-operation extends to joint control centres (JATCRUs) which are staffed by both civilian and military personnel.

In this appendix, attention has been paid only to the needs of civilian traffic. Military ATC has many of the same problems as the civilian side, but Military operations sometimes impose more problems, such as in time of tension or war. Examples of strategic military problems are:

- deciding to which aerodrome an aircraft is to be sent. The aerodrome may not be the one from which the aircraft started out on its sortie;
- the spacing**, in all four dimensions (time and 3 dimensional space), between aircraft may depend upon various factors. If it is necessary to get a squadron off the deck in order to avoid their destruction by enemy activity, the separation between the aircraft will be reduced to a bare minimum. Dogfights also cause separation reductions to occur.

Civilian ATC is far less dramatic. It is also the aspect of ATC which affects the majority of ordinary people.

---

* It might surprise some readers to discover that any military flights which have a filed flight plan and fly within controlled airspace are treated just as if they were civilian flights, and may be controlled by civilian personnel.

** Spacing will hereafter be called *separation*, the correct technical term.

The structure of this appendix is as follows. In the next section, the ATC problem and some of the basic terminology is presented. This presentation will cover some aspects of basic ATC and is intended as a short introduction to the field. In section three, the problems of Area Control will be examined in detail. Area Control is the aspect of ATC which concerns CASSANDRA-II and is about the control of aircraft in sections of airspace, termed areas or sectors. In particular, CASSANDRA-II's problem domain is airway control, which falls wholly within the area control problem.

1.2. A BRIEF INTRODUCTION TO AIR TRAFFIC CONTROL

The fundamental concept of ATC is airspace. Airspace is a volume of air in which aircraft fly. The boundaries of the airspace may be defined by geographical features, such as sea-level, high hills or buildings or by convention (see below, Flight Levels) in the vertical, and by convention in the horizontal. The conventions which apply to horizontal delimitation of airspace are such matters as international agreement (e.g., the boundaries between UK and Irish airspace along the Irish Sea) or by national rules (such as the width and location of the airways within the UK.)

Airspace comes in a number of flavours:

- Uncontrolled airspace. In this kind of airspace, there is no provision of ATC services, and, apart from the laws laid down in the Rules of the Air (a legislative document produced by central government), there is no restiction on what a pilot may do. The airspace directly above Lancaster University is, for example, uncontrolled airspace, which accounts for the large volume of low flying military aircraft;
- Special Rules airspace. As the name suggests, special flying rules apply to this kind of airspace;
- Purple airspace, which is created especially for Royal flights on a one-shot basis;
- Controlled airspace. Controlled airspace is covered by Air Traffic Controllers (ATCOs) who are charged with the monitoring and direction of air traffic through the airspace under their control. Controlled airspace has associated with it a set of regulations and requirements which form the basis of the knowledge encoded in CASSANDRA-II.

In the United Kingdom, airspace is divided into two flight information regions (FIRs.) Each FIR has at least one instance of the airspace types described above: the FIRs are the Scottish FIR (controlled from Atlantic House, Prestwick) and the London FIR (controlled from West Drayton.) Below an altitude of 24,500 feet in each region is the lower flight information region; above 24,500 feet is the upper FIR. In upper FIRs, radar cover is mandatory: in the lower FIRs, radar cover is optional. The FIRs represent administrative and logical divisions of UK airspace. When, in future, references are made to West Drayton, I will use the term *LATCC* (London Air Traffic Control Centre).

Controlled airspace, either in an upper or lower FIR is the normal place for civilian air traffic, particularly those flights which are operated by carriers of various kinds. The bulk of civilian commercial traffic uses the *airways.* An airway is defined by ICAO (International Civil Aviation Organisation) as A control area or part of a control area established in the form of a corridor equipped with radio navigational aids. Airways are artificial divisions of the air above the UK. Their existence and precise location is the result of deliberate decisions, dating back to before 1951. Airways are very much fast highways in the air: their role is to permit traffic to pass as smoothly and as quickly as possible from departure point to destination. The structure of the current airways over the UK is based on an expansion of the airways laid down before 1951.

Each airway has a unique identifier, consisting of a colour (Red, Blue, Amber, White) and a number. Airways, frequently intersect, for example, Amber25 intersects Green1 over central southern Wales. There are also local control areas, control zones and terminal control areas or TMAs (Terminal Management Areas.) For current purposes, the local control areas are of no concern (except for noting that Shanwick oceanic traffic uses the West Scottish Control Area.)

The airways are designed to serve the majority of airline routes. Aircraft going across the Atlantic Ocean will tend to travel along Green1 if the destination (or place of departure) is Washington, New York or Boston, for example. Traffic going to California tends to be routed, from Heathrow, along Amber1 and into the Scottish FIR and then through the West Scottish Control Area. Traffic to Spain will tend to use Amber25.

Each airway is approximately thirty nautical miles wide. Since the boundaries of airways are not physically marked, controlled air traffic is directed to remain within an area twenty-six nautical miles in width within the airway. In other words, there is a two nautical mile (henceforth, mile) border on either side of the airway which serves to separate traffic within the airway from traffic without. The responsibility for making sure that aircraft are within the twenty-six mile corridor rests with the ATCO. Naturally enough, conditions, such as traffic density, weather or an emergency, may dictate that the two mile borders are used for traffic using the airway (en-route traffic), in which case special care must be taken to avoid contact between en-route traffic and traffic in the surrounding airspace.*

Within an airway, traffic is separated horizontally according to the direction in which it is travelling. Eastbound traffic is usually allocated to one side of the airway and westbound traffic the other (the reader may wonder why there is no reference to north and south - this is explained below): for now, let it be taken that there are only these directions, a division which serves to simplify the administrative problem. The reason for this separation by direction is that the two streams are flying in roughly opposite directions and so must be prevented from (roughly) head-on collisions. Figure A1.1 shows an airway and the separation of traffic (this is a hypothetical airway).

The CAA regulations state that traffic in a controlled airspace may not be directed to leave the airway and enter the adjoining airspace unless there are good reasons (e.g., severe turbulence or, perhaps, to make way for an aircraft experiencing an emergency.) Equally, traffic from adjoining airspace may not be directed to enter controlled airspace unless certain conditions are met - for example, an aircraft may start out from uncontrolled airspace - i.e., may depart from an aerodrome in uncontrolled airspace - and then, as part of its flight plan (see below) join an airway or other form of controlled airspace in order to reach its destination.

Within airways there are various kinds of radio aids for determining the location of aircraft and for monitoring progress. These divide into two basic categories: beacons and radars. Beacons are used by aircraft as homing devices. Aircraft usually follow a sequence of beacons through airspace (example locations

* Incidentally, Purple Airspace, that airspace used for Royal flights is always *outside* and immediately adjacent to controlled airspace.

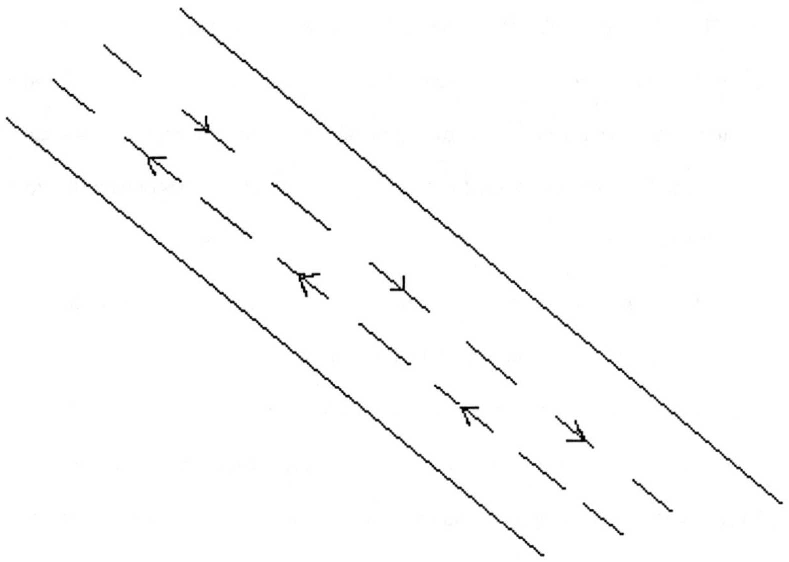

Fig A1.1

Separation of traffic in an airway

are Dane, Cheshire, Lichfield, Staffordshire and Daventry, Northants in the Daventry Sector and Biggin Hill in the Worthing Control sector.) In the UK, there are two types of beacon VOR (VHF Omni-directional Range) and NDB (Non-Directional Beacon); frequently associated with VORs are DME/TACAN stations which measure distances between aircraft and the beacon (DME stands for Distance Measuring Equipment.) The radar coverage in airways is of two types: Primary and SSR (Secondary Surveillance Radar.) The radars are used to plot the positions and altitudes of aircraft. More will be said on beacons and radars below.

The reader should note that there is a growing tendency among the airlines to adopt direct-routing. Instead of following the airways throughout the flight, the pilot selects a heading and follows that, crossing, joining and leaving airways as necessary. This has come about, partly as a result of the increased cost of aviation fuel and of the increased accuracy of onboard inertial navigation systems. This method of routing, although not as popular as it might be with the statutory ATC organisations, is becoming, nevertheless, an increasingly common phenomenon.

1.3. VERTICAL AIRSPACE STRUCTURE

In some areas, controlled airspace is considered to start at ground level or mean sea level (calculated at a standard pressure of 1013.2 mb). In others, controlled airspace is considered to start at some predefined altitude because of hazards such as TMAs,* high ground or buildings. The Rules of the Air specify that the minimum clearance to be observed between aircraft and obstacles of this nature is usually 1,500 feet, although there are exceptions such as the provisions laid down in *The Air Navigation (Restriction of Flying)(Atomic Energy Establishments) Regulations 1983* which specifies a minimum of 2,000 feet for the named Atomic Energy Establishments and *The Air Navigation (Restriction of Flying)(Security Establishments) Regulations 1981* which again specifies a minimum of 2,000 feet. There are other amendments to The Air Navigation Regulations pertaining to various airfields and to areas of land used for military purposes.*

---

* TMA = Terminal Management Area

* There is the Restriction of Flying (Gruinard Island) Regulations, 1981, which specifies a minimum altitude of 450 feet above mean sea level "in the area bounded by a circle having a radius of three-quarters of a nautical mile, whose centre is at 57 53' 20"N 05 28'06"W ". The Secretary of State "for a reason affecting the public interest, deems it necessary in the public interest to restrict flying in the vicinity of Gruinard Island, Ross and Cromarty, by reason of its contamination with anthrax spores." An interesting regulation.

Airspace is divided vertically as well as horizontally. There are three fundamental vertical divisions:

Lower Airspace which extends from ground or sea level (but see below for some qualifications) to eight thousand feet;

Middle Airspace which extends from eight thousand feet to 24,500 feet (24,500 feet is an important altitude, see below);

Upper Airspace which extends from 25,000 feet into space. The vertical limit is undetermined.**

Lower airspace contains free space, or uncontrolled airspace, control zones and TMAs. The latter two are found in this band of altitudes because they are concerned with the control of aircraft in and around aerodromes, and hence, with aircraft which are either landing or taking off.

Middle airspace contains uncontrolled airspace and airways, which are, of course, controlled.

Upper airspace is partly used for commercial flights and is controlled.

Each airway is divided into two components: a lower and an upper airway. Lower airways have a maximum altitude of 24,500 feet; upper airways begin at 25,000 feet and extend, theoretically, into space. In practice, the performance of aircraft determines the maximum altitude which is used in Upper Airspace: Concorde can fly at 60,000 feet, but a 747 is limited to a ceiling of about 40,000.

The vertical division of airspace is shown in fig. A1.2.

1.4. FLIGHT LEVELS

Controlled airspace is divided into *Flight Levels.* A Flight Level (FL or simply level) is a strip of air of determinate thickness and undefined horizontal extension. Flight level zero is at the 1013.2mb pressure level (the standard altimeter setting for mean sea level.) Consecutive flight levels are at intervals of 500 ft. up to FL250 (25,000 ft.) and 1,000 feet above FL 250. The reader should note that levels are specified in terms of hundreds of feet in the standard atmosphere, thus FL35 represents 3,500 ft. and FL245 represents 24,500 ft., and so on. Figure A1.3 shows the flight level structure of airspace.

Aircraft in controlled airspace are allocated to a level. The level at which an aircraft flies is deter-

** Actually, the upper limit is about 60,000 ft. for all practical purposes.

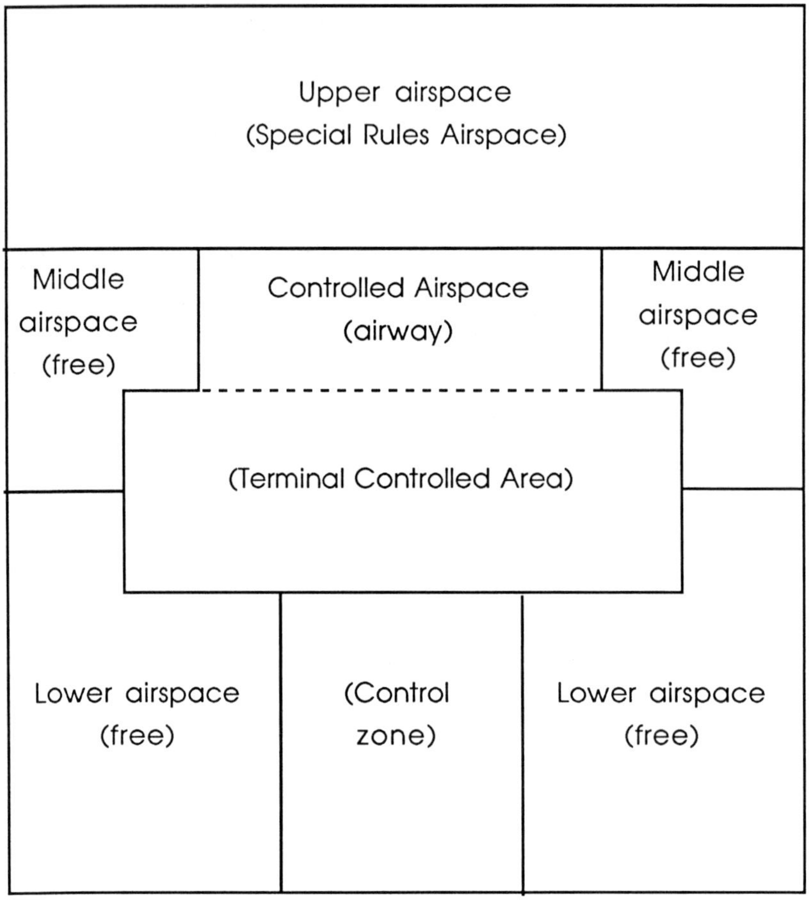

Fig A1.2

Vertical Airspace Structure (n.t.s.)

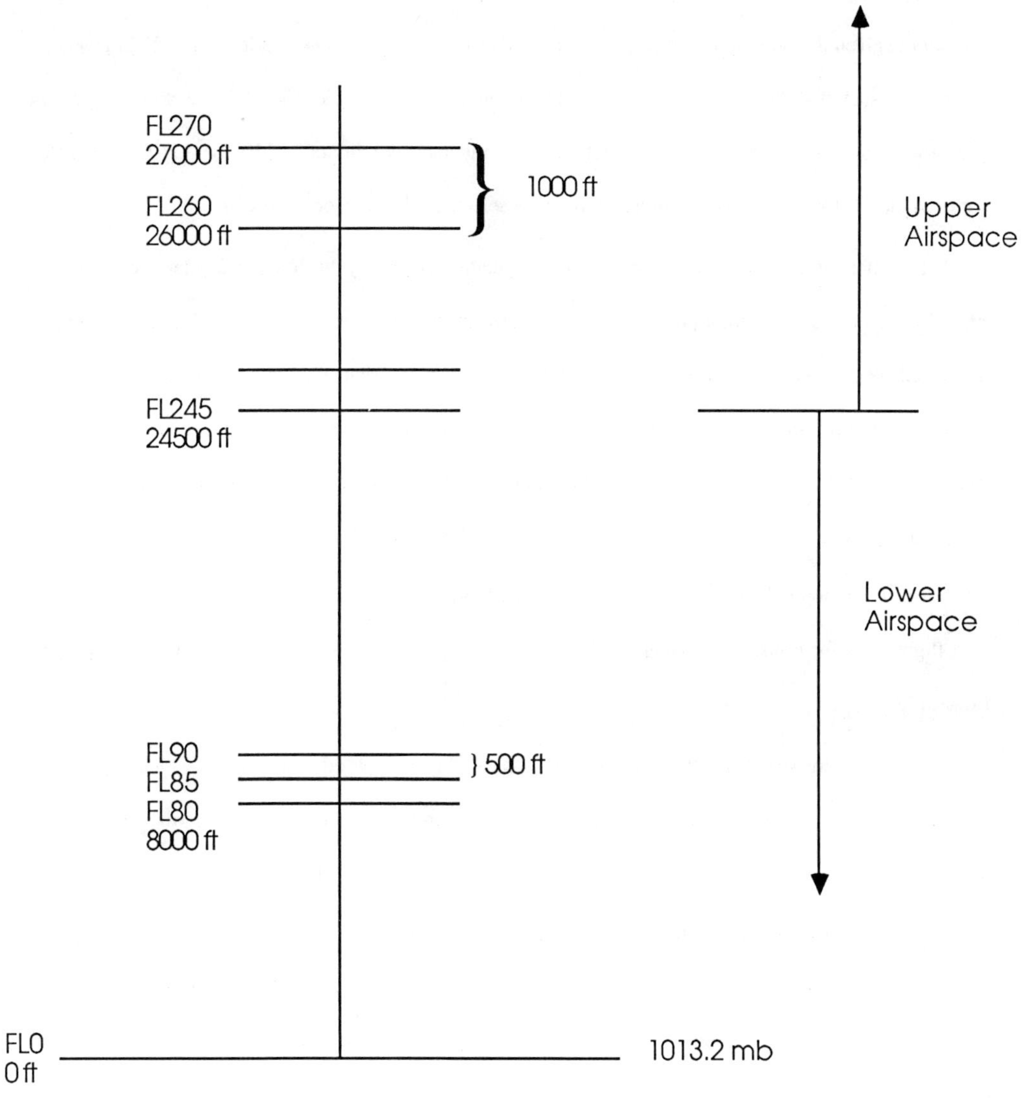

Fig A1.3

Level Structures in Airspace (n.t.s.)

mined by the level requested in the flight plan (see below.) If, for some reason, that level is not available, the pilot is given the opportunity to select an alternative from a set of options. Alternative flight levels are to be given such that they are as close as possible to the originally requested level. Thus, a pilot may have filed a flight plan which requests FL150, but, owing to the unavailability of FL150, the ATCO could offer, for example, FL140 and FL160, from which the pilot selects the level he or she prefers.

The selection of flight levels is partly due to regulation and partly due to the characteristics of the aircraft. The airlines use the flight profiles for each aircraft in their fleets to determine the levels they require. The profile defines a curve over the surface of the Earth which represents the sequence of altitudes at which the aircraft is at its maximum efficiency. The operators do not wish to waste fuel and money by being allocated levels which reduce the efficiency of their aircraft, so when filing flight plans, the profile is used to determine the altitude at which the aircraft will fly during the various phases of its flight.

It is worth noting here that there is a definite prohibition in MATS that FL245 *must not* be allocated as a flight level for cruising (cruising level.) This is because it forms the boundary between Upper and Lower FIRs.

The reason for levels is that aircraft must be separated from each other vertically and the assignment of discrete levels is one way to do this by regulation. In uncontrolled airspace, of course, the level system does not apply.

Rules exist for assigning aircraft to cruising levels (see below.) These rules are not to be taken as expressing a rule of law because of the possibility that levels may not be available. The COM section of the UK Air Pilot gives rules for particular airways and airspaces which, again, are normative rather than wholly prescriptive.

1.5. FLIGHT RULES

Within airspace of any kind within the UK, flights by civilian aircraft can be conducted only according to either visual flight rules (VFR) or instrument flight rules (IFR.) Some airspaces (such as airways) are designated as permitting only IFR flights and all flights in these airspaces must be made in accordance with IFR. Pilots must fly according to IFR if the airspace has been notified as IFR only, or if meteorological conditions preclude VFR flights or if it is a night flight. IFR means quite simply that the pilot uses the aircraft instruments as the source of information rather than by looking out of the windows to see what else is around.

Although a pilot who intends to fly according to VFR is responsible for determining whether meteorological conditions permit such a flight, there are prescribed minima which must be observed. In controlled airspace, a pilot of a VFR flight must remain at least one mile horizontally and 1,000 ft. vertically from cloud and must have at least 5 miles visibility. In uncontrolled airspace, the minima depend upon whether the aircraft is above or below 3,000 ft. amsl (above mean sea level as determined in the standard atmosphere - i.e., mean sea level is at a pressure of 1013.2mb.) If flying above 3,000 ft. amsl, the same minima as for controlled airspace obtain. However, if the flight is below that altitude, then the minima depend upon whether the aircraft is a helicopter or fixed wing; if a fixed wing aircraft, then minima depend upon airspeed. Below 3,000 ft. amsl and at a speed greater than 140 knots (1 knot = 1 nautical mile per hour), the horizontal and vertical distances from cloud are the same, but visibility is reduced to a 3 mile minimum; at speeds less than 140 kts (knots), the horizontal and vertical minima are defined as being clear of cloud and in sight of the surface; the visibility minimum is set to one mile.

IFR flights are those which are monitored by CASSANDRA-II. IFR require a pilot to observe the minimum height rule (in The Rules of the Air) and additional rules according to the type of airspace. Within controlled airspace, pilots must file a flight plan (see below) and obtain clearance (permission to proceed) before proceeding with the flight. Pilots in controlled airspace must also conduct the flight in accordance with instructions and clearances issued by air traffic control; they must maintain a listening watch on appropriate radio frequencies (VHF for civilian flights and for military flights considered as civilian; UHF for military flights) and report the position of the aircraft according to published procedures. Outside controlled airspace, pilots must fly in accordance with either the quandrantal or semi-circular rules for altitude determination (see above) when in level flight above 3,000 ft. amsl.

The CASSANDRA-II system is concerned solely with IFR flights within controlled airspace.

1.6. FLIGHT PLANS

Flight plans are filed with an ATCU (Air Traffic Control Unit) prior to departure from an aerodrome or while in the air. Flight plans contain details of the type of aircraft, route, take-off weight and survival equipment carried (in case of emergency.) The route information for controlled airspace includes information on the airspeed, the route across country (expressed as a sequence of beacons) and the altitude desired for the flight. When under control, the ATCO must try at all times to route an aircraft through airspace as closely as possible in accordance with the requests made in the flight plan. Where this is not possible, the reasons for withholding a clearance or directing an alteration must be given.

There are provisions for the repetitive filing of the same flight plan. Airlines operating scheduled routes would find it excessive to keep filing the same flight plan for each route each time an aircraft were along that route. Under the repetitive flight plan scheme, one flight plan only is filed, but the details are brought forward by Air Traffic Control each time the details of the flight are required.

Once a flight plan has been filed, flight strips (or, simply, strips) are made. Strips are summaries of the flight plan held on paper strips. Strips are to be seen on pictures of ATCOs at work. There are a number of types of strip for various purposes (e.g., en-route control, aerodrome control and so on), but reference here will be made only to en-route strips which describe flights in airways. Strips are held in plastic holders, the colour of which denotes the direction of the flight: blue holders mean westbound en-route and buff (which looks more yellow to me) denote eastbound en-route flights.

When using strips, ATCOs are supposed to maintain them in time order and in order of beacon. Thus, under each beacon in the section of airspace under the ATCOs control, each strip will be ordered according to its arrival time in controlled airspace. Once a strip is no longer required (by virtue of the departure, etc., of the aircraft it represents), it is placed (or thrown) into a tray for collection.

The strip, together with a SSR Mode-C radar display (where provided, and see below for details) is the primary input to the individual ATCO.

1.7. SEPARATION

Separation refers to the maintenance of specified distances between aircraft. The separation may be based on time or on distance and may apply to the horizontal or vertical dimensions. In the vertical, separation is augmented by the level system outlined above. In the horizontal, separation is divided into lateral and longitudinal. Many issues enter into separation: the kind of monitoring performed on the aircraft, the proximity to beacons, geographical factors (there is a special kind of separation for geographical features, called Geographical Separation), proximity to aerodromes and so on. It is crucial that separation of all kinds is maintained between aircraft, for, if it is not, collisions can occur.

Another aspect of separation is the consideration of the vortex-wake effect. When an aircraft moves through the air, it leaves an area of turbulence behind it and there is a vortex effect immediately astern the aircraft. If an aircraft gets too close to the stern of another aircraft, the wake-vortex effect can, in the worst case, 'flip' the following aircraft: that is, the following aircraft might be flipped over, or crushed by the pressure wave in the wake. Consider a light aircraft flying across the wake of a B747 (Jumbo). A B747-200 has an average takeoff weight of some 350 tonnes (for a long range flight), whereas a Short SD3-30 has an average take off weight of about 9.9 tonnes. The effect of flying a 3-30 right across the tail of a Jumbo would be that the 3-30 would be subjected to extreme turbulence, with attendant massive strain on the wings, tail, airframe and control surfaces: the result would be that the 3-30 would, quite literally, disintegrate. Thus, when considering separation, account should be taken of wake-vortex spacing.

MATS specifies separation standards which are *minima.* This entails that ATCOs should try to obtain separations which are greater than the figures given in MATS. The separation minima can be increased when requested by a pilot, when deemed necessary by a controller and when directed by NATS headquarters. Equally, separation may be reduced, but only when either directed by NATS headquarters or when the separation is between search and rescue aircraft. Separation minima may be reduced in the vicinity of an aerodrome under certain, quite specific, conditions. Responsibility for maintaining separation can, for short periods of time, be handed to the pilot of an aircraft, for example, by asking if the pilot can maintain separation by visual methods (e.g., VMC climb and descent). Such a move can, however, only be made when the consent of the pilot has been given: an ATCO cannot simply instruct a pilot to maintain his own separation.

If separation is reduced below the prescribed minima, controllers are to use all and any means at their disposal to obtain the required minimum with the least possible delay and, when considered practicable, give essential traffic information. Essential traffic is traffic flying according to IFR which is separated for any period by less than the specified minimum specified separation. Essential traffic information is information given by the ATCO to essential traffic.

Since essential traffic information will occur later in the presentation of separation rules, it is worth explaining what it entails. MATS specifies that essential traffic information should include the direction of flight of conflicting traffic (a confliction is a violation of a separation minimum); the type of conflicting aircraft; either the cruising level of the conflicting aircraft and the ETA (Estimated Time of Arrival) for the reporting point (see below), or for aircraft passing through the level of another aircraft with less than normal separation, the ETA for the reporting point closest to the point at which the levels are crossed, and any alternative clearance (i.e., any other instructions which are necessary).

Although conflictions are generally to be avoided, part of the skill of the experienced ATCO is the ability to create useful conflictions. These might be used, for example, to provide a window through which another aircraft can pass. The condition on generating conflictions is that they must be such that they can be resolved at a later point without endangering the aircraft in question.

Now that the basics of separation have been dealt with, we can press on with the individual separation classes. These descriptions will lay the foundations for the majority of the KSs in CASSANDRA-II.

1.7.1. Vertical Separation

These are the simplest of all the separation rules to express.

MATS states that vertical separation exists whenever the vertical distance between aircraft is never less than the prescribed minimum. The minima are defined as:

- Below FL290, 1000 ft.;
- Between FL290 and FL450, 2000 ft.;
- Above FL450, if the aircraft are in subsonic flight, 2000 ft.; 4000 ft. otherwise.

Controllers assess the vertical distance between aircraft by using secondary radar Mode C responses (see below) or by obtaining level reports (i.e., reports of the levels at which the aircraft are flying) from pilots.

The altitude at which an aircraft flies may, of course, vary. A change in altitude is referred to as 'level changing'. Controllers may instruct an aircraft to change levels at any place, specified time or at any rate (but subject to the aircraft performance.) There are conditions attached to instructing aircraft to change levels. An aircraft may be instructed to climb or descend to another level which has previously been occupied by another aircraft provided that vertical separation already exists, that the vacating aircraft is proceeding to a level which will maintain vertical separation (as defined in a previous paragraph), and that either the controller observes that the vacating aircraft has left the level (either by pilot report or SSR Mode C return) or the pilot has reported vacating the level. In the case where turbulence is known to exist in the region of the aircraft, instructions to change level are to be delayed until the vacating aircraft is known to be at or through a level 1000 ft. (2000 ft. above FL290) vertically from the level it previously occupied. Further, if two pilots are in direct communication with each other, if they agree, they may be instructed to maintain a specified vertical separation between aircraft during either climb or descent.

1.7.2. Horizontal Separation

Horizontal separation is divided into three types:

- Lateral separation
- Longitudinal separation
- Radar separation.

There are some terms which need to be fixed before explaining the three types of horizontal separation.

- Level change. This means that portion of the climb and descent during which the vertical separation between aircraft of two or more aircraft is less than the prescribed minima. This is determined by the distance between the levels of the aircraft.
- Exact reporting point. This is a position established by a navigational facility which is either overhead a VOR; overhead an NDB; a position which has been notified as a reporting point and which is established by the intersection of VOR radials or a VOR radial and a bearing from an NDB; a position established by a VOR radial combined with a range from a DME, or, a published Decca reporting point.

The reader should refer to these terms and to the provisos for dealing with VOR/DME/TACAN facilities (next paragraph) when reading the horizontal separation rules.

When dealing with a VOR and associated DME/TACAN station, the following points should be remembered.

When measured distance values are being used, each aircraft must be using the same *on track** VOR/DME/TACAN facility. That entails that both aircraft must be flying towards or away from the same facility. Otherwise it would be possible for distances to be measured from different facilities which could, at best, incur measurement errors.

Controllers must maintain communication with the aircraft whose distances are being measured by the VOR/DME/TACAN facility throughout the period that measurements are being used to achieve horizontal separation. Separation is to be checked by obtaining simultaneous readings from aircraft at intervals of not more than ten minutes.

The following terms are used. They refer to tracks determined by VOR radials. 'Same track' refers to tracks to and from the same facility which are separated by less than 20 degrees. 'Reciprocal track' is when the track of one aircraft is separated from the reciprocal track** of the other aircraft by less than 20 degrees.

VOR/DME/TACAN separation criteria are based on the condition that a VOR and the DME/TACAN associated with it are not more than 5 miles apart. If the DME/TACAN and the VOR are separated by a distance greater than 5 miles, special instructions are published.

1.7.2.1. Lateral Separation

1.7.2.1.1. Track Separation

Track separation is established by requiring aircraft to fly on specified tracks which are separated by a minimum amount appropriate to the navigation aid in question. Aircraft must be in the operational cover-

---

* The track of an aircraft is a 2-vector which describes the path followed by the aircraft across the surface of the Earth. 'On track' means that the beacon is at a point which is part of the track of the aircraft.

** Two tracks are reciprocal if and only if the sum of the two tracks expressed in degrees is equal to 180.0 degrees.

age of a VOR or within the protected range of an NDB for track separation to be used. The COM section of the UK Air Pilot specifies these distances. The separation minima are as follows:

- If using a VOR and associated DME/TACAN, both aircraft are established (in fact, are reported to be established) on radials at least 20 degrees apart, then if the aircraft are diverging and one aircraft is 15 miles from the DME/TACAN then minimum separation exists; if aircraft are converging and one is 30 miles from the DME/TACAN station then separation exists; if one aircraft is inbound and the other is outbound from the VOR, and either the outbound aircraft is at least 20 miles from the station or the inbound aircraft is at least 30 miles from the station, then minimum separation exists.
- If using VOR radials and one aircraft is the time equivalent of 15 miles or 4 minutes (whichever is the greater) from the VOR and both aircraft have reported being established on radials which diverge by at least 20 degrees, then minimum separation is established;
- If using VOR radials and both aircraft have passed the VOR on tracks diverging by 45 degrees or more and both aircraft have reported established on the relevant radials, then minimum separation exists;
- If using specified tracks from an NDB, and one aircraft is the time equivalent of 15 miles or 4 minutes (whichever is greater) from the NDB and both aircraft have reported being established on the radials, then minimum separation exists.

The track separation rules are summarised in fig. A1.4. The arrows in the figure represent aircraft.

1.7.2.1.2. Geographical Separation

Geographical separation must be positively indicated by position reports over different geographical locations. These reports must be determined visually or by reference to a navigational aid. Geographical separation must be constant or increasing for the separation minimum to exist.

1.7.2.1.3. Longitudinal Separation - Time and Distance

Longitudinal separation is based either on time or on distance. It is applied such that the spacing between estimated aircraft positions is never less than the prescribed minima. Longitudinal separation is achieved

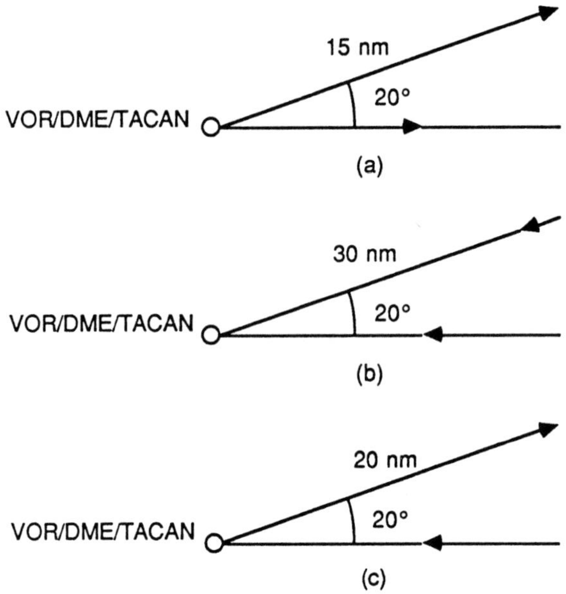

Fig A1.4(a)

Cases:

(a) Aircraft diverge and one is 15 nm from VOR/DME/TACAN

(b) Aircraft converge and one is 30 nm from VOR/DME/TACAN

(c) One inbound, one outbound. Outbound must be ≥ 20 nm from VOR/DME/TACAN; inbound must be ≥ 30 nm from VOR/DME/TACAN.

(N.B. n.t.s.)

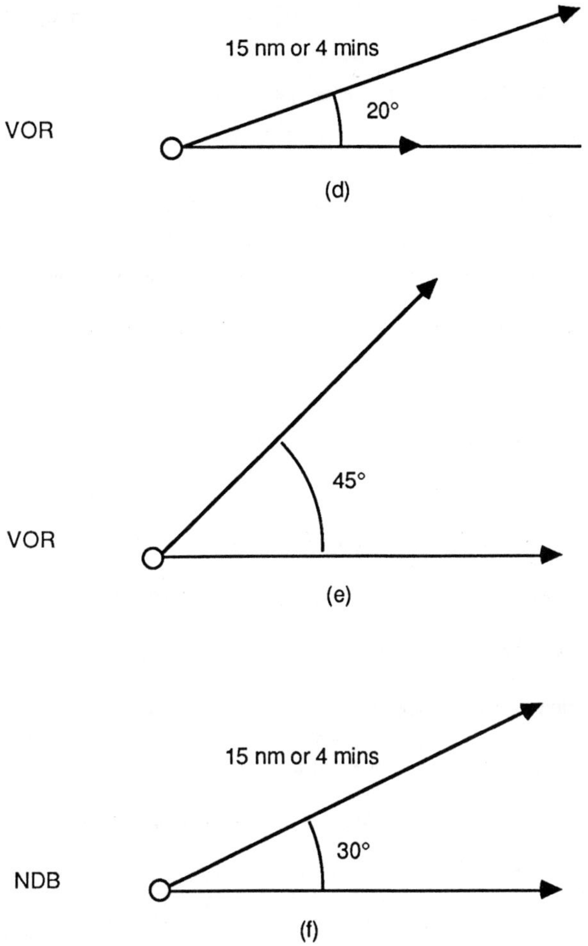

Fig A1.4(b)

Cases:

(d) Aircraft are diverging. One must be the time equivalent of 15 nm or 4 mins (whichever is the greater) from VOR

(e) Aircraft are diverging. They must diverge by ≥ 45°

(f) Aircraft diverging from <u>NDB</u> . One must be the time equivalent of 15 nm or 4 mins (whichever is the greater) from NDB by requiring aircraft

- to depart at specified times, or
- to loose or gain time to arrive at a geographical location at some specified time, or
- to hold over a geographical location until some specified time.

The separation minima based on time are as follows.

If aircraft are en-route and have the same cruising level and same track, then the conditions of this paragraph apply. If 2 minute departure separation has been applied (i.e., aircraft depart at least 2 minutes apart) then the minimum separation is 2 minutes. If one aircraft is following another and the preceding aircraft has filed an airspeed at least 20 kts. or more faster than the following aircraft, then minimum separation is 5 minutes. If NATS headquarters has authorised a 5 minute minimum, then that is the minimum. If both aircraft are equipped with functioning transponders and are monitored by radar and the actual distance between them is never less than 30 miles (this separation has to be authorised by NATS headquarters), the minimum is 5 minutes. Otherwise, the separation minimum is 10 minutes. For all minima except the last, the separation should be based on actual aircraft position reports.

If aircraft are climbing and descending on the same track and are en-route, the conditions of this paragraph apply. If an aircraft is climbing or descending and the level change has commenced within 10 minutes of the time the second aircraft has reported as being over the same exact reporting point, the minimum separation is 5 minutes at the time the levels are crossed. This figure should be based on actual position reports. Otherwise, the minimum is 10 minutes.

If en-route aircaft are crossing tracks, then the condition of this paragraph applies. Separation shall be at least 10 minutes.

If aircraft are on reciprocal tracks* and are en-route, then the minimum separation shall be 10 minutes before and after the estimated passing time.* Furthermore, vertical separation shall be provided for at least 10 minutes both prior to and after the estimated passing time unless both aircraft have actually passed each other and this fact has been confirmed. The source of confirmation can be one or more of the

* See the definition above.

* If aircraft are on reciprocal tracks, then, at some point, they will pass each other.

following: radar derived information, a visual sighting report from both pilots (but only by day), or aircraft position reports over the same exact reporting point - this can be used only if vertical separation is maintained for a time long enough for navigation errors to be taken into consideration.

The rules for longitudinal separation based on distance are now given. When using DME/TACAN facilities, separation is established by maintaining not less than the distances specified in the following paragraphs. The DME/TACAN stations must be on track.

Separation based on DME/TACAN information is not to be used when aircraft are within 15 miles of the overhead of the facility: this is because of slant range errors. Beyond 15 miles, slant range errors can be ignored.

If aircraft are en-route, and are on the same track and cruising level, then the rules of this paragraph apply. The minimum separation is 15 miles if the preceding aircraft maintains a true airspeed (tas) of 20 kts or more faster than the following aircraft and both aircraft are within 100 miles if the DME/TACAN station. If the preceding aircraft maintains a tas of 20 kts or more than the following aircraft and the conditions associated with distance to the DME/TACAN do not hold, then the minimum is 20 miles. The same minimum holds for aircraft which are within 100 miles of the DME/TACAN, but the condition concerning the tas difference of the preceding aircraft does not hold. If none of these rules holds, then the minimum is 25 miles.

If en-route aircraft are climbing or descending on the same track then the minimum is 15 miles at the time levels are crossed. This is provided that one aircraft maintains level flight while vertical separation does not exist.

If en-route aircraft are on reciprocal tracks, then minimum separation is 40 miles. The 40 mile minimum need not apply if it has been established that the aircraft have passed each other and are at least 10 miles apart. The 10 miles can be further reduced to 5 miles when both aircraft are within 100 miles of the DME/TACAN.

Longitudinal separation also pertains to aircraft which are holding, departing aircraft and a mixture of en-route and departing aircraft. These are not included in the current version of CASSANDRA-II and are not, therefore, reported.

1.7.2.1.4. Radar Separation

Although the current version of CASSANDRA-II does not contain radar separation rules, they comprise the next set of rules to be included, so they are presented here.

Horizontal separation based upon radar exists when the distance between the centres of the radar returns does not represent less than the prescribed minima. The following paragraphs present the rules.

The minimum separation shall be 3 miles if the radar is analogue or plot extracted and the conditions of this paragraph apply. If NATS HQ has authorised and both aircraft are below FL245 and are within 40 miles of the radar source provided that both aircraft have been identified or the aircraft are being controlled by adjacent approach control radar units and are operating within areas responsibility which are geographically separated by a buffer zone 3 miles wide.

The separation minimum shall be 5 miles if the conditions of this paragraph obtain. If the radar presentation is analogue then if, in azimuth, the separation between the centres of the returns may be 5 miles provided that the returns are never allowed to touch or overlap. If the presentation is plot extracted, then the minimum holds if, in azimuth, both aircraft are within 80 miles of a known single radar source.

The separation minimum is 5 miles for both plot extracted and analogue presentations provided that, in range, both aircraft are within the coverage of a known single radar souce.

The minimum is 10 miles for plot extracted if, in azimuth, one or both aircraft are more than 80 miles from a known single radar source. This minimum may be reduced if specifically authorised by NATS HQ.

These rules apply under the following conditions. Separation must be determined by using the primary returns if primary radar is being used. Radar separation may not be used between aircraft holding over the same holding point.

SSR alone may be used as a source of information for horizontal separation if the conditions of this paragraph obtain. Pilots must be made aware of the limitations of the service. The circumstances for the application of SSR alone are thus: SSR can be used to overcome the deficiencies within primary radar cover (such as fading or clutter), but the secondary return of only one aircraft may be used to provide separation from another aircraft provided that the primary and secondary displays are correctly aligned; or where primary radar is not available. Reflections, equipment malfunction or other reasons to doubt the accuracy of secondary radar entail that it shall not be used to determine horizontal separation.

The comments conclude the presentation of separation rules.

1.8. CONTROL OF TRAFFIC

Traffic in the airways is notified of permission to perform some course alteration or to move onto the next part of a flight by means of a clearance. A clearance is permission to proceed under conditions specified by an air traffic control unit. The initial request for clearance comes from the flight plan which is filed for every flight in controlled airspace. If a pilot is given a clearance, the fact that it has been issued does not constitute permission to violate any regulation or law established by ministerial or statutory agency.

Even when a clearance has been given, there is a limit to it. The limit of a clearance is specified by naming an aerodrome, a reporting point (a beacon, a navigational aid or other exact point) or an airspace boundary. When an aircraft has reached a reporting point and has not been cleared to proceed further along its route, the aircraft must hold at that point (by flying a triangular course with each side of each triangle about 5 nautical miles long).

Clearances can be amended when necessary. If a clearance is amended, it automatically cancels any previous clearance. Clearances can also be witheld if conditions so dictate. A reason for witholding clearance for take off might be that an aircraft is to be detained by police or customs.

Traffic control is also concerned with flight priorities. Normally, clearances are to be dealt with in the order in which they are received and are issued in accordance with traffic conditions. However, certain flights are given priority over others. When two or more flights of different priorities request clearance, the flight with the highest priority (category) is dealt with first.*

The highest category is A. Aircraft in emergency (e.g., engine failure, fuel shortage, seriously ill passenger), aircraft in the service of the police which are empowered to declare a police emergency, ambulance aircraft when the safety of life is involved and the pilot has declared an emergency due to the condition of the passenger - all of these are cases of category A flights.

* This is a regulatory fiction. Aircraft are dealt with, in practice, in the order in which they contact the ATCO.

Category B flights (the next highest priority) are those involving post accident incident flight checks carried out by CAFU (Civil Aviation Flying Unit) aircraft at the request of AIB (Accident Investigation Branch).

Flights which are either Royal Flights or are carrying visiting heads of state and which have been notified by NOTAM (NOtice to AirMen) form category C flights.

Flights which have been notified by NATS HQ and are not subjects of NOTAM action and which carry members of the Royal Family, government ministers whether of HM Government or of another state and other VIPs fall into category D. Supplementary flight checks by CAFU aircraft, MoD secret flights or any other flights notified by NATS HQ are also of category D.

The category of most flights is Normal. Normal Flights are scheduled services, executive, private and positioning flights which have filed a flight plan.

Below Normal Flights in decreasing priority order are categories X, Y and Z.

Category X flights are preferred flights. A preferred flight is a Special Flight upgraded to meet a deadline.

Special Flights such a photographic surveys, parachute drops, police helicopters and so on, and test flights fall within category Y.

The lowest category is Z. These are training flights. Since training flights have the lowest category, they must be fitted into the normal traffic pattern as the opportunity occurs.

Flights have to be notified to the receiving centre, sector or unit to permit analysis prior to co-ordination. Notification in controlled, special rules or advisory airspace consists of either a current flight plan, or an estimate and control information. This information is necessary for clearances to be given and so that airspace can be managed effectively. Co-ordination occurs when control of an aircraft is handed from one ATCU to another.

1.9. RADAR OPERATIONS

Airways are provided with radar cover. Radar is used for vectoring, derivation of position information, monitoring of traffic to provide information to non-radar controllers and to assist aircraft crossing controlled airspace.

1.9.1. Identification

Aircraft can be identified by either primary or secondary radar. If using primary radar, distance measuring equipment should be used to assist identification, provided that it has been approved for such use.

There are three methods of identification by primary radar: the turn method, the departing aircraft method and the position reporting method. The turn method requires an aircraft to alter heading by at least 30 degrees once its heading and track have been observed. The turn method involves correlating the radar return from the aircraft with either an acknowledged or observed return. The departing aircraft method involves the observation and correlation of a radar return for a departing aircraft with a known airborne time: unless otherwise authorised by NATS HQ, the identification must be achieved within one mile of the end of the runway from which the aircraft has taken off. The final method, the position report method, operates by matching a radar return with a report from the pilot that the aircraft is either over an exact reporting point displayed on the radar map (the specified track must be consistent with the route of the flight) or a specified distance on a specified radial from a co-located VOR/DME or TACAN (DME) which, again, must be displayed on the radar map. If using the position reporting method, aircraft must not be descended below the appropriate minimum sector altitude until identification has been made by a method other than the position reporting method.

If, using radar, there is any doubt about the accuracy of the equipment, radar methods should not be used.

If secondary methods are available, then it can be used for identification. There are four SSR methods which can be used:

- observing the pilot's compliance with the instruction to set a discrete four digit code;
- recognising a validated four digit code previously assigned to an aircraft call sign;
- observing an IDENT feature when it has been requested. Misidentification can occur due to simultaneous requests for SPI* transmissions;

* SPI = Special Position Identification.

- instructing the pilot to switch the transponder to STANDBY and then back to ON. This method may only be used when no other SSR method is available. It must be used with some caution, however, because the same effect can be caused by temporary shading of the aircraft radar antenna or the simultaneous use of the same procedure by another aircraft.

When an aircraft is operating in controlled airspace, the controller need not inform the pilot of a positive SSR identification.

Controllers are to assign discrete codes to aircraft according to the code allocation plan. The plan lists the codes which are allocated to individual service units for assignment to aircraft. The plan consists of domestic codes which are assigned to aircraft flying within the unit's area of responsibility and ORCAM** codes which are assigned to international flights and are retained by the aircraft beyond the limits of the area of the assigning unit's responsibility.

Mode C must be selected in conjunction with Mode A unless otherwise directed. Mode A codes must be checked whenever they are used. Verification is achieved by one of three methods:

- instructing the aircraft to squawk* the assigned code and observing that the code appears correctly on the radar display;
- instructing the aircraft to 'squawk IDENT' and checking the code numbers associated with the radar return;
- matching a radar return already identified by primary radar with the assigned code for the flight.

If the check fails, the pilot must be instructed to recycle the assigned code. If this fails then the pilot must be instructed to select code A0000. If a corrupt code still exists, the pilot is normally instructed to switch off the transponder. If Mode C is verified, and the procedure is approved by NATS HQ, the corrupt code may be retained to assist identification and tracking. Associated units must be informed of the corrupt code.

** ORCAM = Originating Region Code Assignment Method. The idea behind ORCAM is that an aircraft should be assigned a unique SSR code for use throughout its flight. The codes used by ORCAM are formed into blocks and these are used by the countries (participating areas) to assign unique codes within their own areas. When an aircraft moves from one participating area to another, it may have to change its code: within an area, aircraft wear the same code from takeoff to touchdown. The UK, Belgium, France, Germany, Ireland, Luxembourg, Netherlands, Switzerland and parts of Spain and Italy are the five participating areas within the ICAO EUR region. Scandinavia forms a different participating area.

* squawk = transmit

There are special purpose codes which may be selected under the appropriate conditions. Codes 7500, 7600 and 7700 are assigned as Emergency codes. Code 2000 is selected by pilots entering UK airspace from adjacent regions where transponder operation has not been required. There is also the conspicuity code 4321 which must be used in conjunction with Mode C which should be displayed by all suitably equipped aircraft unless they have been assigned a discrete code or unless they are flying in an aerodrome traffic pattern below 3000 ft. or unless they are transponding on one of the special purpose codes.

Mode C radar can also be used for vertical separation and level assessment.

1.9.2. Using Mode C for Vertical Separation

When using SSR for vertical separation, the responses are to be continuously monitored to ensure that the vertical separation is never less than the prescribed minima. Minimum separation may be applied between verified Mode C transponding aircraft if the intentions of both aircraft are known to the controller because they are both under his/her control, or they have been co-ordinated or because they are operating in accordance with established agreements. If the intentions of both aircraft are not known, the minimum vertical separation shall be 5000 ft.. If Mode C returns are not verified (by, for example, transponding the conspicuity code 4321) then a minimum separation of 5000 ft. must be maintained between aircraft and the radar returns must not be allowed to merge. If an aircraft is transponding Mode A0000, i.e., has a faulty transponder, then Mode C vertical separation must not be used.

Mode C accuracy is checked by verifying that the readout indicates 200 ft. or less from the level reported by the pilot: if the aircraft is climbing or descending, then the pilot must be instructed to give a precise report as the aircraft passes through a level. Mode C is assumed to be verified if it is associated with a deemed validated Mode A code. There is, however, no need to monitor level readouts when Mode C information is not being used to provide verical separation.

1.9.3. Using Mode C for Level Assessment

Mode C can be used for level assessment if the following criteria apply.

- An aircraft can be considered to be at an assigned level provided that the Mode C readout indicates 200 ft. or less from that level;

- an aircraft known to have been instructed to climb or descend can be considered to have left a level when the readout from Mode C indicates that there has been a change of 400 ft. or more from the level and that the aircraft is continuing in the anticipated direction;
- an aircraft can be considered to have reached an assigned level if the Mode C readout indicates 200 ft. or less from that level.

1.9.4. Vectoring

Vectoring is the instruction of an aircraft to fly along a specified bearing for any specified time. This means that, when vectoring instructions have been given to a pilot, he or she is to change the heading of the aircraft to that specified in the vectoring instructions. It means that the aircraft must change its heading.

Radar controllers have complete freedom to instruct aircraft to turn in any direction as directed by circumstances. When avoiding unknown aircraft, the Rules of the Air should be observed if practicable.

This consideration of SSR concludes this section.

2. APPENDIX 2: CASSANDRA-II KNOWLEDGE SOURCES

This Appendix contains details of the Knowledge Sources currently used in CASSANDRA-II. Some KSs are notated in a pseudo-code, while others are expressed as a short paragraph of English: in general, the exemplary KSs or those which best give a flavour of the task are represented in pseudo-code. The reader should note that CASSANDRA-II does not contain any clauses which specify that aircraft should be within 100nm of a DME/TACAN: this is because most of the sectors in the mainland UK are so small that this clause is totally redundant (it applies only to the Western Approaches and to the North Sea sectors in the London FIR): the avarage sector is 40nm square and there is ample coverage of each sector by VOR/DME/TACAN beacons.

- input Level Manager,
- cruise level allocation Level Manager (upper, then lower Level Manager),
- vertical separation Level Manager (upper, then lower Level Manager),
- lateral separation Level Manager (upper, then lower Level Manager), and finally
- longitudinal separation Level Manager (upper, then lower Level Manager).

The reader should compare these KSs with the corresponding statements of the basic rules (Appendix 1).

2.1. INPUT LEVEL MANAGER

There are six KSs in this Level Manager. The database local to this Level Manager is referred to as the 'input level'.

2.1.1. PruneAircraftOutsideAirspace

This KS side-effects the entry on which it was triggered.

```
IF the entry is of type List
   AND the entry contains aircraft
THEN
   FOREACH aircraft in the entry DO
      remove aircraft from entry;
```

2.1.2. CreatePairList

This KS creates the list of all pairs of aircraft mentioned in the entry which caused it to be triggered.

```
IF  the entry is of type List
   AND the entry contains aircraft
THEN
   LET new-entry BE
      create all possible pairs of aircraft
   IN
      post new-entry on input level;
```

2.1.3. PostCruiseLevelEntry

This KS posts an entry to the Cruise Level Allocation upper Level Manager for every aircraft in the entry which caused it to be triggered.

```
IF  the entry is of type List
   AND the entry contains aircraft
THEN
   FOREACH aircraft in entry DO
      LET cl-entry BE
         create an entry containing the aircraft
      IN
         send cl-entry to cruise level upper Level Manager;
```

2.1.4. CreateVerticalPrioList

This KS creates a list of aircraft pairs ordered by increasing vertical distance and posts an entry for each pair to the Vertical Separation upper Level Manager.

```
IF  the entry is a PairList
   AND there are pairs in the entry
THEN
   order pairs by vertical distance;
   FOREACH pair in ordered pairs DO
      LET v-ent BE
         create an entry
      AND LET the prioritisation BE
         vertical
      IN
         send v-ent to Vertical Separation
         upper Level Manager;
```

2.1.5. CreateHorizontalPrioList

This KS is exactly analogous to CreateVerticalPrioList, but the separation is horizontal and not vertical and message-sending is to the Lateral and Longitudinal Separation upper Level Managers. Prioritisation is horizontal.

2.1.6. HaveCrashed

This aircraft detects crashes between aircraft. If a crash has occurred, the KS informs the user.

```
IF the entry is of type PairList
   AND there are aircraft in the entry
THEN
   FOREACH aircraft pair DO
      IF vertical distance between aircraft is
        less than crash minimum
        AND horizontal distance between aircraft
        is less than horizontal crash minimum
      THEN
         inform user: these aircraft have crashed!;
```

2.2. CRUISE LEVEL ALLOCATION

2.2.1. UPPER LEVEL MANAGER

There is one KS on the upper Level Manager.

2.2.1.1. PutCruiseLevTestEntries

This KS sends an entry on the lower Level Manager for each aircraft in the entry which caused the KS to be triggered.

```
IF the entry is of type List
   AND there are aircraft in the entry
THEN
   FOREACH aircraft DO
      LET cl-ent BE
         create entry
         WITH
            e-aircraft = aircraft
      IN
         send cl-ent to lower Level Manager;
```

2.2.2. LOWER LEVEL MANAGER

There are two KSs in the lower Level Manager.

2.2.2.1. CheckFL245NotAlloc

This KS checks that the aircraft mentioned in the triggering entry has not been allocated FL245 as a cruise level.

```
IF the entry is of type SingleAircraft
   AND there is an aircraft
THEN
   IF the aircraft has been allocated
      FL245 as a cruise level
   THEN
      inform user: FL245 allocated
               for this aircraft;
```

2.2.2.2. CheckCruiseLevel

This KS checks that the aircraft mentioned by the entry which caused it to trigger is on the correct flight level for its heading as specified by the semi-circular rule.

```
IF the entry is of type SingleAircraft
   AND there is an aircraft
   AND the heading of the aircraft is h
   AND the level of the aircraft is l
THEN
   IF l is not the correct level for
     the heading h according to the
     semi-circular rule
   THEN
      inform user: aircraft on wrong
               flight level;
```

2.3. VERTICAL SEPARATION

2.3.1. UPPER LEVEL MANAGER

There are two KSs for the upper Level Manager.

2.3.1.1. Prune5000ftVerticalSep

This KS removes all aircraft which have a vertical separation greater than or equal to 5000 ft.. The KS side-effects the entry on which it was triggered.

```
IF the entry is a PrioList
   AND there are aircraft in the entry
   AND the entry is prioritised by vertical distance
THEN
   FOREACH aircraft pair in the entry DO
      IF the vertical separation is greater than
         or equal to 5000 ft
      THEN remove the aircraft pair;
```

2.3.1.2. PutVerticalSepTestEntries

This KS sends an entry to the lower Level Manager for every aircraft pair which remains in the entry on which it was triggered.

```
IF the entry is PrioList
   AND there are aircraft pairs in the entry
THEN
   FOREACH aircraft pair in the entry DO
      LET ent BE
         create an entry for the aircraft pair
      IN
         send ent to Vertical Separation lower Level Manager;
```

2.3.2. LOWER LEVEL MANAGER

There is one KS in this Level Manager (CheckVerticalSep). The KS tests to see if there is vertical separation between the aircraft in the pair found in the entry on which it was triggered. If there is not vertical separation (as defined for the altitudes at which the aircraft are flying), a message is sent to the user.

```
IF the entry is of type AircraftPair
   AND there is a pair
THEN
   FOREACH pair in the entry DO
      IF vertical separation does not exist
      THEN
         inform user:
           vertical separation does not exist for these aircraft;
```

2.4. LATERAL SEPARATION

2.4.1. UPPER LEVEL MANAGER

There is one KS in the upper Level Manager. The KS sends an entry to the lower Level Manager for every pair of aircraft in the entry on which it triggered.

```
IF the entry is of type PrioList
   AND there are aircraft pairs
   AND the priotisation is horizontal
THEN
   FOREACH aircraft pair DO
      LET l-ent BE
         create an entry of type beacon
         WITH
            beacon = the nearest beacon on which
                  the aircraft are converging or diverging
      IN
         send l-ent to lower Level Manager;
```

2.4.2. LOWER LEVEL MANAGER

There are six KSs in the lower Level Manager. The form of the KSs are very similar, and so only three examples are given in detail.

2.4.2.1. LateralSepKS1

This KS applies the rule that if two aircraft are on diverging tracks from a DME/TACAN and they are established on radials at least 20 degrees apart, minimum lateral separation is 15 nm.

```
IF the aircraft are diverging from a beacon
   AND the beacon is a VOR/DME/TACAN
   AND they are established on radials at least
      20 degrees apart
   AND the distance between the beacon and
      either aircraft is less than 15 nm
THEN
   inform user: these aircraft do not have minimum separation;
```

2.4.2.2. LateralSepKS2

This KS represents the rule: if using a VOR, there are two aircraft established on radials at least 20 degrees apart and one aircraft is outbound and the other is inbound, one aircraft must be at least 30nm from the beacon for lateral separation to exist.

```
IF the beacon is a VOR
   AND one aircraft (a1) is outbound
      from the beacon
   AND the other aircraft (a2) is
      inbound to the beacon
THEN
   IF the distance between a1 and the
      beacon is less than 30nm
      OR the distance between a2 and
      the beacon is less than 30nm
   THEN
      inform user: lateral separation does not exist;
```

2.4.2.3. LateralSepKS3

This KS represents the rule: if using a VOR, there are two aircraft and the aircraft are established on radials at least 20 degrees apart and one aircraft is outbound and the other inbound the outbound aircraft must be at least 30nm from the beacon and the inbound aircraft must be at least 20nm for separation to exist.

2.4.2.4. LateralSepKS4

This KS represents the rule: if using a VOR, there are two aircraft and the aircraft are established on radials at least 20 degrees apart and both aircraft are diverging from the VOR, one aircraft must be the time equivalent of 15nm or 4 minutes (whichever is the greater) from the beacon.

2.4.2.5. LateralSepKS5

This KS represents the rule: if using a VOR, there are two aircraft established on radials at least 45 degrees apart and both aircraft are diverging from the beacon, lateral separation exists.

2.4.2.6. LateralSepKS6

This KS represents the rule: if using specified tracks from a NDB, one aircraft is the time equivalent of 15nm or 4 minutes (whichever is the greater) from the beacon and both aircraft have reported established on tracks which diverge by at least 30 degrees, lateral separation exists.

2.5. LONGITUDINAL SEPARATION

2.5.1. UPPER LEVEL MANAGER

There are two KSs in the upper Level Manager. One of the KSs, Put LongitudinalSepTestEntries is analogous to the single KS in the upper Level Manager of the Lateral Separation Level Manager pair and, so, is not presented; the other KS, however, is presented.

2.5.1.1. PruneLongitudinalSepItems

This KS removes all references to aircraft pairs in the entry which caused it to be triggered if one or both of the aircraft in a pair is within 15nm of the overhead of a VOR and if the aircraft in a pair are separated by more than 50nm. This KS side-effects the entry on which it was triggered.

```
IF  the entry is of type PrioList
    AND the prioritisation is horizontal
    AND there are aircraft pairs
THEN
    FOREACH aircraft pair DO
       IF one or both aircraft is within 15nm
          of the overhead of the VOR
          OR the aircraft are separated by more than 50nm
       THEN remove the pair from the entry;
```

2.5.2. LOWER LEVEL MANAGER

There are eight KSs in the lower Level Manager. As was the case with Lateral Separation, only the exemplar KSs are presented.

2.5.2.1. LongitudinalSepKS1

This KS represents the rule: if one aircraft is following another and the leading aircraft maintains a tas of 20kts or more greater than the following aircraft and both aircraft are on the same track and cruise level, the minimum separation is 20nm.

```
IF  a1 is following a2
   AND a1 and a2 are on the
      same track
   AND a1 and a2 are on the
      same level
   AND the tas of a1 is t1
   AND the tas of a2 is t2
   AND a2 >= a1 + 20
   AND the distance between a1 and a2 is less than 20nm
THEN
   inform user: separation does not exist;
```

2.5.2.2. LongitudinalSepKS2

This KS represents the rule: if there are two aircraft and they are on the same track and cruise level and both aircraft are within 100nm of a DME/TACAN and the aircraft are separated by at least 20nm, minimum separation exists.

2.5.2.3. LongitudinalSepKS3

This KS represents the rule: if there are two aircraft and they are on the same track and are on the same level and one aircraft is following the other and both aircraft are within 100nm of a DME/TACAN, minimum separation is 15nm.

2.5.2.4. LongitudinalSepKS4

This KS represents the rule: if there are two aircraft on the same level and track and rules 1 to 3 above do not hold, minimum separation is 15nm.

2.5.2.5. LongitudinalSepKS5

This KS represents the rule: if there are two aircraft on the same track and one aircraft is climbing or descending while the other maintains level flight, minimum separation is 15nm at the time levels are crossed.

```
IF a1 and a2 are on the same track
   AND
      OR (a1 is climbing
         AND
         a2 is in level flight)
        (a2 is climbing
         AND
         a1 is in level flight)
   AND a1 is separated from a2
      by less than 15nm at the time
      the levels are crossed
THEN
   inform user: separation does
            not exist;
```

2.5.2.6. LongitudinalSepKS6

This KS represents the rule: if two aircraft are on reciprocal tracks and the aircraft have passed, minimum separation is 10nm.

2.5.2.7. LongitudinalSepKS7

This KS represents the rule: if two aircraft are on reciprocal tracks and have passed and both aircraft are within 100nm of a DME/TACAN, minimum separation is 15nm.

2.5.2.8. LongitudinalSepKS8

This KS represents the rule: if two aircraft are on reciprocal tracks and the two previous rules did not apply, minimum separation is 40nm.

3. APPENDIX 3: CASSANDRA-II TRACES

3.1. INTRODUCTION

This Appendix presents an edited trace of the CASSANDRA-II system. The version of the system from which the trace was generated contained entry deletion KSs in each Level Manager. The trace represents the monitoring activity of the system during a simulated one minute period in an airspace fifty miles square (that is, of the same order of size as many sectors in UK airspace). The one minute monitoring period was chosen so that the important features of the system were demonstrated without generating an execssive amount of data. It should be noted that the run traced in this Appendix is one of the simpler and shorter runs: this is so that the reader does not become confused with masses of Air Traffic Control details.

3.2. AIRSPACE CONFIGURATION

The airspace simulated for this run of CASSANDRA-II was square in shape, each side being 50 nm long. Horizontally, the airspace is represented by cartesian 2-space co-ordinates and the origin can be though of as being in the bottom left-hand corner. Vertically, the airspace stretches from 0 ft. to infinity, although none of the aircraft simulated for this run actually fly higher than 17,500 ft.. The transition altitude for the airspace is 3,000 ft.. The airspace is declared to the simulator to be an airway, so the semi-circular rule is used to define legal cruise levels for aircraft. There is one beacon, a VOR/DME/TACAN, in the airspace: it is located at co-ordinate <10.0, 10.0>.

Four aircraft traverse the airspace. Two are Boeing 747s and two are Boeing 727s. The 747s have the callsigns BA283 and BA194; the 727s have callsigns PA1 and PA12. BA283 begins the simulation at an altitude of 15,000 ft. (FL150), on a heading on 270 degrees and with a speed of 450 kts: its initial position is <4.8, 5.0>. BA194 begins the simulation at an altitude of 17,000 ft. (FL170), on a heading of 270 degress and with a speed of 450 kts: its initial position is <0.0, 5.0>. PA1 begins at 17,500 ft., on a heading of 90 degress at 450 kts: its initial location is <0.0, 4.0>. The final aircraft is PA12 which begins at location <4.0, 5.0>, on FL170 with a heading of 90 degrees. PA12's initial speed is 250 kts. All aircraft are **NORMAL** category flights and all are flying according to Instrument Flight Rules (IFR): this means that they are all just ordinary commercial flights.

The reader should note a few things about the simulation used for this run of CASSANDRA-II. The aircraft are bunched together in a very small region of the simulated airspace. No aircraft is separated from any other by more than the legal minimum horizontal separation when the simulation starts and there are vertical separation conflicts between aircraft. The point of placing the aircraft so close together is that it tests the monitor's abilities to detect conflicts. The aircraft are flying on headings designed to reduce the effects of some conflicts. Basically, there are two pairs of aircraft each of which is flying away from the other. Within each pair, the aircraft are flying on the same heading.

Also, the simulator is run before CASSANDRA-II is invoked: this provides data for the monitor. If one assumes that at the start of the run, the time is 0, then the first data received by CASSANDRA-II represents the airspace at time 60 (assuming the clock is set to 60). Since the system is meant to run continuously, the running of the simulator before execution of the monitor really amounts to the creation of an airspace state which represents what has gone on before the monitor is used.

The aircraft callsigns and types were chosen at random for the run. They are not intended to indicate the presence of all of the actual flights in the same airspace at the same time (unless airline route codes have been changed since the simulation was performed, this is impossible).

3.3. EXAMPLE SESSION

This section presents an edited version of the trace generated by CASSANDRA-II using the simulated airspace described above. Explanatory text is printed in Roman (this font) and output from CASSANDRA-II is printed in Helvetica Bold-Oblique (***this font***). The reader should note that the original trace has been severely edited down to size. The general approach followed in presenting the trace is that information is generally given only once unless it provides a context for some interesting behaviour. For example, the system prints a warning on the terminal when it is about to check for warning messages -- sometimes messages are generated, sometimes not -- the trace will usually contain the warning only when a message is to be presented.

Welcome to CASSANDRA-II - An Intelligent Airspace Monitor

>What is the current time (in seconds) for the simulator?
A non-numeric value sets the clock to zero
0
>What is the clock rate (in seconds) ?
60
>Current time is 0

At startup, CASSANDRA-II prints a welcome banner. It then asks the user to set the system clock so that simulations operate correctly. The clock is used in the distance calculations made by the simulator and be the deletion Knowledge Sources. The clock can be set to any arbitrary time, but in this run was set to zero. The clock rate has also to be specified. For this run, the clock 'ticks' every sixty seconds, so each interpreter cycle represents one minute of real time. In other words, the clock rate determines the radar sweep time. The radar in the simulated airspace will make one complete revolution in a time equal to the clock rate: in the current case, the radar will make one complete sweep every minute.

The simulator now executes and generates input for CASSANDRA-II.

When CASSANDRA-II gives the user information or asks a question, it prints a greater-than symbol ('**>**') on the terminal as a flag.

>What do you wish to do?
>Clear aircraft (c), inspect airspace (i),
>get parameters for one or more aircraft (p),
>have a ks explained (k), general projection (g),
>display the blackboard (d),
>show the process status (u),
>carry on with Cassandra-II monitoring (m), or stop (s)?
>enter your choice - c, i, p, d, k, g, m, u or s
m

With the clock time and rate set, CASSANDRA-II asks the user what it is to do. The system can perform a number of operations on the aircraft in its simulated airspace -- clearing (giving permission for a manoeuvre to take place), obtaining parameters relating to the simulated airspace (e.g., obtaining the 2-space co-ordinates of its four corners), obtaining aircraft parameters (e.g., finding the current true air speed), and so on. The choice to display the blackboard prints the contents of each Level Manager's local database. The user enters the choice ***m*** and a monitoring session begins.

When monitoring the airspace, CASSANDRA-II examines aircraft parameters on each radar sweep -- this is determined by the clock rate -- and prints messages informing the user of conflicts between aircraft.

During the operation of CASSANDRA-II, internal information is printed. This information is concerned with the contents of the Level Managers in the system and with the currently scheduled task. For each Level Manager, the contents of the entry database are printed as well as the names of each KS it owns. On each system cycle, the system prints the current clock time.

```
clock time = 0
Level Manager = l1
Level Manager contents :---
Entries
    ((item0))
Knowledge Sources :---
    (PruneAircraftOutsideAirspace
    CreatePairList
    CreateHorizontalPrioList
    CreateVerticalPrioList
    PostCruiseLevelEntry
    HaveCrashed
    IPGarbageCollectKS1
    IPGarbageCollectKS2)

Precondition Matcher: fclosure[4]
Number of Entries 1
Action Interpreter Type: SingleInterpreter
Scheduler Type: sched
Local Control Database: vector[2]
```

The Level Manager being displayed is the Input LM (the internal and external Level Manager names are different, it should be noted). Currently, there is only one entry (or item) in the local entry database: that entry is called *item1*. The number of entries thought by the system to be in the local database is also printed as a check. The names of the Knowledge Sources needed for the Input Level Manager are displayed so that the user can verify that all is correct.

The reader may care to note the KSs named *IPGarbageCollectKS1* and *IPGarbageCollectKS2* are present: they are deletion KSs which remove entries when they are no longer required. There are two deletion KSs: one for time- and the other for match-triggered deletion.

In addition, the local scheduler name is printed (actually, all schedulers have the same name in this implementation even though they are, in fact, different pieces of code -- more will be said on this in a while), as is the type of the local action interpreter and the local precondition matcher. Finally, the local control database is printed in brief form: again, this is to check that all is well at runtime.

Level Managers in CASSANDRA-II contain pieces of LISP code. One can view a Level Manager as being related to an object in an object-oriented language such as Smalltalk ([Goldberg, 1983]). The pieces of code included directly in Level Managers (Knowledge Sources are accessed via properties) perform precondition matching, local scheduling and action interpretation. Because the precondition matcher must have access to information which is related directly to the Level Manager in which it resides, it is represented as a *function closure* and this accounts for the somewhat un-informative name displayed by the Level Manager print routines. The other functions stored in each Level Manager are able to make use of the regular Level Manager structure -- they can access LM contents by name, that is -- and they are represented as instances of functions with no free variables. The local scheduler, which is always represented in displays as *sched* actually resides in the local action interpreter and is accessed via a property of the symbol *sched* (the property is the name of the appropriate Level Manager).

CASSANDRA-II now prints the control database contents for this Level Manager cycle.

```
((item0 0 Real CreatePairList)
 (item0 0 Real PruneAircraftOutsideAirspace)
 (item0 0 Real PostCruiseLevelEntry))
```

The control information just presented is the contents of the local control database's real airspace partition. Each control database is divided into two partitions: one for real, the other for projected airspace. Since this run has not, so far, generated any projections, the real airspace partition only is printed. It contains three tasks. Each task contains the name of the entry which triggered the Knowledge Source given as the last entry in each list. The entry identifier is the first element of each task, the creation time is the second, the airspace type is shown as the third element and the KS name is shown as the last element. The structure of tasks varies with Level Manager. Some LM's contain scheduling information, but, since the Input Level Manager has no prioritisation scheme, there is no priority data held in its tasks: instead, its scheduler operates on pre-determined sequences -- this is handled by the schedule table.

Schedule Table:
(PruneAircraftOutsideAirspace
CreatePairList
HaveCrashed
PostCruiseLevelEntry
CreateVerticalPrioList
CreateHorizontalPrioList)

The schedule table is used to determine which Input Level Manager KS should execute. The table basically records which KSs have yet to be executed. When a KS has been executed by the local controller, its name is removed from the schedule table. The Level Manager can wait for new input when all its KSs have been executed in the correct sequence.

Scheduled Task =
(item0 0 Real PruneAircraftOutsideAirspace)
Deletion Tasks =
nil

Since there are tasks in the control database which can be executed, the local controller finds one to execute. The selection process involves using the schedule table (as described above) to enforce a sequence. The first task to be performed whenever there is new input from the simulator is to remove all references to aircraft outside the monitored region of airspace. The Knowledge Source *PruneAircraftOutsideAirspace* is executed to perform this task. The KS is executed on item0, the first entry generated from simulator data in the run. When making a scheduling decision, the local controller also checks to see if there are any entry deletion tasks which are to be performed. In CASSANDRA-II, the rule is that all deletion tasks (that is, tasks which have been created by the triggering of an entry deletion KS) should be executed as soon as the chosen problem (airspace attending) task has been executed.

The execution of a KS can cause new entries to be posted in the local entry database. Because the simulation for this run was set up to contain no aircraft other than those inside the monitored airspace, *PruneAircraftOutsideAirspace* does not remove any aircraft references from item0, the current entry.

On the next Level Manager cycle (it should be noted that there can be many Level Manager match-deliberate-act cycles for one radar sweep or clock cycle), there are still tasks in the Input Level Manager's control database. In fact, there are two tasks:

((item0 0 Real CreatePairList)
(item0 0 Real PostCruiseLevelEntry)).

At this stage, the system examines the user interface message queue. This operation is performed after each monitoring KS has been executed so that the message queue never becomes large. There are as yet no messages, so the following is displayed to the user:

Checking Messages
-- No Messages

The Level Manager is now about to execute another task and the local control database is printed, as is the summary of the Level Manager's internals. Since the Level Manager has not changed, it is not reproduced here. The control database contents are the same as those displayed prior to examination of the message queue, so the control database is not reproduced. In general, if there is an interesting change in a Level Manager, it will be shown; if, on the other hand, there is no change or the change is only minor, it will either be ignored or else summarised.

The schedule table is printed before the next task is executed.

```
Schedule Table:
    (CreatePairList
     HaveCrashed
     PostCruiseLevelEntry
     CreateVerticalPrioList
     CreateHorizontalPrioList)
```

The first entry in the schedule table is always the name of the next KS to execute. Since *CreatePairList* is a KS mentioned by a task in the control database, it can be selected by the scheduler.

```
Scheduled Task =
    (item0 0 Real CreatePairList)
Deletion Tasks =
    nil
```

The local controller has selected the task whose KS is first on the scheduler table list. The task is executed and the scheduler looks for deletion tasks to execute. Since there are no deletion tasks, none can be executed.

CreatePairList creates a list containing all possible pairs of aircraft references, as has been explained. A new entry is created which holds the list of pairs. The new entry is added to the Input Level Manager's local database. The addition of the new entry, called item1, is crucial to the operation of the

Input Level Manager: since many of the other Level Managers operate on pairs of aircraft references (for example, the vertical and longitudinal separation Level Managers), Input Level Manager KSs which send messages to these other LM's can only trigger after this entry has been added to the local database.

The task in the control database at this point in the run is *PostCruiseLevelEntry*. Since the scheduler operates a sequential strategy and since this KS is not the next task named in the schedule table, other tasks triggered by the addition of item1 to the local database will be preferred. The control database and the schedule table at this point look as follows.

```
((item1 0 Real CreateVerticalPrioList)
 (item0 0 Real PostCruiseLevelEntry)
 (item1 0 Real CreateHorizontalPrioList)
 (item1 0 Real HaveCrashed))

Schedule Table:
    (HaveCrashed
     PostCruiseLevelEntry
     CreateVerticalPrioList
     CreateHorizontalPrioList)
```

The control database now contains a variety of tasks, the most important of which is *HaveCrashed*. *HaveCrashed* examines the aircraft references for pairs representing aircraft which have crashed. This KS is important for it is essential that the user be informed of crashes immediately so that the emergency services can be directed to the probable crash site. The task which the schedule table says should be executed next is *HaveCrashed* and so it is executed.

```
Scheduled Task =
    (item1 0 Real HaveCrashed)
Deletion Tasks =
    nil
```

Again, there are no deletion tasks.

When *HaveCrashed* executes, it finds that there are no aircraft which have crashed. No warning messages are sent to the user and the Level Manager begins another cycle. Since *HaveCrashed* does not produce any new entries, no new tasks are triggered.

After *HaveCrashed* is executed, *PostCruiseLevelEntry* is executed. *PostCruiseLevelEntry* is a message-passing KS which sends a message to the Cruise Level Allocation Upper Level Manager. The KS sends the Level Manager a message which contains an entry holding the identifiers of all the aircraft currently in the monitored airspace. The entry contains a list of single identifiers (they are not combined into pairs) because cruise level allocation is a property of each aircraft considered as an individual, and is not a property of pairs of aircraft. Since the selection and execution of this KS proceeds in a manner identical to all KSs discussed so far, it is not reproduced from the trace.

At this point, the control database contains three tasks as shown below.

```
((item1 0 Real CreateHorizontalPrioList)
 (item1 0 Real CreateVerticalPrioList)
 (item0 0 Real IPGarbageCollectKS2))

Schedule Table:
     (CreateVerticalPrioList
      CreateHorizontalPrioList)
```

The first two tasks in the control database have triggered on item1, the most recently added entry. The third task has triggered on item0, the original entry which was passed from the simulator. The third task in the database was created by triggering *IPGarbageCollectKS2*, a match-triggered deletion Knowledge Source. This is the first time that a deletion KS has been triggered. *IPGarbageCollectKS2* triggers when it finds an entry with a complete set of match-tags: that is, item0 has been successfully matched once by each KS in the Level Manager which should trigger on it -- it can now be deleted from the Level Manager by this KS.

```
Scheduled Task =
     (item1 0 Real CreateVerticalPrioList)
Deletion Tasks =
     ((item0 0 Real IPGarbageCollectKS2))
```

The print routine displays the scheduled task -- as is to be expected from the schedule table, the task is an instance of the *CreateVerticalPrioList* KS. This KS creates a list of aircraft pairs ordered by the vertical distance separating them. The list is put into an entry and sent to the Vertical Separation Upper Level Manager. This task is executed.

For the first time, a deletion task has been triggered and placed in the Input Level Manager's local control database. The deletion task is executed immediately after the scheduled domain task has completed. The rule in CASSANDRA-II is that all deletion KSs are executed as soon as possible: here *IPGarbageCollectKS2* is executed immediately after *CreateVerticalPrioList*.

Eventually, the Input Level Manager's control database becomes empty. When this happens, the Level Manager conceptually goes into a wait state and remains in that state until new input is received from the simulator. In the CASSANDRA-II implementation shown here, control passes to another Level Manager -- upper Cruise Level Allocation Level Manager. As has been stated elsewhere, the order in which upper Level Managers are activated is arbitrary, though fixed, in this version of CASSANDRA-II.

Here, for information is the Upper Cruise Level Allocation Level Manager contents.

```
Level Manager = ucl1
Entries
      ((item2))
Knowledge Sources :---
      (PutCruiseLevTestEntries
      CruiseLevelUpperGCKS1
      CruiseLevelUpperGCKS2)

Precondition Matcher: fclosure[4]
Number of Entries 1
Action Interpreter Type: SingleInterpreter
Scheduler Type: sched
Local Control Database: vector[2]
```

The reader will readily see that the structure of this Level Manager is the same as the of the Input Level Manager. This Level Manager has three KSs: two are deletion KSs (*CruiseLevelUpperGCKS1* and *CruiseLevelUpperGCKS2*) and the other is a domain KS. The domain KS, *PutCruiseLevTestEntries*'s basic task is to send one message per aircraft reference to the Cruise Level Allocation Lower Level Manager where it will be tested to see if it is on the correct flight level for its heading.

Since the Cruise Level Upper Level Manager executes *PutCruiseLevTestEntries* as its first scheduled KS and there are no deletion KSs executed during this run, the operations of this Level Manager and those of its corresponding lower Level Manager will be ignored, and we will jump to the point in the run where CASSANDRA-II detects the first conflict.

The currently active Level Manager is the Cruise Level Allocation lower Level Manager. This Level Manager examines aircraft to see if they are flying on the correct flight level for their heading. The Level Manager has three KSs, one for problem solving and two for entry deletion. At the point the trace resumes, there are three entries in the local database.

```
Level Manager = lcl1
Level Manager Contents :---
Entries
      ((item8 item7 item6))
Knowledge Sources :---
      (CheckFL245NotAlloc
      CheckCruiseLevel
      CruiseLevelLowerGCKS1
      CruiseLevelLowerGCKS2)

Precondition Matcher: fclosure[4]
Number of Entries 3
Action Interpreter Type: SingleInterpreter
Scheduler Type: sched
Local Control Database: vector[2]
```

A task is now selected for execution.

```
Scheduled Task =
      (item6 0 Real CheckCruiseLevel)
Deletion Tasks =
      nil
```

The execution of this task results in a warning message. There is a conflict.

```
Checking Messages
>Do you want to see the next message? (y or n)
y

Message0:
Real Airspace Conflict
CheckCruiseLevel
BA283 is on level 150 on heading 270.0


Type c to continue
c
```

The user is asked if the warning is to be displayed. The response is in the affirmative, so the system prints the message. The message says that there is a conflict in real airspace (as opposed to projected airspace -- if the message related to a projection, it would have ***Projected Airspace Conflict*** as its first line. The message says that BA283 is flying on flight level 150 with a heading of 270 degrees. For this heading, the aircraft should, according to the semi-circular rule, be flying on an even flight level (FL160 or FL140, for example). The conflict was detected by KS *CheckCruiseLevel* The system then asks the user to type ***c*** so that CASSANDRA-II may continue processing.

The next conflict is detected by the KS *CheckVerticalSep*, one of the Vertical Separation lower Level Manager Knowledge Sources. This KS checks that vertical separation exists between each pair of aircraft within 5 nm of each other inside the airspace. The aircraft pairs inspected by this KS are what remain after two pruning operations: the first operation removes aircraft outside airspace (this is done in the Input Level Manager) and the second removes aircraft which are either separated by more than 5 nm in the horizontal or by more than 5,000 ft. in the vertical (or both). The second pruning operation is performed by the single domain KS in the Vertical Separation upper Level Manager. The aircraft pairs sent to the Vertical Separation lower Level Manager are all vertical separation conflict candidates.

```
Checking Messages
>Do you want to see the next message? (y or n)
y

Message1:
Real Airspace Conflict
CheckVerticalSep
Vertical Separation Conflict
Involving PA12 PA1
On levels 170 175
Vertical Separation is 5


Type c to continue
c
```

This message again says that the conflict is in real airspace (there are no projections in this run, it should be remembered) and that it is a vertical separation conflict. The conflict was detected by the KS *CheckVerticalSep* (the domain KS for the Vertical Separation lower Level Manager). The conflict is between PA1 and PA12. PA1 is on flight level 170 (17,000 ft.) and PA12 is on FL175 (the order of the levels corresponds to the order in which the aircraft callsigns are printed). The vertical separation is 5, that it 500 ft. (vertical separation is printed in units of one hundred feet -- this corresponds to the terminology for naming flight levels).

A separation of 500 ft. violates the vertical separation rules because both aircraft are in flight below FL245 and in an airway. The rules state that minimum separation for aircraft below FL245 in an airway is 1,000 ft.

The user is invited to type ***c*** to resume CASSANDRA-II when s/he has finished reading the message.

The final message generated in this run is a longitudinal separation conflict. The conflict is detected by KS *LongitudinalSepKS4*, the catchall KS in the Longitudinal Separation lower Level Manager. The dialogue is as follows.

Checking Messages
>Do you want to see the next message? (y or n)
y

Message3:
Real Airspace Conflict
LongitudinalSepKS4
Longitudinal Separation Conflict
Involving PA12 PA1
PA12 and PA1 are on reciprocal tracks

LongitudinalSepKS1 LongitudinalSepKS2 LongitudinalSepKS3
do not apply

Separation distance is 4.121309089309661

Type c to continue
c

The two aircraft, PA12 and PA1 are on reciprocal tracks (i.e., the difference of the two headings is 180). The message states that the other longitudinal separation KSs do not apply (this is, in effect, the justification for this message because the KS *LongitudinalSepKS4* does not respond to conflicts unless the three other KSs have failed to apply). The separation distance is fractionally over 4 nautical miles and the rule requires aircraft to be separated by at least 15 nautical miles for longitudinal separation to exist. Perhaps this message ought also to tell the user to pray -- the situation described by the message is a near-miss.

The user once again types ***c*** to resume CASSANDRA-II.

At the end of the cycle, the system prints the menu we saw at the start of the trace. It also prints the current time (in seconds): one minute of simulated time has elapsed since the start of the run. Everything in the trace presented above has conceptually been generated at time 60 -- this should clear any confusion about running the simulator before executing CASSANDRA-II at start-up. This time, however, the user decides to stop the execution of the program, and so enters the choice ***s*** (stop) and the program terminates.

```
>Current time is 60
>What do you wish to do?
>Clear aircraft (c), inspect airspace (i),
>get parameters for one or more aircraft (p),
>have a ks explained (k), general projection (g),
>display the blackboard (d),
>show the process status (u),
>carry on with Cassandra-II monitoring (m), or stop (s)?
>enter your choice - c, i, p, d, k, g, m, u  or s
s
```

Before terminating, CASSANDRA-II prints a termination message, the amount of cpu used and then, politely, says goodbye.

```
CASSANDRA-II execution terminates
CPU time used = 23.35 seconds
Goodbye
```

GLOSSARY

This appendix contains a glossary of terms and abbreviations used in Air Traffic Control. The contents have been extracted from MATS Vol. 1: the wording has been changed to make terms more accessible.

The glossary is organised as follows. Terms are presented first: where a term is attributable to ICAO, it is noted. After the definition of terms, a setion of abbreviations is provided.

1. TERMS

- **AERODROME.** An airfield, airport or a strip of water which provides facilities for the landing and departure of aircraft.
- **AIR TRAFFIC.** All aircraft which are in flight or operaiting on the manoeuvering areas of an aerodrome.(ICAO)
- **AIRWAY.** A control area or part of a control area in the form of a corridor and equipped with navigational aids.(ICAO)
- **ALTITUDE.** The vertical distance of a level, a point or object (considered as a point), measured from the standard mean sea level.(ICAO)
- **CONFLICT.** A violation of separation minima.
- **CONFLICTION.** See **CONFLICT** (synonymous term).
- **CONTROL AREA.** A controlled airspace extending vertically upwards from a specified limit above the earth's surface.(ICAO)
- **CONTROLLED AIRSPACE.** An airspace of defined dimensions within which an air traffic control service is provided for IFR flights.
- **CRUISING LEVEL.** A level maintained for a significant part of a flight.(ICAO)
- **FLIGHT LEVEL.** A surface of constant atmospheric pressure which is related to the specific pressure constant of 1013.2mb and which is separated from all other such surfaces by specific pressure intervals.

- **FLIGHT PLAN.** Speicified information provided to air traffic service units concerning the intentions of a pilot with regard to a flight or portion of a flight.
- **HOLDING POINT.** A specified location which is identified by visual or other means in the vicinity of which an aircraft in flight will maintain its position in accordance with air traffic control procedures.(ICAO)
- **HOLDING PROCEDURE.** A predetermined manoeuvre which keeps an aircraft within a specified airspace while waiting for further clearances.(ICAO)
- **LEVEL.** A generic term which relates to the vertical position of an aircraft in flight: this term can mean height, altitude of flight level.
- **MINIMUM SECTOR ALTITUDE.** The lowest safe altitude for instrument flights.
- **NIGHT.** The time between half an hour before sunset and half an hour before sunrise. Sunset and sunrise are determined at surface level.
- **PRIMARY RADAR.** A radar system which uses reflected radio signals.(ICAO)
- **RADAR VECTORING.** The provision of navigational guidance to aircraft in the form of specific headings based on radar use.(ICAO)
- **RADIAL.** A magnetic bearing extending from a VOR/DME/TACAN.
- **REPORTING POINT.** A specified geographical location which is used as a datum point for the reporting of the position of an aircraft.
- **SECONDARY SURVEILLANCE RADAR.** A radar system using ground interrogators and airborne transponders to determine the position of aircraft in range and azimuth. When modes and codes are agreed, SSR can be used to determine identity and height.
- **TERMINAL CONTROL AREA.** A control area usually established at the confluence of airways in the vicinity of one or more majore aeridromes.
- **TRACK.** The direction of the path of an aircraft over the ground. This is usually expressed in degrees from north. True or magnetic north may be the determining point for the determination of a track.

- **TRANSPONDER**. A transmitter/receiver which replies with a signal to a proper interrogation. The interrogation and reply are transmitted on different frequencies.

1.1. ABBREVIATIONS

- **amsl**. Above Mean Sea Level.
- **ATC**. Air Traffic Control.
- **ATCC**. Air Traffic Control Centre.
- **ATCO**. Air Traffic Control Officer. (An air traffic controller.)
- **ATCU**. Air Traffic Control Unit.
- **ATSU**. Air Traffic Service Unit.
- **CAA**. Civil Aviation Authority.
- **DME**. Distance Measuring Equipment. Equipment associated with a navigational beacon which is used to determine the distance between an aircraft and the beacon.
- **EUR**. Europe (used as an ICAO area designator).
- **FIR**. Flight Information Region. A geographical region (consisting of number of sectors in the UK) for which air traffic control facilities are provided.
- **FL**. Flight Level. A horizontal band of airspace 1000 ft high. Flight levels are used to denote the height at which an aircraft in controlled airspace is flying.
- **ft**. Foot (feet).
- **GMT**. Greenwich Mean Time (Also called "Zulu").
- **ICAO**. International Civil Aviation Organisation. The international regulatory body for civil aviation.
- **IFR**. Instrument Flight Rules. Rules which must be obeyed when not using visual information for avoiding obstacles and for making correct and safe progress through the air.
- **kts**. Knots (= nautical miles per hour).

- **mb**. Millibars.
- **NATS**. National Air Traffic Services. The organisation which controls all air traffic in the UK.
- **nm**. Nautical Mile. A distance of 6080 feet.
- **NOTAM**. Notice To AirMen.
- **ORCAM**. Originating Region Code Assignment Method. A method for assigning callsigns to aircraft in such a way that they need not be changed when an aircraft moves from, say, British to French airspace.
- **SPI**. Speed Position Indicator. The radar 'scope' used by air traffic controllers to view aircraft movements.
- **SSR**. Secondary Surveillance Radar. A radar system which interrogates all aircraft in range for call sign and altitude. This information is presented to the air traffic controller on the SPI (see above), together with an indication of the aircraft's location and its speed (speed is judged by watching the SPI and estimating how fast the aircraft's icon is moving).
- **TACAN**. Tactical Air Control And Navigation.
- **tas**. True Air Speed.
- **TMA**. Terminal Control (Management) Area. A region of airspace immediately surrounding a large airport (e.g., London Heathrow) within which special rules apply.
- **VMC**. Visual Meteorological Conditions. Conditions under which visual observations of other aircraft and surface features can be made: this is done simply by looking out of the window.
- **VOR**. VHF Omni-directional Range. A type of navigational beacon, often found in controlled airspace sectors. A VOR emits a signal on a number of 'raidals'. The signal is received by equipement in aircraft and allows the pilot to determine the angle of approach to the beacon of his/her aircraft. Typically, aircraft fly through controlled airspace by following a sequence of beacons of this kind.

BIBLIOGRAPHY

(Aiello, 1983) Aiello, N A comparative study of control strategies for expert systems: AGE implementation of three variations of PUFF. Proceedings of the National Conference on Artificial Intelligence (AAAI-83), 1 - 4, 1983

(Aikens, 1980) Aikens,J.S. Protypes and Production Rules: A Knowledge Representation for Computer Consultations. Rept. STAN-CS-80-814, Stanford University, 1980

(Aikens, 1983) Aikens, J.S. Prototypical Knowledge for Expert Systems. AIJ, Vol. 20, No. 2, pp. 163 - 210, Feb. 1983

(Anderson, 1983) Anderson, J.R., The Architecture of Cognition. Harvard University Press, London, 1983

(Austin, 1962) Austin, J.L. How To Do Things With Words. Oxford University Press, 1962

(Balzer, 1980) Balzer, R., Erman, L., London, P. and Williams, C. HEARSAY-III: A Domain Independent Framework for Expert Systems. Proc. First Annual Conference on Artificial Intelligence, pp. 108 - 110, 1980

(Bobrow, 1979) Bobrow, D.G. and Winograd, T. An Overview of KRL, A Knowledge Representation Language. Cognitive Science, Vol. 1, pp. 3 - 46, 1979

(CAA, 1) Civil Aviation Authority, Manual of Air Traffic Services, Vol. 1

(Chomsky, 1980) Chomsky, N. Rules and Representations, Blackwell, Oxford, 1980

(Clancey, 1985) Clancey, W.J. Heuristic Classification. AIJ, Vol. 27, pp. 289-350, 1985

(Clocksin, 1982) Clocksin, W and Mellish, C, Programming in Prolog. Springer-Verlag, Berlin, 1981

(Coffman, 1971) Coffman, E.G., Elphick, M. and Shoshani, A. System deadlocks, Computing Surveys Vol. 3, pp. 67 - 78

(Colmerauer, 1975) Colmerauer, A. Les grammaires de metamorphose. Groupe d'Intelligence Artificielle, Marseille-Luminy, 1975

(Craig, 1985) Craig, I.D. Cassandra: a real time knowledge based airspace monitoring system. Internal Report, Dept. of Computing, University of Lancaster, June, 1985

(Craig, 1986) Craig, I.D. The Ariadne-1 Blackboard System. Computer Journal, Vol. 29, No. 3, pp. 235 - 240, 1986

(Craig, 1987) Craig, I.D. BB-SR. Technical Report No. 94, Department of Computer Science, University of Warwick, February, 1987

(Davis, 1980) Davis, R. Meta-rules: Reasoning about control. AIJ, Vol. 15, pp. 179 - 222.

(Davis, 1983) Davis, R. and Smith, R.G. Negotiation as a Metaphor for Distributed Problem Solving. AIJ, Vol. 20, pp. 63 - 109, 1983

(Doyle, 1979) Doyle,J., A Truth Maintenance System. AIJ, Vol. 12, pp 231 - 272, 1979

(Duda, 1978) Duda, R.O., and Hart, P.E., Nilsson, N.J., and Southerland, G.L. Semantic Network Representation in Rule-based Inference Systems. In Waterman, 1978, pp. 203 - 222.

(Erman, 1975) Erman, L.D. and Lesser, V.R., A Multi-level Organisation for Problem Solving Using Many, Diverse, Cooperating Sources of Knowledge. Proc. IJCAI 4, Vol. 2, pp. 483 - 490, 1975

(Erman, 1981) Erman, L.D., London, P. and Fickas, S. The Design and an Example Use of HEARSAY-III. Proc. IJCAI 7, Vol. 1, pp. 409 - 415, 1981

(Ernst, 1969) Ernst, G. and Newell, A. GPS: A Case Study in Generality and Problem Solving, Academic Press, New York, 1969

(Fagan, 1980) Fagan, L.M. VM: Representing time-dependent relations in a medical setting. Doctoral Dissertation, Heuristic Programming Project, Dept. of Computer Science Stanford University, 1980

(Feigenbaum, 1978) Feigenbaum, E. and Nii, H.P., Rule-based Understanding of Signals. Pattern -Directed Inference Systems, D.A. Waterman and F. Hayes-Roth (Eds.), Academic Press, 1978

(Feigenbaum, 1982) Feigenbaum, E., Nii, H.P., Anton, J.J. and Rockmore, A.J. Signal-to-signal transformation: HASP/SIAP case study. AI Magazine, Vol. 3, pp 23 - 35, 1982

(Fodor, 1983) Fodor, J.A. The Modularity of Mind. Bradford Books, MIT Press, 1983.

(Forgy, 1977) Forgy, C.L. and McDermott, J. OPS, A Domain-independent Production System Language. Proc. IJCAI 5, pp 933 - 939

(Forgy, 1979) Forgy, C.L. On the efficient implementation of production systems. Dept. of Computer Science, Carnegie-Mellon University, 1979

(Forgy, 1980) Forgy, C.L. RETE: A fast algorithm for the many pattern/many object pattern match problem. Tech. Report, Dept. of Computer Science, Carnegie-Mellon University, 1980

(Forgy, 1981) Forgy, C.L. The OPS5 User's Manual. Tech. Rep. CMU-CS-81-135, Dept. of Computer Science, Carnegie-Mellon University, 1981

(Genesereth, 1984) Genesereth, M.R. Partial Programs. Memo HPP-84-1, Heuristic Programming Project, Dept. of Computer Science, Stanford University, 1984

(Genesereth, 1983) Genesereth, M.R. The MRS Casebook. Memo HPP-83-26, Heuristic Programming Project, Dept. of Computer Science, Stanford University, 1983

(Goldberg, 1983) Goldberg, A. and Robson, D. Smalltalk-80 The Language and Its Implementation, Addison-Wesley, Reading, MA, 1983

(Goldman, 1978) Goldman, N. AP3 User's Guide. USC/ISI, Marina del Rey, CA, 1978

(Graham, 1972) Graham, G.S. and Denning, P.J. Protection - Principles and Practice, Proc. AFIPS Spring Joint Computer Conference, Vol. 40, pp. 417 - 429, 1972

(Hayes-Roth, 1977) Hayes-Roth, F. and Lesser, V.R., Focus of Attention in the Hearsay-II speech understanding system. Proc. IJCAI 5, pp. 27 - 35, 1977

(Hayes-Roth, 1979) Hayes-Roth, B. and Hayes-Roth, F., A Cognitive Model of Planning. Cognitive Science, Vol. 3., pp. 275 - 310, 1979

(Hayes-Roth, 1983) Hayes-Roth, B. The Blackboard Architecture: A General Framework for Problem Solving? Report No. HPP-83-30, Heuristic Programming Project, Computer Science Dept., Stanford University, Palo Alto, CA, May 1983

(Hayes-Roth, 1984) Hayes-Roth, B. A Blackboard Model of Control. Report No. HPP-83-38, Heuristic Programming Project, Computer Science Department, Stanford University, Palo Alto, CA.,

June 1983 (Revised December, 1984)

(Hayes-Roth, 1984b) Hayes-Roth, B. BB1: An Architecture for blackboard systems that control, explain, and learn about their own behavior. Technical Report HPP-84-16, Stanford University, 1984

(Hayes-Roth, 1985a) Hayes-Roth, B and Hewett, M. Learning Control Heuristics in BB-1. Technical Report HPP-85-2, Stanford University, 1985

(Hayes-Roth, 1985b) Hayes-Roth, B. A Blackboard Model for Control. Artificial Intelligence, Vol. 26, pp. 251 - 322, 1985

(Hayes-Roth, 1986) Hayes-Roth, B., Garvey, A., Johnson, M.V. and Hewett, M. BB*: A Layered Environment for Reasoning about Action. Technical Report No. KSL 86-38, Knowledge Systems Laboratory, Stanford University, 1986

(Hempel, 1966) Hempel, C.G. Philosphy of Natural Science. Foundations of Philosophy Series, Prentice-Hall, NJ, 1966

(Hewitt, 1972) Hewitt, C. Description and Theoretical Analysis (using schemata) of PLANNER. MIT AI Lab., TR-258, 1972

(Hoare, 1985) Hoare, C.A.R. Communicating Sequential Processes. Prentice-Hall, Englewood Cliffs, N.J., 1985

(Konolige, 1980) Konolige, K. and Nilsson, N., Multiple Agent Planning Systems, Proc. First Annual Conference of the American Association for Artificial Intelligence, Stanford, CA, 1980

(Kowalski, 1979) Kowalski, R. Logic for Problem Solving. North Holland, Oxford, 1979

(Kunz, 1978) Kunz,J., Fallet, R., McClung, D., Osborn, J., Votteri, B., Nii, H.P., Aikens, J.S., Fagan, L. and Feigenbaum, E. A physiological rule based system for interpreting pulmonary function test results. HPP-78-19 (Working Paper), Heuristic Programming Project, Dept. of Computer Science, Stanford University, 1978

(Kunz, 1983) Kunz,J., Kehler, T.P. and Williams, M.D. Applications Development Using A Hybrid AI Development System. AI Magazine, Vol. 5, No. 3, pp. 41 - 54, 1983

(Lagally, 1978) Lagally, K. Synchronisation in a Layered System, in Operating Systems: An Advanced Course, Ed. Bayer, R., Graham, R.M. and Seegmüller, G., Lecture Notes in Computer Science, Springer-Verlag, pp. 252 - 281, Berlin, 1978

(Laird, 1985) Laird, J.E., Rosenbloom, P.S. and Newell, A. Chunking in Soar: The Anatomy of a General Learning Mechanism. Knowledge Systems Laboratory Report No. KSL-85-34, Department of Computer Science, Stanford University, Palo Alto, CA, Spetember 1985

(Lenat, 1982) Lenat, D.B. The Nature of Heuristics. AIJ, Vol. 19, pp. 189-249, 1982.

(Lenat, 1983) Lenat, D.B., Threory Formation by Heuristic Search.The Nature of Heuristics II: Background and Examples. AIJ, Vol. 21, Nos. 1,2, pp. 31 - 60, March, 1983

(Lesser, 1983) Lesser, V.R. and Corkhill, D.D. The Distributed Vehicle Monitoring Testbed: A Tool for Investigating Distributed Problem Solving Networks, AI Magazine, Vol. 3, No. 3, pp. 15 - 33, 1983

(Lieberman, 1981) Lieberman, H. A Preview of Act 1. MIT AI Laboratory Memo 625, June, 1981

(Marr, 1982) Marr, D. Vision. W.H. Freeman, San Francisco, CA, 1982

(McCarthy, 1969) McCarthy, J. and Hayes, P.J. Some Philosophical Problems from the Standpoint of Artificial Intelligence, in Machine Intelligence 4, Meltzer, B. and Michie, D., Eds., Edinburgh University Press, pp. 463 - 502, 1969

(McClelland, 1981) McClelland, J.L. and Rumelhart, D.E. An interactive activation model of context effects in letter perception: Part 1. An account of basic findings. Psychological Review, Vol. 88, pp. 375-401, 1981

(McDermott, 1974) McDermott, D. and Sussman, G.J. The CONNIVER Reference Manual. MIT AI Laboratory Memo 259a, 1974

(McDermott, 1982) McDermott, J. R1: A Rule-Based Configurer of Computer Systems. AIJ, Vol. 19, pp. 39 - 88, 1982

(McDermott, 1978) McDermott, J. and Forgy, C.L. Production System Conflict Resolution Strategies. In Waterman, 1978, pp 177 - 199

(McDermott, 1984) McDermott, J. R1 Revisited: Four Years in the Trenches, AI Magazine, Vol. 5, No. 3, pp. 21 - 32, 1984

(Minsky, 1980) Minsky, M. The Society Theory of Thinking. In Artificial Intelligence: An MIT Perspective, ed. Winston, P.H. and Brown, R.H., MIT Press, Cambridge, MA, 1980

(MITRE, 1984) Shively, C. and Schwamb, K.B. AIRPAC: Advisor for the Intelligent Resolution of Predicted Aircraft Conflicts. MTR-84-W164, MITRE Corp., Metrek Div., McLean, VA, 1984

(Mycroft, 1984) Mycroft, A. and O'Keefe, R.A. A Polymorphic Type System for Prolog. AIJ, Vol. 23, No. 3, pp 295 - 308, August, 1984

(Newell, 1973) Newell, A. Production systems: models of control structures. In W.G. Chase (ed.), Visual Information Processing, Academic Press, New York, 1973

(Nii, 1979) Nii, H.P. and Aiello, N. AGE: A knowledge-based program for building knowledge-based programs. Proc. IJCAI 6, pp. 645 - 655

(Nii, 1986a) Nii, H.P. The Blackboard Model of Problem Solving. Artificial Intelligence Magazine, Vol. 7, No. 2, pp. 38 - 53, 1986

(Nii, 1986b) Nii, H.P. Blackboard Systems Part Two: Blackboard Application Systems. Artificial Intelligence Magazine, Vol. 7, No. 3, pp. 82 - 106, 1986

(Rice, 1986) Rice, J. P. POLIGON: A System for Parallel Problem Solving, Technical Report No. 86-19, Knowledge Systems Laboratory, Stanford University, 1986

(Roberts, 1977) Roberts, R.B. and Goldstein, I.P. The FRL Manual. MIT AI Lab., Memo 409, 1977

(Rumelhart, 1982) Rumelhart, D.E. and McClelland, J.L. An interactive model of context effects in letter perception: Part 2. The contextual enhancement effect and some tests and extensions of the model. Psychological Review, Vol. 89, pp. 60-94, 1982

(Rychener, 1978) Rychener, M.D. and Newell, A. An instructable production system: basic design issues. In Waterman, 1978

(Sacerdoti, 1974) Sacerdoti, E.D. Planning in a Hierarchy of Abstraction Spaces. AIJ, Vol. 5, pp. 115 -135, 1974

(Sacerdoti, 1977) Sacerdoti, E.D. A Structure For Plans and Behavior. Elsevier, New York, 1977

(Schank, 1982) Schank, R.C., Dynamic Memory. Cambridge University Press, London, 1982

(Searle, 1965) Searle, J.R. What Is A Speech Act? In Philosophy In America, ed. M. Black, pp. 221-239, Allen and Unwin, 1965

(Searle, 1969) Searle, J.R. Speech Acts. Cambridge University Press, 1969

(Shortliffe, 1976) Shortliffe, E. Computer-Based Medical Consultations: MYCIN. Elsevier, New York, 1976

(Simon, 1969) Simon, H.A. Sciences of the Artificial, MIT Press, Cambridge, MA, 1969

(Stefik, 1982) Stefik, M., Aikens, J., Balzer, B., Benoit, J., Birnbaum, L., Hayes-Roth, F and Sacerdoti,E. The Organization of Expert Systems: A Prescriptive Tutorial. Xerox, PARC, VLSI-82-1, 1982

(Stoy, 1977) Stoy, J.E., Denotational Semantics: The Scott-Strachey Approach to Programming Language Theory. MIT Pressm 1977

(Sussman, 1977) Stallman, R.M and Sussman, G.J. Forward Reasoning and Dependency Directed Backtracking. AIJ, Vol. 9, pp 135 - 196, 1977

(Teitelman, 1975) Teitelman, W. Interlisp Reference Manual. Xerox Corp., Palo Alto, CA, 1975

(Terry, 1983) Terry, A. The CHRYSALIS Project: Hierarchical Control of Production Systems. Memo HPP-83-19, Heuristic Programming Project, Computer Science Dept., Stanford University, Palo Alto, CA., May, 1983

(van Melle, 1979) van Melle, W. EMYCIN: A domain-independent production-rule system for consultation programs. Doctoral dissertation, Heuristic Programming Project, Dept. of Computer Science, Stanford University, 1980

(Warren, 1977) Warren, D.H.D. Implementing Prolog. DAI Research Report No. 39, Edinburgh University, 1977

(Waterman, 1978) Waterman, D.A. and Hayes-Roth, F. (eds) Pattern-directed inference systems. Academic Press, New York, 1978

(Wilensky, 1983) Wilensky, R. Planning and Understanding. Addison-Wesley, London, 1983

(Williams, 1984) M.A. Williams, H. Brown and T. Barnes. TRICERO Design Description. Technical Report ESL-NS539, ESL Inc., Sunneyvale, CA, 1984.

(Woods, 1975) Woods, W.A. What's in a link? In Bobrow, D.G. and Collins, A., Representation and Understanding, Academic Press, 1975

(Xerox, 1983) Xerox Corporation Interlisp-d Manual. Xerox Corp., Palo Alto, CA, 1983